AFFIRMATIVE ACTION

A Reference Handbook

Other Titles in ABC-CLIO's
CONTEMPORARY
WORLD ISSUES
Series

Books in the Contemporary World Issues series address vital issues in today's society such as terrorism, sexual harassment, homelessness, AIDS, gambling, animal rights, and air pollution. Written by professional writers, scholars, and nonacademic experts, these books are authoritative, clearly written, up-to-date, and objective. They provide a good starting point for research by high school and college students, scholars, and general readers, as well as by legislators, businesspeople, activists, and others.

Each book, carefully organized and easy to use, contains an overview of the subject; a detailed chronology; biographical sketches; facts and data and/or documents and other primary-source material; a directory of organizations and agencies; annotated lists of print and nonprint resources; a glossary; and an index.

Readers of books in the Contemporary World Issues series will find the information they need in order to better understand the social, political, environmental, and economic issues facing the world today.

AFFIRMATIVE ACTION

A Reference Handbook

Lynne Eisaguirre

**CONTEMPORARY
WORLD ISSUES**

ABC-CLIO

Santa Barbara, California
Denver, Colorado
Oxford, England

Acknowledgments

This book would not have been written without the help of many people. My assistant, Debra L. Harris, provided timely and extensive research and editorial and word processing expertise. O.C. O'Connell contributed her excellent research and editorial skills as did Alyssa Graves. Thank you all for your dedication and professionalism.

My husband, John Evans, provided support and encouragement, as always, and my children, Nicholas and Elizabeth, the inspiration to try to make the world a better place.

Copyright © 1999 by Lynne Eisaguirre

Library of Congress Cataloging-in-Publication Data

Eisaguirre, Lynne, 1951–
    Affirmative action : a reference handbook / Lynne Eisaguirre.
       p. cm.
    Includes bibliographical references and index.
    ISBN 0-87436-854-5 (alk. paper)
    1. Affirmative action programs—United States—History.
    2. Affirmative action programs—Law and legislation—United States.
HF5549.5.A34E39   1999
331.13'3'0973—dc21
                                                   99-35720
                                                  CIP

05 04 03 02 01 00   10 9 8 7 6 5 4 3 2

ABC-CLIO, Inc.
130 Cremona Drive, P.O. Box 1911
Santa Barbara, California 93116-1911

This book is printed on acid-free paper ∞ ·
Manufactured in the United States of America

Contents

How to Read Case and Statute Citations

A case may be reported by several different reporting services, which are generally found in law libraries. If a case is decided by the United States Supreme Court, it will be found first in a loose-leaf service entitled *U.S. Law Week* (U.S.L.W.) and then, later, in either the *United States Reports* (U.S.) or the *Supreme Court Reporters* (S. Ct.). If it is a federal case decided by a court other than the U.S. Supreme Court (either a federal district or federal appeals court), you can find the case soon after it has been decided in *U.S. Law Week* and then in either the *Federal Reporter, Second Series* (F.2d) or the *Federal Supplement* (F. Supp.).

Most state courts print their own official state reports. In addition, all published state court decisions are included in the West Reporter System. The West Company has divided the country into seven regions. A particular state's court decisions will be reported in the reporter for the region to which that state had been assigned. The abbreviations for these reporters are:

- A. and A.2d: The *Atlantic Reporter (First and Second Series)*, which includes decisions from Connecticut, Delaware, the District of Columbia,

Maine, Maryland, New Hampshire, New Jersey, Pennsylvania, Rhode Island, and Vermont.

- N.E. and N.E.2d: *Northeastern Reporter (First and Second Series)*, which includes decisions from Illinois, Indiana, Massachusetts, New York (except for decisions from New York appellate courts, which are published in a separate volume, *New York Supplement [N.Y.S.]*), and Ohio.
- N.W. and N.W.2d: *Northwestern Reporter (First and Second Series)*, which includes decisions from Iowa, Michigan, Minnesota, Nebraska, North Dakota, South Dakota, and Wisconsin.
- P. and P.2d: *Pacific Reporter (First and Second Series)*, which includes decisions from Alaska, Arizona, California (except California appellate decisions, which are published in a separate volume, the *California Reporter* [Cal. Rptr.]), Colorado, Hawaii, Idaho, Kansas, Montana, Nevada, New Mexico, Oklahoma, Oregon, Utah, Washington, and Wyoming.
- S.E. and S.E.2d: *Southeastern Reporter (First and Second Series)*, which includes decisions from Georgia, North Carolina, South Carolina, Virginia, and West Virginia.
- So. and So.2d: *Southern Reporter (First and Second Series)*, which includes decisions from Alabama, Florida, Louisiana, and Mississippi.
- S.W. and S.W.2d: *Southwestern Reporter (First and Second Series)*, which includes decisions from Arkansas, Kentucky, Missouri, Tennessee, and Texas.

A case citation provides the names of the people, schools, government agencies, or companies on each side of a case (the plaintiff[s]) and defendants[s]); the volume of the reporter in which the case can be found; the page number on which the case begins; and the year in which the case was decided. For example: *Ellison v. Brady, 924 F.2d 872 (9th Cir. 1991)*. Ellison and Brady are the names of the parties involved in the case. Ellison is the plaintiff, and Brady is the defendant. The case is reported in volume 924 of the *Federal Reporter, Second Series* beginning on page 872. The Ninth Circuit (a federal court of appeals) decided the case in 1991.

Introduction 1

Affirmative action has been defined as "public or private actions or programs that provide or seek to provide opportunities or other benefits to persons on the basis of, among other things, their membership in a specified group" (Jones 1985, 903). Affirmative action began in the 1960s as attempts by Presidents John F. Kennedy and Lyndon B. Johnson to assist minorities in realizing equal employment opportunities. Local and state governments later joined in that effort, as did private businesses. Still later, the federal government added affirmative action requirements to federal funding for educational institutions.

Today, affirmative action has become one of the most controversial issues in the United States. The issue emphasizes the tension between individual and group rights as well as a clash between conflicting American values. Americans tend to believe that fairness involves treating everyone the same and that, conversely, we should do everything possible to overcome past discrimination and provide equal opportunities.

Proponents of affirmative action claim that affirmative action is the best means of defeating the inequality produced by historical discrimination. This inequality, advocates claim, is not a manifestation of a "conscious bigotry but a situation that will occur regardless of good-faith efforts to eliminate bias from employment and education practices because of deep-seated and largely unconscious biases and stereotypes (Bernhardt 1993, 24). Proponents further argue that affirmative action has accomplished its goals, but that reducing its application will result in a new onslaught of discrimination. In contrast, opponents view affirmative action as divisive and injurious to individual rights and assert that it impinges on individual freedoms (Bernhardt 1993, 34). They contend "either that it has worked so well it is no longer needed or that it has failed to work, it is ill-conceived, and has served only to worsen racial divisions in society" (Schuldinger 1996, 133).

Manning Marable, author and director of the Institute for Research in African-American Studies at Columbia University, is among those who believe that "a higher ideal" is at stake. According to Marable, we should strive for nothing less than "the ultimate elimination of race and gender inequality, the uprooting of prejudice and discrimination, and the realization of a truly democratic nation" (Guernsey 1997, 25).

Do Americans support this goal? Public opinion polls reveal conflicting results about the issue. Yet, in general, since the 1970s, opinion surveys have shown increasing hostility toward affirmative action (Eastland 1997, 2).

In 1995, A *Wall Street Journal*/NBC News poll found that two out of three Americans opposed affirmative action. But when the polls were divided along racial lines, the results were more instructive. A 1995 *Newsweek* poll suggests that whites oppose racial preferences in employment or college admissions by a margin of 74 percent to 14 percent; minorities supported these policies by a 50 to 46 percent margin (Guernsey 1997, 27).

However, how the questions in the polls are worded makes a difference in the results. If the pollsters use the term "affirmative action," larger percentages support the policy. But if other terms are used, such as "preferences" or "quotas," the respondents tend to reject the policy. Similarly, public opinion often depends on which groups the affirmative action programs help. Some people believe that these programs should only compensate African Americans to redress them for slavery, oppression, and discrimination. According to many others, however, affirmative action should also benefit other groups that have historically been and continue to be discriminated against, including women and racial minorities or even white Americans of limited means.

Supporters of affirmative action argue that the idea of "merit" in employment, contracting, and hiring is elusive, pointing to companies run by family relations and colleges where students are given preferences if their parents or siblings attended the institution. In addition, many colleges have traditionally limited the number of students from certain geographic locations in the name of increasing diversity. A few students may have grumbled about these policies, but they have not led to the controversy raised by affirmative action programs.

Why? Perhaps because these traditional policies have not been as openly known or debated. Yet experts point to another issue: the affirmative action issue involves race. Because of our history on race relations in the United States, any discussion about affirmative action can raise a welter of emotions: guilt, anger, grief, sadness, and pain.

What Is Affirmative Action?

Even the supporters of affirmative action disagree about this question since the reality is that there is a spectrum of affirmative action solutions, depending upon which specific program is being debated.

There seems to be little disagreement that when it was originally envisioned, the program entailed casting a wider net—making sure that potential students, employees, and government contractors from minority backgrounds were made aware of and considered for positions. Various government agencies, legal battles, and in some cases the organizations themselves moved from this version of affirmative action to different versions of goals, timetables, and quotas.

President Bill Clinton in a 1995 speech on the subject recommended mending, not ending, affirmative action. His high-level government commission on the subject agreed, although their proposal received little popular support or notice.

Other supporters, such as law professor Lani Guinier, argue that the policy should go further, that affirmative action should be used as an opportunity for all organizations to look at the whole question of merit, testing, selection, and promotion to determine if current methods will provide the best mix of people for the job or school. She questions whether the traditional methods of tests, subjective performance criteria, and nepotism have ever done this.

Guinier, for example, suggests that both workplaces and schools should move to what she calls "performance-based selection." This would require them to rely on long interviews and/or probationary periods that are meant to set up real workplace situations or simulations. For example, if someone is being considered for a promotion at work, Guinier suggests the employer should have him or her actually work at the position for some period of time before the decision is made.

This would reduce reliance on standardized tests as well as the more subtle forms of prejudice, which, in most cases, "do not enable institutions to identify the most successful applicants. This approach would instead focus decision makers' attention on creating scenarios and contexts necessary to make informed judgments about performance. This would improve the capacity of institutions to find people who are creative, adaptive, reliable, and committed, rather than just good at test taking" (Guinier and Sturm 1996, 974).

Guinier suggests that aside from holding a lottery each time someone is to be hired or promoted, this is the only way our "testocracy"—a system that emphasizes test scores—can be eliminated. She argues that the emphasis on test scores favors students who have enjoyed expensive and privileged educations and other advantages. "Conventional selection methods fail because they give preferences to people based on socioeconomic positions, and allocate positions in ways that do not reflect functional capacity" (Guinier 1996, 1035).

A Historical Perspective: The Roots of Affirmative Action

Understanding the roots of affirmative action in the United States may help readers clarify their own thoughts about the debate. The current debate over affirmative action doesn't occur in a historical vacuum. The controversy is best understood as an outgrowth and continuation of our national effort to remedy discrimination against racial and ethnic minorities and against women. Although some affirmative action efforts began before the great burst of civil rights statutes in the 1960s, affirmative action efforts didn't really begin until it became clear that antidiscrimination statutes alone wouldn't dislodge long-standing patterns of discrimination.

For example, although most students study how African Americans came to the United States as slaves, not everyone is aware that as late as 1857, the U.S. Supreme Court declared that no black person could claim United States citizenship. Even when the Civil War ended slavery, the government still held African Americans in a different status, finding, for instance, in the Supreme Court decision *Plessy v. Ferguson*, that there could be "separate but equal" facilities for blacks and whites and implicitly sanctioning continued segregation in schools, transportation, the armed services, and public accommodations. Similarly, all women were denied the right to vote until 1920.

For much of the twentieth century, racial and ethnic minorities and women have faced legal and social exclusion. African Americans and Hispanic Americans were segregated into low-wage jobs, usually agricultural. In the early part of this century, Asian Americans were forbidden by law from owning land, while working fields to which they couldn't hold title. In many states, women were barred by law from entering occupations in mining, fire fighting, bartending, law, and medicine.

African Americans and women began to make progress in employment opportunities during the labor shortages of World War II and immediately afterward. Yet racial separation in employment continued, and African Americans were still segregated into low-wage jobs into the 1960s. For Hispanic Americans, employment opportunity remained seriously restricted into the 1970s. Whole industries were, in effect, all white, all male; women and minorities were forbidden to even apply.

In grocery and department stores, clerks were white, and janitors and elevator operators were black. Generations of African Americans swept the floors in factories while being denied the opportunity to become higher-paid machine operators. In businesses such as the canning industry, Asian Americans were not only precluded from becoming managers but were housed in physically segregated living quarters. Stereotypical assumptions that women would be only part-time or temporary workers resulted in their exclusion from many job opportunities. Newspapers' job listings were segregated by gender. Women also faced sexual harassment at work and lost their jobs if they married or became pregnant.

Even college-educated African Americans worked as bellboys, porters, and domestics unless they could manage to get a scarce teaching position in an all-black school. In higher education, most African Americans attended predominately black colleges, many established by states as segregated institutions. Most black colleges concentrated on teacher training to the exclusion of professional education. Students who were interested in business were offered courses in business education rather than business administration. A few black students attended predominately white institutions; by 1954, about 1 percent of first-year students at white colleges and universities were black.

Asian Americans and Hispanic Americans were legally barred from attending some public schools, and women were systematically excluded from some private and state-funded colleges, universities, and professional schools well into the 1970s.

The Civil Rights Movement

Blacks continued to be sent to separate schools, typically with less funding and substandard facilities, until the 1954 U.S. Supreme Court decision *Brown v. Board of Education of Topeka, Kansas*. Even though that decision would theoretically apply to other forms of government services, it wasn't until 1955—when Rosa Parks, a courageous black woman tired from a long day's work, defied the Montgomery Alabama law requiring segregation on city buses and refused to give up her seat to make room for a white man—that the country began to struggle with the real issues behind the laws.

That one act served as a springboard to the civil rights movement of the 1960s, which included a series of nonviolent sit-ins at segregated restaurants, the "Freedom Riders," a group of black and white activists who demonstrated against segregated bus lines, and numerous other marches and protests throughout the southern states and beyond.

For example, James Meredith, who four years earlier had been accompanied by federal marshals when he enrolled as the first black student at the University of Mississippi, set out on a 220-mile "March against Fear." He was shot along the way and recovered in a Memphis hospital while hundreds joined his walk. Stokely Carmichael, the chairman of the Student Nonviolent Coordinating Committee (SNCC), first introduced the nation to the slogan "Black Power." He told his largely black audience that they couldn't count on whites for support but must do it on their own.

As the country continued to erupt in protests and demonstrations, often met with violence by racist southern police officers and others during the early 1960s, Congress finally responded in 1964 and passed the Civil Rights Act. In 1965, Congress passed the Voting Rights Act, which gave blacks their first meaningful access to the ballot in southern states. That same year, President Johnson delivered a historic speech on civil rights at Howard University, called the "black Harvard," declaring: "Freedom is not enough. You do not take a person who, for years, has been hobbled by chains and liberate him, bring him to the starting line of a race, and then say, 'You are free to compete with all others' and still justly believe you have been completely fair" (Lawrence and Matsuda, 1997, p. 132). The speech presented Johnson's view that equalizing the "playing field" isn't enough; special help is also needed.

Fairness

More urban uprisings occurred and escalated in 1968, when Dr. Martin Luther King, Jr.—the leading inspiration for the non-violent civil rights movement—was assassinated in Memphis, Tennessee. Partly as a response to King's death, Congress finally passed the Fair Housing Act in 1968 as an effort to end discrimination in housing.

In the late 1960s and early 1970s, Chicano (Americans of Mexican descent) activists, inspired by the slogans of black power, studied Chicano history and constructed a politics demanding voices and places for Mexican Americans in venues of power, as well as pressuring for larger enrollments in colleges, curricular changes, voter registration drives, and so on.

In 1969, nearly 600 American Indians, representing more than 50 tribes, took up their own cause in the civil rights renaissance. The Native Americans occupied Alcatraz Island in San Francisco Bay and issued a Proclamation to the Great White Father and All His People. They reclaimed the island as a symbol of their claim to all the lands taken from them and set out a plan to develop on it several Indian institutions, including a center for Native American studies, an American Indian spiritual center, an Indian center of ecology, a great Indian training school, and an American Indian museum.

During the 1970s, young Japanese Americans in California started to organize to demand redress for the losses experienced by their parents when they were interned in concentration camps during World War II. They helped organize a movement to insist that the nation apologize and pay reparations.

Similarly, during the 1970s, advocates of women's rights sought passage of the Equal Rights Amendment and repeal of anti-abortion laws, started to raise the issue of sexual harassment in the workplace and schools, and pushed for an end to other forms of discrimination.

Executive Orders:
Contracting and Employment

The longest standing federal affirmative action program has its roots in World War II. An executive order barring discrimination in the federal government and by war industries was issued by President Franklin D. Roosevelt in 1942. The action was taken to forestall a planned march on Washington, D.C., organized by A. Philip Randolph, the president of the Brotherhood of Sleeping Car Porters. Roosevelt's order barred discrimination against blacks by defense contractors and established the first Fair Employment Practices Committee. Federal compliance programs, however, were routinely understaffed, underfunded, and lacking enforcement authority.

After World War II, gains that had been made by women and blacks receded as returning GIs reclaimed their jobs. By 1960, the 10 million workers on the payrolls of the 100 largest defense contractors included few blacks. The $7.5 billion in federal grants-in-aid to the states and cities for highway, airport, school, and public housing construction went almost exclusively to whites. The U.S. Employment Service, which provided funds for state-operated employment bureaus, encouraged skilled blacks to register for unskilled jobs, accepted requests only from white employers, and made no efforts to get employers to accept African American workers. President Dwight D. Eisenhower's Committee on Government Contracts, chaired by Vice-President Richard M. Nixon in 1959, blamed the "indifference of employers to establishing a positive policy of nondiscrimination," stated that such indifference was more prevalent than overt discrimination, and called for remedial steps.

In response to the growing civil rights movement, President Kennedy in 1961 created the Committee on Equal Employment Opportunity and issued Executive Order 10925, which used the term "affirmative action" to refer to measures designed to achieve nondiscrimination.

Soon after his Howard University speech in 1965, President Johnson issued Executive Order 11246, aimed at requiring firms conducting business with the federal government to take affirmative action to attain equal employment opportunity. Firms across the country were to set "good faith goals and timetables" for employing "underutilized" minority group members available and qualified for hire. Federal contractors were to take affirmative action to ensure equality of employment opportunity without regard to race, religion, and national origin. In 1968, gender was added to the protected categories.

During the Johnson administration, the Department of Labor started to make the race of its employees a part of personnel records so that it could begin to evaluate hiring practices, opened the Office of Federal Contract Compliance Programs (OFCCP), and strengthened its affirmative action requirements. Recipients of government contracts in excess of $1 million were required, for the first time, to formulate and present a "written affirmative action compliance program" that would "provide in detail for specific steps to guarantee equal employment opportunity keyed to the problems and needs of minority groups, including, when there are deficiencies, the development of specific goals and timetables." The OFCC began with construction contractors, who as of 1968 were required to set goals and timetables under a regulation issued to implement Johnson's executive order. However, under pressure from unions and the General Accounting Office, which found the process too vague, the OFCC discontinued the effort.

Local governments and private business enthusiastically followed the federal government's lead. For example, in 1967, the City of New York, the Roman Catholic Church in Michigan, and the Texas-based retailer Neiman Marcus announced plans requiring their suppliers and contractors to take affirmative steps toward hiring African Americans.

In 1969, President Nixon appointed George Shultz as Secretary of Labor, and together they pushed through the first official government affirmative action program—the Philadelphia Plan. Shultz made demands on the segregated Philadelphia construction industry and required more minority hiring and even the setting of percentages or goals. In issuing the so-called Philadelphia Order, Assistant Secretary of Labor Arthur Fletcher said:

> Equal employment opportunity in these [construction trades] in the Philadelphia area is still far from a reality. The unions in these trades still have only about 1.6 percent minority group membership and they continue to engage in practices, including the granting of referral priorities to union members and to persons who have work experience under union contract, which result in few Negroes being referred for employment. We find, therefore, that special measures are required to provide equal employment

opportunity in these seven trades. (Lawrence and
Matsuda 1997, 49)

President Nixon later remembered, "A good job is as basic
and important a civil right as a good education. . . . I felt that
the plan Shultz devised, which would require such [affirmative]
action by law, was both necessary and right. We would not impose quotas, but would require federal contractors to show 'affirmative action' to meet the goals of increasing minority employment" (Lawrence and Matsuda 1997, 67). Order No. 4 in
1970 extended the plan to nonconstruction federal contractors.

Fair Employment: Enforcement of Title VII

In July 1963, in the midst of the civil rights campaign in Birmingham, Alabama, President Kennedy appeared on national television to propose a civil rights bill. The measure proposed outlaw-
ing discrimination in public accommodations, permitting a
cut-off of federal funds to discriminating institutions, and expanding the equal employment opportunity committee he had
established.

Following Kennedy's assassination, Title VII was enacted as
part of the Civil Rights Act of 1964, seeking to end discrimination
by large private employers whether or not they had government
contracts. The Equal Employment Opportunity Commission
(EEOC), established by the Civil Rights Act, was charged with
enforcing the antidiscrimination laws through prevention of employment discrimination and the resolution of complaints. The
act was designed to compensate employees for lost wages and
other employment benefits because of illegal discrimination and
to encourage employers to end discrimination. Title VII was substantially strengthened in the 1972 amendments signed by President Nixon. As Supreme Court holdings concluded, the legislative history to the 1972 amendments made clear that Congress
approved of race- and gender-conscious remedies that had been
developed by the courts in enforcing the 1964 act.

Civil rights activists claimed that these judicial and legislative victories were not enough to overcome long-entrenched discrimination. They cited several reasons: first, these measures frequently focused only on issues of formal rights (such as the right
to vote) that were particularly susceptible to judicial or statutory
resolution. In addition, formal litigation-related strategies were
inevitably resource-intensive and often dependent upon clear

"smoking gun" evidence of overt bias or bigotry, whereas prejudice can take on myriad subtle, yet effective, forms. Both private and public institutions often seemed impervious to the winds of change, remaining all white or all male long after court decisions or statutes formally ended discrimination.

As a result, in the 1970s, both the courts and Republican and Democratic administrations as well as some private businesses turned to race- and gender-conscious remedies as a way to end entrenched discrimination. These "affirmative remedies" evolved into what we now call "affirmative action." These remedies were developed after periods of experimentation had shown that other means too often failed to correct the problems. Here are some examples:

- In July 1970, a federal district court enjoined the state of Alabama from continuing to discriminate against blacks in the hiring of state troopers. The court found that "in the thirty-seven year history of the patrol there has never been a black trooper." The order included detailed, nonnumerical provisions for assuring an end to discrimination, such as stringent controls on the civil service certification procedure and an extensive program of recruitment of minority job applicants. Eighteen months later, not a single black had been hired as a state trooper or into a civilian position connected with the troopers. The district court then entered a further order requiring the hiring of one qualified black trooper or support person applicant for each white hired until 25 percent of the force was black. By the time the case reached the Court of Appeals in 1974, 25 black troopers and 80 black support personnel had been hired. The U.S. Supreme Court ultimately affirmed the orders.
- In 1979, women represented only 4 percent of the entry-level officers in the San Francisco police department. By 1985, under an affirmative action plan ordered in a case in which the Department of Justice sued the city for discrimination, the number of women in the entry class had risen to 175, or 14.5 percent.
- Similarly, a federal district court review of the San Francisco Fire Department in 1987 led to a consent decree that increased the number of blacks in officer positions from 7 to 31, Hispanics from 12 to 55, and Asians from 0 to 10; women were admitted as firefighters for the first time.

- In 1975, a federal district court found that Local 28 of the Sheet Metal Workers' International Association had discriminated against nonwhite workers in recruitment, training, and admission to the union. The court found that the union had (1) adopted discriminatory admission criteria, (2) restricted the size of its membership to deny access to minorities, (3) selectively organized shops with few minority workers, and (4) discriminated in favor of white applicants seeking to transfer from sister locals. The court found that the record was replete with instances of bad-faith efforts to prevent or delay the admission of minorities. The court established a 29 percent membership goal, reflecting the percentage of minorities in the relevant labor pool. The Supreme Court affirmed the order.
- Prior to 1974, Kaiser Aluminum hired only persons with prior craft experience as craft workers at its Gramercy, Louisiana, plant. Because blacks traditionally had been excluded from the craft unions, only 5 of 273 skilled craft workers at the plant were black. In response, Kaiser, together with the union, established its own training program to fill craft jobs with the proviso that 50 percent of new trainees were to be black until the percentage of black craft workers in the plant matched the percentage of blacks in the local labor pool. The Supreme Court held this program to be lawful.
- On March 23, 1973, the Nixon administration's Department of Justice, Department of Labor, Equal Employment Opportunity Commission, and Civil Service Commission issued a joint memorandum titled "State and Local Employment Practices Guide." The guide points out that "the Nixon Administration . . . since September of 1969, recognized that goals and timetables . . . are a proper means for helping to implement the nation's commitment to equal employment opportunity." The memorandum stressed that strict quotas are unacceptable but that goals and timetables are entirely different and reasonable tools. (Attorney General John Mitchell led the legal defense of the distinction between goals and quotas.) In July 1986, Supreme Court Justice Sandra Day O'Connor referred to this document, and the merits of fair and effective affirmative action goals, in the concurring portion of her opinion in *Local 28, Sheet Metal*

Workers v. EEOC. In doing so, she joined the Court majority's support for numerical guidelines in affirmative action programs.

Court-ordered affirmative action to remedy violations of Title VII developed on a parallel track with the executive order program as another remedial effort to stop existing discrimination and prevent its recurrence. The Supreme Court's most comprehensive review of affirmative action has occurred in the employment area.

Affirmative Action in Education

Discrimination in education was the target of the original breakthrough civil rights cases. Indeed, because education is the gateway to opportunity, education has consistently been a central focus of civil rights efforts. But for nearly two decades following the original court decisions, educational institutions—particularly colleges and graduate schools—remained predominately white and male. In 1955, only 4.9 percent of college students ages 18–24 were black. This figure rose to 6.5 percent during the next five years but by 1965 had slumped back to 4.9 percent. Only in the wake of affirmative action measures in the late 1960s and early 1970s did the percentage of black college students begin to climb steadily: in 1970, 7.8 percent of college students were black; in 1980, 9.1 percent; and in 1990, 11.3 percent.

In 1967, the Department of Health, Education, and Welfare began requiring colleges and universities receiving federal funds to establish affirmative action goals for hiring female and minority faculty members.

Under President Nixon's tenure, universities also came under affirmative action scrutiny. Columbia University, for example, submitted three different affirmative action plans before obtaining the $13 million in federal funding that had been taken away because of the school's hiring policies regarding women and minorities.

The 1978 *Regents of the University of California v. Allan Bakke* case set the parameters of educational affirmative action. The University of California at Davis Medical School had reserved 16 available places for qualified minorities. In a splintered decision with Justice Lewis Powell casting the deciding vote, the Supreme Court essentially decided that setting aside a specific number of places in the absence of proof of past discrimination was illegal, but that minority status could be used as a factor in admission. The desire to obtain a "diverse" student body was found to be a compelling goal in the educational context in Justice Powell's controlling opinion.

Increased educational opportunity has, in fact, revolutionized education, although some gaps persist. Although the enrollment of women in higher education has risen steadily, with women now earning nearly 50 percent of all bachelor's and master's degrees, they earn only one-third of doctorate and first professional degrees and continue to lag in math, engineering, and the physical sciences at both the undergraduate and the doctoral levels.

Through the availability of student aid programs and aggressive recruitment and retention programs, the college-bound rate for blacks and whites who graduated from high school was about equal by 1977. Since 1977, however, the proportion of black high school graduates age 18 to 24 enrolled in college has not kept pace with that of white students. Although the percentage of black students who have graduated from high school has increased approximately 20 percent in the past 25 years, the portion of black high school student graduates attending college is now 25 percent less than that of white students.

The story is similar for the Hispanic enrollment rate. In 1976, the college-going rate for Hispanics age 16 to 24 who had recently graduated from high school (53 percent) actually exceeded the white rate (29 percent). Since then, the Hispanic college enrollment rate has stagnated while the white rate has increased significantly. By 1994 the white college enrollment rate had risen to 64 percent, whereas the Hispanic rate had fallen to 49 percent.

The 1980s: Backlash against Affirmative Action

Ronald Reagan was elected president in 1984, setting the stage for a counterrevolution of the 1980s. As a conservative Republican candidate and former California governor, Reagan promised to end affirmative action if he was elected. "We must not allow," Reagan declared, "the noble concept of equal opportunity to be distorted into federal guidelines or quotas which require race, ethnicity, or sex—rather than ability and qualifications—to be the principal factor in hiring or education" (Bowen and Bok, 1998, p. 124).

As president, Reagan appointed Supreme Court justices who opposed affirmative action. He also cut the budgets of the Equal Employment Opportunity Commission and the Office of Federal Contract Compliance, limiting their ability to pursue affirmative action and discrimination cases. Many experts now claim that the Reagan administration, in effect, killed the federal policy of affirmative action.

Conversely, by the mid-1980s, so many companies had found affirmative action "good for business" that the National Association of Manufacturers adopted a policy statement supporting affirmative action as "good business policy," and some companies filed amicus briefs and sent telegrams to the White House opposing the Reagan administration's efforts to curtail affirmative action. The chief executive officers (CEOs) of *Time* and Pillsbury publicly stated that they would retain their affirmative action programs even if the government did not require them to do so.

In the 1980s, the Supreme Court continued to issue confusing and sometimes contradictory opinions about affirmative action. In *Local 28, Sheet Metal Workers' International Association v. EEOC*, in 1986, for example, the court approved a court-ordered hiring goal for another union of 29 percent nonwhite members, again based on the share of nonwhites in the local labor pool.

In 1987, the Supreme Court decided in the case of *United States v. Paradise* that the Alabama Department of Public Safety had systematically excluded blacks from employment as state troopers throughout its history, flouting several court orders and failing to keep commitments it repeatedly made in court. The Court approved the quota as meeting the compelling interest test, ruling that the plan was needed to remedy persistent discrimination in hiring and promotion, and that no other remedy would work.

That same year, the Supreme Court ruled in *Johnson v. Transportation Agency of Santa Clara County* that in order to correct "a manifest imbalance in traditionally segregated job categories," a woman was entitled to a job dispatching road crews in California, making it clear that affirmative action plans should take into account the gender of underrepresented workers as well as their race.

Meanwhile, feminist activists pushed for approval of the Equal Rights Amendment as well as for enforcement of laws against sexual harassment.

The 1990s: A New Act, a New President, and New Cases

In 1990 and 1991, civil rights groups regained some of their earlier power and pressured the administration of President George Bush to support additional legislation. In 1990 a new civil rights act was proposed in reaction to several Supreme Court decisions. The Court had begun to show more leniency toward employers; minorities and women who might have won their discrimination cases prior to 1989 increasingly found themselves on the losing side. After much opposition and discussion, Congress finally passed the Civil Rights Act of 1991. Although Bush initially opposed the act, after the turmoil in the country over racial and gender issues sparked by the appointment of Clarence Thomas to the Supreme Court and the sexual harassment accusations against Thomas by Anita Hill, Bush decided that he needed to prove to the American people that he was not racist or sexist. He signed the Civil Rights Act of 1991.

The same year, the Supreme Court decided the important case of *Metro Broadcasting, Inc., v. FCC*, which deals with Federal Communications Commission (FCC) policies established to enhance minority ownership and management of radio and television stations. Writing for the majority of five, Justice William Brennan declared that when the purpose of an affirmative action program is benign, the courts should inspect it less closely. In a compromise, the Court employed the intermediate level of scrutiny they had first proposed in *Bakke*, as opposed to either a strict or deferential measure. In terms of evidence, the Court relied upon a conclusion of the FCC that there was "an empirical nexus" between minority ownership and greater diversity rather than requiring proof of discrimination in every case or accepting a general assertion of a benefit to society. In sustaining the program, the Court found that the program was launched after long study, was aimed directly at well-documented barriers to minority control, and was limited in its extent and duration by the requirement that the program be reassessed before it could be renewed.

In the final debate of the 1992 campaign, Democratic presidential candidate Bill Clinton declared, "I don't think we've got a person to waste. I owe the American people a White House staff, a cabinet, and appointments that look like America, but that meet high standards of excellence, and that's what I'll do" (Lawrence and Matsuda, 1997, p. 176). After his election, Clinton appointed the most diverse cabinet to date—three women, four African Americans, and two Hispanic Americans.

Clinton also appointed a federal commission to study the issue of affirmative action. In 1995 the commission issued what has come to be known as the Glass Ceiling Report, claiming that "White men, while constituting about 43 percent of the workforce, hold about 95 percent of senior management positions." Although the diverse 20-member commission included ten Republicans and ten Democrats in the fields of law and labor, and its chair, Secretary of Labor Robert Reich, hailed the report as a "step toward bipartisanship," the report appeared just in time to have an impact on the 1996 elections, causing affirmative action to emerge as one of the most important "wedge" issues—a controversial issue on which the two parties are separated by their opposing views.

In 1995, the Supreme Court decided on the case of *Adarand Constructors, Inc., v. Pena*, which considered a government program that offered some contractors an incentive to grant subcontracts to small businesses owned by members of underrepresented minority groups. For the first time, the Supreme Court held that all government affirmative action programs—whether federal, state, or local—must meet the most exacting standard of analysis under the U.S. Constitution. The "strict scrutiny" test means that any race-conscious program must "promote a compelling state interest" and be "necessary" or "narrowly tailored" to reach that end. Because the Court expanded the application of that standard in *Adarand,* experts assume that fewer forms of affirmative action will be judged constitutional.

On July 19, 1995, President Clinton, partially in response to *Adarand,* gave a major speech in support of affirmative action. "Mend it, don't end it," the president declared, with an emphasis on reforms implied by the "mend." He also called for a government-wide review of federal programs in light of the rulings, as an extension of an ongoing inquiry about the rights and wrongs of affirmative action.

Clinton's promised government-wide review of federal programs turned out to be a limited effort. When a portion of the report was released in 1996 and roused only passing interest, the administration considered itself victorious. The controversy over affirmative action temporarily died down.

Late the same year, the controversy heated up again when the U.S. Court of Appeals for the Fifth Circuit struck down an affirmative action program at the University of Texas School of Law in *Hopwood v. State of Texas*. The majority opinion held that Justice Powell's holding in *Bakke*—that securing the benefits of a diverse student body was a compelling interest for a public university—was no longer good law. The Supreme Court chose not to review the case.

In response to *Hopwood*, the U.S. Department of Education issued guidelines advising that *Bakke* still holds, but that colleges and universities in the states that make up the Fifth Circuit—Louisiana, Mississippi, and Texas—must follow *Hopwood*. For schools in Louisiana and Mississippi, which operate under desegregation decrees by federal courts that remain good law, *Hopwood* was not strictly binding. For public schools in Texas, however, it was now illegal to consider race as a factor; for private schools the law was unsettled. Since this ruling, Texas political leaders have proposed an alternative plan to address the underrepresentation of women and people of color. The new plan gives entry to Texas universities all students in the top 10 percent of their Texas high school.

Ward Connerly, a conservative black activist and University of California regent appointee of former California governor Pete Wilson, led a drive in the 1996 elections in California to end affirmative action in employment, hiring, and contracting. After much public debate, California voters passed Proposition 209, ending state affirmative action programs. In December 1996, a court in northern California entered a preliminary injunction that barred enforcement of the referendum until the case was tried on its merits. After appeal, a three-judge panel lifted the Proposition 209 injunction and declared the referendum constitutional. The matter may not be decided until—or if—it reaches the Supreme Court (the Court may decide not to hear the issue).

In the same year, as another controversial case headed to the Supreme Court, a coalition of civil rights groups raised money to settle the Piscataway case (*Board of Education of the Township of Piscataway v. Sharon Taxman*), which centered on allegations of a white secondary school teacher that she was laid off because of reverse discrimination. The groups felt that the case would create an unfavorable precedent on the issue of affirmative action.

In early 1998, voters in the city of Houston defeated an antiaffirmative action referendum; in November 1998, voters in the state of Washington passed an antiaffirmative action initiative.

All of these efforts affect state and local affirmative action laws rather than federal laws or orders.

Do We Still Have Prejudice and Discrimination?

In deciding which candidate should be hired, promoted, or paid more, even well-meaning decision makers may believe they are focusing on merit while using biased methods. One researcher who has supported this view is psychologist Faye Crosby, who created fictitious information about male and female managers, all working for the same company. The records contained a mixture of ratings on different areas of efficiency and experience, making sure they equaled out for male and female; the men were given higher salaries by the experiment participants. The complex and interesting experiments produced a predictable result: people see what they want to see. The reviewers participating in the experiment constructed many other reasons for the differences in salary other than discrimination. The majority refused to identify or believe that prejudice was a factor (Bergmann 1996, 73). Other researchers have found that African Americans and women receive worse offers in the marketplace for cars and other high-ticket items, even when they have been trained in and use the same negotiating methods as the white males in the same group.

In addition, evidence of continuing discrimination is offered by many young African Americans who say they still have trouble finding employment, and some statistics support this view. According to the Urban Institute, 53 percent of black men ages 25 to 34 are either unemployed or earn too little to lift a family of four out of poverty (Guernsey 1997, 32).

Some experts, such as Ann Morrison, author of the book *Breaking the Glass Ceiling,* warn that if the government abandons affirmative action, women will also continue to suffer. "[Companies] are going to shove it on the back burner, because it's difficult and it's draining. The progress that has been made is still so fragile" (Guernsey 1997, 39).

Experts rely upon conflicting statistics. In a 1996 special issue of *The New Yorker,* "Black in America," authors Hendrik Hertzberg and Henry Louis Gates, Jr. point to the achievements of many African Americans, including those in artistic and cultural endeavors, and offer an encouraging statistic: "The successes of integration and affirmative action created a substantial black middle class: there are now four times as many black families with incomes above $50,000 a year as there were in 1964" (Hertzberg and Gates 1996, p. 56).

But the authors go on to point out that the same programs that have lifted the income of middle- and upper-income blacks "have contributed to a distillation of ever more concentrated pools of poverty and despair in the inner cities." Other experts counter with the argument that affirmative action programs were never meant to solve all of the problems of race and poverty in this country. Even if such efforts have mostly benefited the middle or upper classes, the proponents suggest, that is no reason to abandon affirmative action; it simply shows that we need additional efforts to address other and deeper issues of poverty and discrimination.

Surveys of popular attitudes reveal additional discouraging results. *USA Weekend* surveyed 250,000 students in grades 6 to 12 from all over the country. When asked if people their age held some racial prejudice, 84 percent of the teenagers answered "yes." When asked if they believed that racial tensions will always exist, 86 percent said "yes." As one 15-year-old African American put it, "I feel accepted by my peers, but some people tell me it's because I 'act white.' What does that mean?" Many black students expressed their opinion that prejudice and discrimination haven't changed in the past 30 years (Guernsey 1997, 56).

Other writers, such as Bob Herbert, a columnist for the *New York Times*, point to a recent report from the Southern Poverty Law Center, an Alabama-based organization that tracks hate crimes and hate groups across the country as evidence of the intractability of prejudice and hate. The report details horrible examples of crimes that occurred in 1998. The writers recount the widely reported death in Jasper, Texas, of James Byrd, Jr., a 49-year-old black man who was chained to a pickup truck and dragged along a country road until his body was literally torn apart. After Byrd's convicted murderer, James King, was sentenced to death, he grinned and uttered a sexual obscenity. In 1997 in downtown Denver—a city where race relations have been less acrimonious—Oumar Dia, an African immigrant, was murdered while waiting for a bus by members of a racist "skinheads" gang.

In addition, the Law Center report told of a dark-haired woman, Amy Robinson, who was abducted in Texas and murdered by two white men who used her for target practice because they wanted to "go out and shoot black folks." She was chosen because the men thought she was biracial; in fact, she was white. In San Diego, California, a black Marine was paralyzed from the neck down after being attacked by a group of whites "armed with brass knuckles and chanting 'white power.'"

Morris Dees, the chief trial counsel of the Southern Poverty Law Center, said he is surprised by what appears to be the increasing frequency and viciousness of such attacks. They are being committed by whites and blacks, he said, fueled by the growing number of organized hate groups and the proliferation of Internet sites devoted to racism, anti-Semitism, homophobia, and other forms of intolerance.

In workplaces, additional debates prevail. For example, affirmative action supporters point out that if white males really are falling victim to reverse discrimination, why is there still double-digit unemployment in the African American community but not in the white community? Why do women continue to be in the minority in senior management, and why do women who make it to the top earn one-third less than male executives with the same job? In light of this evidence of continuing discrimination, supporters claim it is too soon to argue that the country is ready for color-blind and gender-blind social policies.

Economist Barbara Bergmann, for example, rebuts the argument about the sense of grievance white males feel by pointing out that they still enjoy the highly favored position they had in the labor market in 1964, the year employment discrimination by race and sex was made illegal. In 1994, among those working full time, pay for white males was 49 percent higher than pay for other labor force participants. Differences in skill levels account for some, not all, of this pay difference. Segregation on the job by race and sex remains a common pattern. Opening access for all to the highest-paying and most prestigious jobs that are now the preserves of white males would take a far more rigorous application of affirmative action techniques than has yet occurred. It would take the introduction of vigorous affirmative action programs into the many workplaces where they have been absent or ignored, Bergmann asserts (Bergmann 1996, 27).

Supporters of affirmative action also argue that the policy has become essential to our future since it is projected that, by the year 2000, two out of three new workers will be either women or members of minority groups. Some educators also argue that they need to prepare students for work in a multicultural world and that the best way to do so is to include a representative number of minorities and women in faculty, staff, and students. Additionally, as the population of people of color in the United States increases, supporters believe affirmative action ensures that traditionally underserved communities receive equal access to jobs, education, and business contracts.

Even some who oppose affirmative action see reasons to support programs that enhance diversity. They want schools and work to reflect the diversity among American citizens, but they believe affirmative action laws or policies are unnecessary. Business leaders are realizing that the workers and consumers of American products and markets abroad are increasingly nonwhite. For example, Robert M. Teeter, a Republican pollster who is a member of the board of United Parcel Service, suggested that "Diversity isn't a slogan—it's a reality when you're hiring people everywhere. . . . You could abolish affirmative action tomorrow and not much would change." The CEOs of major companies in a poll conducted by *Fortune* magazine agreed: 96 percent insist that their companies would not change their affirmative action efforts even if all federal enforcement were abolished (Guernsey 1997, 23).

Are There Other Remedies?

Critics of affirmative action say there are other remedies that will help address the issues without creating new problems. They suggest, for example, that we should simply better enforce the current civil rights laws. Proponents respond that we need to do that also, but that the expense and time necessary to spur agency enforcement of those laws is not possible in the current political climate, particularly when many antiaffirmative action activists had supported past funding costs of enforcement agencies.

Similarly, a popularly suggested alternative is to select people based upon class, rather than race, gender, or ethnicity. Proponents of this solution suggest that it is fundamentally unfair to grant a preference to a woman or a person of color if they have never suffered any economic discrimination or hardship. Opponents of this proposal counter by stating that low-income whites have not and do not suffer from racial prejudice.

Authors William Bowen and Derek Bok point to the surprise of one strong supporter of Proposition 209—John Yoo, an acting professor at Boalt Hall, the Berkeley law school. He has been quoted as saying, "I had never looked to see what the effect of 209 would be on admissions. I didn't realize the score gaps were so huge." Other, less direct, effects also surprised Yoo:

What I didn't realize was how entrenched the desire
to have racial diversity for its own sake was in the university system, and how much pressure was going to
be asserted to preserve that goal. . . . I didn't realize
until Proposition 209 went into effect that affirmative
action, as it was applied by the schools, allowed you
to have some racial diversity and at the same time to
maintain intellectual standards for the majority of
your institutions. It was a form of limiting the dam-
age. Now that you have to have race-neutral methods,
if you still want to get African-Americans and Hispanics in, you have to redefine the central mission of
the research university in a way that lowers standards
for everybody. That's an unintended consequence of
Proposition 209, and it's unfortunate. (Bowen and Bok
1998, 228)

Similar situations have been advanced by three University
of Texas law professors in a brief filed in the *Piscataway* case in
which they argued that the Court should preserve affirmative action because "If affirmative action is ended, inevitable political,
economic, and legal forces will pressure the great public universities to lower admission standards as far as necessary to avoid
resegregation" (Bowen and Bok 1997, p. 228).

Does Affirmative Action Harm Its Intended Beneficiaries?

One of the more interesting and recently popular arguments
about affirmative action has been put forth by critics who claim
that the intended beneficiaries are hurt by being placed into education or workplace situations where they are doomed to fail
or are labeled as affirmative action candidates. In his highly personal book *Confessions of an Affirmative Action Baby*, Stephen
Carter honestly examines his own anger when he learned that
Harvard offered him a law school slot—after initially rejecting
him—only after the school learned that he was an African
American.

Opponents argue that the policy undermines respect for its
intended beneficiaries because they may be stigmatized by the
common assumption that they did not make it on their own, and

Carter—who admits his own ambivalence in his book—suggests that he is forced to live in a world where people assume that he received his positions because of his race.

Others, most notably William Bowen and Derek Bok (former university presidents at Princeton and Harvard, respectively) in their 1998 book *The Shape of the River,* have examined the long-term effect of affirmative action admissions on prestigious colleges and found that by measures of career success, community involvement, and personal satisfaction, the intended beneficiaries gained rather than lost, as did the broader community, because of their admissions to these universities.

Shelby Steele, a conservative African American author, has argued that the program's very existence encourages blacks to believe whites have victimized them and has led to an increase in black anti-Semitism. Yet proponents, such as economist Bergmann, point out that blacks did not need affirmative action to convince them that they were oppressed, having taken part in the civil rights movements of the 1950s and 1960s.

Some critics of affirmative action respond by pointing to the University of California at Berkeley, often touted as a model of affirmative action because it has long recruited a higher percentage of diverse students than most other prestigious colleges. According to author Dinesh D'Souza, a former editor of the conservative *Dartmouth Review* newspaper, the results have been a failure. He claims that only 22 percent of Hispanics and 18 percent of blacks admitted through affirmative action programs graduated in 1987. For those black and Hispanic students not admitted through affirmative action programs, however, he claims the graduation rate was 42 percent and 55 percent respectively (D'Souza 1991, 253).

Writer Viet D. Dinh also opposes affirmative action and claims that the push to admit other minorities has closed many doors for Asian American students and created serious tension among the races at Berkeley. He cites vandalism of the African Student Center and graffiti on bathroom walls saying "Nip go home" as evidence of this tension. He decries limiting Asians in affirmative action programs: "Asian Americans have as valid a claim of racial victimization as other minorities. Just as Africans were brought to America as slaves, Chinese were dragged here as indentured laborers." He also points out that they were forced to work in inhuman conditions to build the railroads and were interred during World War II (Guernsey 1997, 59).

Chang Lin Tien, the former chancellor of the University of California at Berkeley, disagrees with Dinh's statements about the school. First, he argues, the academic quality at Berkeley has not declined as the student population has diversified. "Of the freshmen admitted to our campus," he writes, "95 percent continue to rank among the top 12.5 percent of the statewide high school graduates. More important . . . our academic standards are higher than ever, and each entering class is more talented than the last" (Guernsey 1997, p. 60).

He also debunks the myth that a diverse student body doesn't succeed, arguing that the percentage of those who graduated within five years leaped from only 50 percent during the 1940s and 1950s (when the overwhelming majority of students were white) to 60 percent in the 1970s and to 70 percent in the late 1980s and 1990s. Moreover, the "graduation rate for all ethnic groups has improved significantly" (Guernsey 1997, 60).

Conclusion

As the reader may see, there are no easy answers to the question of affirmative action. Almost everyone would agree that in a perfect world, race would be irrelevant. As authors Bowen and Bok quote a black friend, "Our ultimate objective should be a situation in which every individual, from every background, feels unselfconsciously included" (Bowen and Bok 1998, 289).

Although proponents of affirmative action frequently cite Supreme Court Justice Harry Blackmun's proposition that "To get beyond racism, we must first take account of race," they would still be glad to embrace a time when that is not necessary. Yet they caution that trying to arbitrarily limit mandated solutions to the issue fails to address how deep and divisive the issues of race are in America.

Part of the problem in resolving the issue is that so much of the current debate relies on anecdotes, biases, and assumptions about "facts" or on unapologetic opinions or politics. It is easy, too, for those who have benefited from affirmative action to be offended by what they may regard as unjustified assaults on their competence or character. Some of the critics of affirmative action also feel defensive, sensing that they are unjustly dismissed as racist, sexist, or heartless. This book, then, serves as a chance for the reader to step back from the uninformed rhetoric and think carefully about the record, the facts, and the history behind the debate. It is hoped that you may make an educated and enlightened decision about your own stance on the issue of affirmative action.

References

Bergmann, Barbara R. 1996. *In Defense of Affirmative Action.* New York: Basic Books.

Bernhardt, David S. 1993 "Affirmative Action in Employment: Considering Group Interests while Protecting Individual Rights." *Stetson Law Review* 23, 11: 34.

Bowen, William G., and Derek Bok. 1998. *The Shape of the River: Long-term Consequences of Considering Race in College and University Admissions.* Princeton, N.J.: Princeton University Press.

D'Souza, Dinesh. 1991. *Illiberal Education: The Politics of Race and Sex on Campus.* New York: Free Press.

Eastland, Terry. 1997. "Support Is Fading for Racial, Gender, Ethnic Preferences." *San Diego Union-Tribune*, 7 July, p. 2, col. 1.

Guernsey, Joann Bren. 1997. *Affirmative Action: A Problem or a Remedy?* Minneapolis: Lerner Publications Company.

Guinier, Lani, and Susan Sturm. 1996. "The Future of Affirmative Action: Reclaiming the Innovative Ideal." *California Law Review* 84: 953.

Hertzberg, Hendrix, and Henry Louis Gates Jr. 1996. "Black in America." *New Yorker* (July).

Jones, James E. 1985. "The Genesis and Present Status of Affirmative Action in Employment: Economic, Legal and Political Realities." *Iowa Law Review* 70: 901–903.

Lawrence, Charles R. III, and Mari J. Matsuda. 1997. "We Won't Go Back: Making the Case for Affirmative Action." New York: Houghton-Mifflin Company.

Schuldinger, Henry. 1996. "Still Searching for the Limits of the Permissible Use of Affirmative Action: *United States v. Board of Education of the Township of Piscataway.*" *George Mason University Civil Rights Law Journal* 6, 97, p. 133.

Save the Dream MARCH
Selma 1965 - Sacramento
OCTOBER 27, 1997

Chronology 2

As outlined in other sections of this book, confusion over the definition of affirmative action has clouded the debate. In addition, a few important cases and legislative developments have substantially changed the legal complexion of affirmative action, often wiping out all of the decisions and developments that came before. Keep in mind that some information presented in the following chronology may be affected or become irrelevant due to such changes.

Pre–Twentieth Century

Thomas Jefferson inadvertently starts the debate on affirmative action by declaring in the Declaration of Independence that "We hold these truths to be self-evident . . . that all men are created equal, that they are endowed by their Creator with certain unalienable rights, that among these are Life, Liberty, and the pursuit of Happiness." Ironically, Jefferson himself owns African American slaves. During the course of the debate on slavery, discrimination, and affirmative action, most Americans have agreed with

Jefferson's statement as an ideal. Putting the ideal into practice has turned out to be much more difficult, however.

In 1857, for example, the Supreme Court declares that no black person can claim U.S. citizenship. The decision also holds that Congress cannot prohibit slavery in U.S. territories.

When the Civil War ends and slavery is abolished, the government still keeps most African Americans in a different status. In 1896, for instance, the Supreme Court decision *Plessy v. Ferguson* calls for "separate but equal" facilities, and this leads to countless forms of segregation sanctioned by the government, including schools, transportation, the armed services, and public accommodations.

Similarly, women are denied the right to vote and, in many states, the right to own property, until 1920.

Twentieth Century

1920   The suffragist movement (supporters of a woman's right to vote) wins passage of the Nineteenth Amendment to the U.S. Constitution.

1954   The Supreme Court decides the case of *Brown v. Board of Education of Topeka, Kansas,* making it illegal to require racial segregation in any school or government-run facility, such as public beaches and city buses.

1955   Rosa Parks, a 43-year-old African American woman, defies Montgomery, Alabama, law requiring segregation on city buses and refuses to move from her seat to make room for a white man.

Early   Inspired by the black civil rights movement, Chicano
1960s   activists push for an increased Mexican American voice in government and business and demand larger enrollments in colleges as well as the inclusion of Chicano studies programs.

1960   Four freshmen at A & T College—an African American school in Greensboro, North Carolina—take seats at a Woolworth lunch counter restricted to whites. When denied service, they refuse to leave—beginning the sit-in movement, which within a matter of weeks spreads to fifteen cities in five southern states. By the end of the year, tens of thousands of young people have participated in demonstrations and over 3,600 are jailed. These "new abolitionists" see agitation and disruption as the essence of democracy.

In the South, the "Freedom Riders" demonstrate against segregated facilities on interstate bus lines. They are attacked by mobs with iron bars and jailed. Meanwhile, throughout the South, the Student Nonviolent Coordinating Committee (SNCC) and the Southern Christian Leadership Conference are organizing local black people to register to vote and protest against racism; these protests are also met with mobs, violence, and jail. In the space of only three months during 1963, the Department of Justice records 1,412 civil rights demonstrations.

1961   President John F. Kennedy is probably the first person to use the term "affirmative action" and link the term to civil rights shortly after he takes office. By signing Executive Order 10925, he establishes the Equal Employment Opportunity Commission (EEOC) and declares that people in the construction industry have certain obligations when doing business with the government. The order states, in part: "The contractor will take affirmative action to ensure that applicants are employed, and employees are treated during their employment, without regard to their race, creed, color, or national origin." The language is broad in its scope and offers no detailed definition of affirmative action.

1964   The militant, nonviolent protest movement turns north, erupting in demonstrations in Cleveland, New York, Chicago, Philadelphia, and Jersey City. In Los Angeles, the black community of Watts erupts in the most violent urban outbreak since World War II.

In response to the massive rebellion and consciousness-raising within the black community, Congress finally responds. In July, Congress considers signing into legislation the Civil Rights Act, originally proposed by President Kennedy before his death. The act would outlaw

1964
cont.

discrimination in employment and create the Equal Employment Opportunity Commission. As originally introduced, the bill prohibits discrimination based upon race, color, religion, or national origin. A group of southern senators desiring to kill the bill attaches an amendment barring discrimination based upon gender, assuming that adding sexual equality is so radical that the amendment will scuttle the bill. Although the idea of prohibiting sex-based discrimination engenders mirth on the floor of Congress and in the editorial pages of major newspapers, the Johnson administration pushes the bill through, and the virtually all-male Congress passes it into law. As with Executive Order 10925, the act does not address affirmative action and, in fact, declares that no part of it is designed "to grant preferential treatment to any group because of race, color, religion, sex, or national origin."

1965

Congress passes the Voting Rights Act that gives southern blacks their first meaningful access to the ballot. In June, President Lyndon B. Johnson delivers a historic speech at Howard University commencement, entitled "To Fulfill These Rights." After praising Americans for passing legislation to eliminate racial barriers, Johnson emphasizes that equalizing the "playing field" isn't enough; special help is also needed.

In September, Johnson issues Executive Order 11246, regarded as the originating document of federal affirmative action, aimed at requiring firms conducting business with the federal government to take affirmative action to attain equal employment opportunity.

1966

The Department of Labor begins to include employees' race in their personnel records in an attempt to begin to evaluate hiring practices. The department also creates the Office of Federal Contract Compliance (OFCC) and begins to tighten its affirmative action requirements. Contractors engaged in government work are required to present a "written affirmative action compliance program" that details steps guaranteeing equal employment opportunity for minorities, including the development of specific goals and timetables.

1967   The City of New York, the Roman Catholic Church in Michigan, and the Texas-based retailer Neiman Marcus announce plans requiring their suppliers and contractors to take affirmative steps toward hiring African Americans.

James Meredith, who four years earlier had been accompanied by federal marshals when he enrolled as the first black at the University of Mississippi, sets out on a 220-mile "March against Fear." Shot along the way, he recovers in a Memphis hospital while hundreds join his walk. On June 16, Stokely Carmichael, the chairman of the SNCC, introduces the nation to the slogan "Black Power," pushing for blacks to advance their civil rights agenda without the help of whites.

1968   The Department of Health, Education, and Welfare begins requiring colleges and universities receiving federal funds to establish affirmative action goals for hiring female and minority faculty members.

More urban uprisings occur, escalating when civil rights leader Martin Luther King, Jr. is assassinated.

The Fair Housing Act is passed in an effort to end discrimination in housing.

The Kerner Commission report argues that the United States is moving toward two separate and unequal societies of black and white and puts the burden of that conclusion on white racism, recommending a massive redistribution of wealth.

1969   The first official government affirmative action program—the Philadelphia Plan—is devised by President Richard M. Nixon and newly appointed Secretary of Labor George Shultz. Shultz makes demands on the segregated Philadelphia construction industry, requiring more minority hiring and even setting percentages and goals.

In February, the Labor Department, with Shultz at the helm, issues a new set of affirmative action plans.

1969 *cont.*	Order No. 4 takes aim at large government contractors and speaks in terms of requiring proportionate representation of minorities among their employees.

Early
1070s
Having found that affirmative action can help raise profits, companies such as Dow Chemical make voluntary efforts to diversify their workforce.

1970
American Indians from more than 50 tribes occupy Alcatraz Island in San Francisco Bay and issue a proclamation reclaiming the island as a symbol of their claim to all the lands taken from them. Although their plan to develop on it several Indian institutions never sees fruition, their cause achieves unprecedented coverage of and support for Native American civil rights.

1971
In March, the Supreme Court rules in *Greggs v. Duke Power Company* that requiring an applicant to have a high school diploma or pass an intelligence test to work creates "built-in headwinds" against minorities, making the requirements illegal under Title VII of the 1964 Civil Rights Act.

In December, the Labor Department makes permanent a Revised Order No. 4 that specifically includes women in the "affected class" it was designed to protect.

Universities also come under affirmative action scrutiny. Columbia University, for example, submits three different affirmative action plans before obtaining the $13 million in federal funding that had been taken away because of the school's hiring policies regarding women and minorities.

1973
The Equal Employment Opportunity Commission takes the position that all employers within its jurisdiction—not just those receiving federal funds—must institute result-oriented affirmative action programs.

Mid-
1970s
Young Japanese Americans in California organize to demand redress for the losses experienced by their parents when they were interned in concentration camps during World War II. They help organize a movement

to demand that the nation apologize and pay reparations. They also call for Asian studies programs in colleges and universities.

1975   At the University of California at Berkeley, the faculty of the law school votes to eliminate Japanese and Chinese Americans from the minority admissions program, arguing that a sufficient number of Asian Americans are being admitted through the regular admissions process. This move starts a national trend toward excluding Asian Americans from affirmative action programs.

1978   The Supreme Court decides *Regents of the University of California v. Bakke*. Allan Bakke, a white medical school applicant, charged that he had been discriminated against by the University of California's admission program since several students had been admitted under a social program for members of minority groups. Bakke had been rejected even though his test scores were higher.

In a two-part, complex decision (5 to 4) the Court sides with Bakke, yet goes on to state that schools can consider race or ethnic background as one factor among others. The confusing decision is widely interpreted as a compromise that doesn't help schools determine how to achieve a desired racial mix of students without imposing racial quotas. The Court in *Bakke* tries to distinguish between a goal and a quota, between a voluntary plan and a required plan, and between what the Civil Rights Act allows and what it prohibits.

1979   *United Steelworkers of America v. Weber* is decided by the Supreme Court. The case approves a voluntary plan adopted by a union and aluminum manufacturer that calls for half of the openings in training programs to be reserved for blacks until such time as the share of black craft workers approximates that of blacks in the local labor force.

1984–   President Ronald Reagan severely undercuts the work
1989   of previous administrations to develop and strengthen

1984–
1989
cont.

affirmative action: he appoints two Supreme Court justices who are known to oppose affirmative action, and he cuts the budgets of the EEOC and the OFCC, seriously limiting their ability to pursue affirmative action cases.

Despite Reagan's efforts to kill the federal policy of affirmative action, by the mid-1980s many companies have found affirmative action to be a good business policy, and top executives state that they will retain their affirmative action programs even if the government does not require them to do so.

1986

The Supreme Court decides on *Local 28, Sheet Metal Workers' International Association v. EEOC,* approving a court-ordered hiring goal for another union of 29 percent nonwhite members, again based on the share of nonwhites in the local labor pool.

1987

The Supreme Court decides in *United States v. Paradise* that a quota for black Alabama state troopers is needed to remedy persistent discrimination in hiring and promotion within the Alabama Department of Public Safety.

On March 25, the Supreme Court rules in *Johnson v. Transportation Agency of Santa Clara County* that in order to correct an imbalance in traditionally segregated jobs, the plaintiff, a woman, is entitled to a job dispatching road crews in California. The Court's decision underscores that the sex of underrepresented workers should also be taken into account in affirmative action plans.

1990–
1991

In 1990, a new civil rights act is proposed in reaction to several Supreme Court decisions favoring employers. After initial opposition by President George Bush, the Civil Rights Act of 1991 is passed.

1991

The Supreme Court decides in *Metro Broadcasting, Inc., v. FCC* that when the purpose of an affirmative action program is benign, the courts should inspect it less closely. The Court employs the intermediate level of scrutiny it had first proposed in *Bakke,* as opposed to either a strict or deferential measure.

1992 In the final debate of the 1992 presidential campaign, Democratic candidate Bill Clinton declares that he owes the nation "a White House staff, a cabinet, and appointments that look like America but that meet high standards of excellence." After his election, Clinton appoints three women, four African Americans, and two Hispanic Americans to his cabinet.

1995 A federal commission issues the 1995 Glass Ceiling Report claiming that white men still far outnumber minorities and women in senior management positions.

    The Supreme Court decides in *Adarand Constructors, Inc., v. Pena* that all government affirmative action programs—whether federal, state, or local—must meet the most exacting standard of analysis under the U.S. Constitution and that any race-conscious program must "promote a compelling state interest" and be "necessary" or "narrowly tailored" to reach that end.

    On July 19, President Clinton, partially in response to *Adarand,* gives a major speech in support of affirmative action. "Mend it, don't end it," he urges. He also calls for a government-wide review of federal programs in light of the Court's ruling.

1996 Clinton's promised review of federal programs turns out to be a limited effort. A portion of the report is released and garners only passing interest.

    The U.S. Court of Appeals for the Fifth Circuit strikes down an affirmative action program at the University of Texas School of Law. The majority opinion rules that an earlier ruling—that securing the benefits of a diverse student body is a compelling interest for a public university—is no longer good law. The Supreme Court chooses not to review the case. The U.S. Department of Education advises colleges and universities in the states that make up the Fifth Circuit—Louisiana, Mississippi, and Texas—that they must follow the new ruling. For schools in Louisiana and Mississippi that operate under desegregation decrees by federal courts that remain good law, the recent holding is not strictly

1996
cont.
binding. For public schools in Texas, however, it is now illegal to consider race as a factor; for private schools the law is unsettled.

California passes Proposition 209, which limits affirmative action in California. In December 1996, a court in northern California enters a preliminary injunction that bars enforcement of the referendum until the case is tried on the merits.

1997
A three-judge panel lifts the Proposition 209 injunction and declares that the referendum is constitutional. The matter may not be decided until (if?) it reaches the Supreme Court.

1998
A coalition of civil rights groups antes up enough money to settle *Board of Education of the Township of Piscataway v. Sharon Taxman* out of court. The case centered on allegations by a white secondary school teacher that she was laid off because of reverse discrimination. The groups feel the case would create unfavorable precedent on the issue of affirmative action.

1999
The Center for Individual Rights (CIR), a Washington, D.C., public interest law firm, files lawsuits against the law schools of the University of Michigan and the University of Washington, challenging their affirmative action in their admissions programs.

ave the Dream MARCH
Selma 1965 ~ Sacramento
OCTOBER 27, 1997

Biographical Sketches 3

To list all of the people who have contributed to the debate on the issue of affirmative action would be impossible because so many people have written just a few important articles or given several speeches on the issue rather than making the subject of affirmative action the focus of their careers. This is particularly true of those who criticize the idea of making affirmative action a legally actionable wrong. It has been difficult to identify representatives on both sides of the issue as there is currently no organized opposition to either the legal or social movements to eliminate affirmative action. Therefore, because an attempt is made in this book to present all points of view, some critics of affirmative action laws and policies may be featured more prominently in these biographies than might appear warranted by their involvement in the issue. Conversely, some proponents of the movement to make affirmative action illegal have necessarily been omitted. The list is not meant to be comprehensive but rather represents a sample of persons related to the issue. The list profiles some of the important writers, researchers, attorneys, politicians, lawsuit plaintiffs, political activists, and others who have figured in the issue of affirmative action.

Judith C. Appelbaum (1952–)

Judith Appelbaum is currently the vice president and director of employment opportunities at the National Women's Law Center (NWLC), a nonprofit organization dedicated to advancing and protecting women's legal rights. The center focuses on major policy areas that are of importance to women and their families, including employment, family economic security, education, health, and reproductive rights. Particular emphasis is given to the concerns of low-income women. Appelbaum's energies are primarily directed toward participating in litigation, advocacy, and public education activities, with a strong focus on employment-related issues such as sex discrimination in the workplace, affirmative action, and child care policy.

She joined the NWLC in 1995 after serving as counsel to Senator Edward M. Kennedy on the Senate Judiciary Committee staff and acting as his chief advisor on women's rights issues. In that capacity, she assisted with Supreme Court confirmation proceedings and was ultimately responsible for drafting and moving to enactment several major pieces of legislation involving sex discrimination, domestic violence, and women's health and reproductive rights.

Appelbaum is a frequent speaker and writer on the issue of affirmative action on behalf of the NWLC as well as for Americans for a Fair Chance. The latter is a consortium of six civil rights legal groups, including the National Women's Law Center, that have joined forces in a nationwide effort to educate the public about how affirmative action benefits women and minorities.

Previously, Appelbaum served as attorney-advisor to the chairman of the Federal Trade Commission and was in private practice in Washington, D.C. She received her law degree from Stanford University in 1977 and her undergraduate degree from the University of Pennsylvania in 1974.

Barbara Bergmann (1927–)

Barbara Bergmann began a long and distinguished career as an economist and a feminist even before she received her Ph.D. from Harvard University in 1959. Throughout her storied career, Bergmann has studied and written about economics and social policy, particularly as it relates to women, families, and African Americans. From 1949 to 1953, Bergmann served as an economist with the Bureau of Labor Statistics. She later was a senior staff member of the President's Council of Economic Advisors during the Kennedy administration. She has held numerous prestigious positions including that of senior staff member at The Brookings Institute, senior economic advisor with the U.S. Department of State, and professor emerita at the University of Maryland and American University.

Renowned within government, public policy, and academic arenas, Bergmann gained public acclaim with her 1996 book, *In Defense of Affirmative Action.* Bergmann methodically counterattacks affirmative action to make a compelling case in favor of its continued use. Bergmann's book focuses on discrimination in the workplace rather than in university admissions and contract awards. She examines the implementation of affirmative action in 50 large corporations and makes the case that when systematically applied, affirmative action creates economic gains and justice. She challenges critics who claim that rigid enforcement of antidiscrimination laws or affirmative action based on economic disadvantage rather than race or gender can remedy the ills that affirmative action is designed to correct.

Bergmann concedes that affirmative action brings quota problems as well as problems specific to white males. However, she contends that allowing racial and sexual discrimination to go unchecked is a far worse problem. Bergmann writes in *In Defense of Affirmative Action* that "Just as all potent medicines have side effects, affirmative action may well have some results that are bad. . . . To fight a war, you generally have to suffer some casualties." She believes that improving the status of women and minorities yields far greater dividends by reducing poverty and improving race relations.

In addition to *In Defense of Affirmative Action,* Bergmann has written extensively on the issues of economics, comparable worth, child care, unemployment, race and gender inequities, and the economic value of housework. In 1986 she authored *The Economic Emergence of Women,* and a decade later she wrote *Saving Our Children from Poverty: What the United States Can Learn from France.* She is currently president-elect of the International Association for Feminist Economics.

Clint Bolick (1958–)

A relative newcomer to the affirmative action debate, Clint Bolick has arrived with enough panache and preparation to create history in this debate. Bolick is a devout libertarian fervent in his opposition to affirmative action. He is a former Reagan administration Justice Department official best known for his assault on affirmative action. He was instrumental in torpedoing Lani Guinier's nomination to the top civil rights post in the Justice Department in 1993.

In his book *The Affirmative Action Fraud: Can We Restore the American Civil Rights Vision?* (1996), Bolick contends that affirmative action has deteriorated into a system of racial and gender preferences that has given way to quotas causing increasing racial strife and undermining the country's commitment to individual rights. Bolick believes that focusing on group rights, instead of individual empowerment, derailed the civil rights movement. *The Affirmative Action Fraud* outlines a civil rights vision based on the removal of barriers to opportunity that impede individuals from controlling their own destinies. According to Bolick, the two cornerstones of individual empowerment are economic liberty and school choice. He argues that making quality education available to low-income citizens through school vouchers and reducing economic regulations will produce the results that affirmative action cannot.

Bolick received his law degree from the University of California at Davis in 1982 and his undergraduate degree from Drew University in 1979. He currently is vice president and director of litigation at the Institute for Justice, which he cofounded in 1991. The institute engages in constitutional litigation to protect individual liberty and teaches public interest litigation skills to lawyers, law students, and policy activists. Bolick is widely considered the architect of legal strategies for defending school voucher programs and a national expert in that arena. He also wrote the book *Grassroots Tyranny: The Limits of Federalism* (1993).

Ellen Bravo (1944–)

Ellen Bravo credits personal observation and extensive research as the catalysts for her own involvement with affirmative action. Bravo is the codirector of 9to5, National Association of Working Women, which is a national grassroots membership group committed to strengthening women's economic status and eliminating all forms of discrimination. Bravo says that 9to5 chapters and activists across the country have made a priority of opposing all attacks on affirmative action and working instead to strengthen it.

Bravo's organization successfully fought efforts to repeal affirmative action in Colorado in 1996 and in Georgia in 1998. In both cases 9to5 worked with its local chapters to rally like-minded volunteers and similar organizations to speak at committee hearings, press conferences, and television interviews. They flooded the phone lines to key legislators to voice opposition. In Colorado, the opposition was quelled without ever having raised enough signatures to get the issue on the ballot; in Georgia 9to5 celebrated a very narrow victory.

9to5's hallmark is its ability to leverage its grassroots network to make noise on a national level. Its members are dedicated to dispelling what they call "the myths about affirmative action." Bravo says that affirmative action is as essential today as it ever was. The assumption that women and people of color have equal access and opportunity is simply not true. The group cites substantially higher rates of unemployment among African Americans and the gender gap in pay equity as prime examples of the need for affirmative action. Bravo, who has worked with 9to5 since 1982, is a long-time ardent supporter of affirmative action.

Bravo holds a B.A. from Cornell University and a master's degree from Cambridge University. In addition to her work with 9to5, she has taught courses on women's studies and women and work, and she has been an activist and writer.

Stephen L. Carter (1954–)

Stephen L. Carter launched himself squarely in the middle of the affirmative action debate with the publication of his 1991 book, *Reflections of an Affirmative Action Baby*. As a beneficiary of affirmative action, he shares his ambivalence about the merits of the program. After graduating with honors from Stanford University in 1976, he applied to a half-dozen law schools. Every one accepted him, save Harvard University. Shortly after receiving the Harvard rejection letter, Carter received a phone call from Harvard offering him admission. Carter says in his book, "I was told by one official that the school had initially rejected me because 'we assumed from your record that you were white.'" Carter was deeply insulted by his interaction with Harvard.

Ultimately, Carter rejected Harvard's offer and chose to attend Yale, although he acknowledges that his race probably influenced his acceptance there. He wrote about it, saying, "I may embrace this truth as a matter of simple justice or rail against it as one of life's great evils, but being a member of the affirmative action generation means that the one thing I cannot do is deny it." When Carter later became one of Yale's youngest tenured professors in the school's history, he was offended when campus newspapers reported that he was the first black law professor at the university. In *Reflections of an Affirmative Action Baby*, he wrote, "I felt oppressed by this vision of tenure as an extension of affirmative action."

Carter found that affirmative action resulted in the emergence of racial-preference programs that caused him not to be judged on his merits but to be viewed as "the best black." He explains that affirmative action is "not merely something manufactured by racists to denigrate the abilities of professionals who are not white. On the contrary, the durable and demeaning stereotype of black people as unable to compete with white ones is reinforced by advocates of certain forms of affirmative action."

Carter also argues vehemently that affirmative action has helped only middle-class blacks instead of the poor. Carter would like to see affirmative action eliminated or radically overhauled to assist genuinely disadvantaged individuals garner the opportunity to access the educational system. In his view, the playing field needs to be leveled without preferential treatment that is insulting. He also objects to the fact that affirmative action looks at blacks as a group instead of as individuals. This creates pressure on blacks to have a unified perspective, hindering the dialogue between blacks because there is no room for dissension.

Carter has written three other books that examine a variety of cultural issues. In *The Culture of Disbelief: How American Law and Politics Trivialize Religious Devotion* (1993), Carter looks at the separation of church and state. He contends that faith should be part of public life and that God should not be considered a hobby. He went on to write about the flaws in the federal appointment process in *The Confirmation Mess: Cleaning Up the Federal Appointments Process* (1994). In 1996 he penned the first volume of a trilogy when he wrote *Integrity*. In it, Carter takes a provocative look at the erosion of integrity in American culture and exhorts the nation to reclaim this elemental trait.

Linda Chavez (1947–)

Linda Chavez is the founder and president of the conservative think tank and public policy research group Center for Equal Opportunity in Washington, D.C. She has spent most of her professional career immersed in the civil rights milieu. After obtaining a B.A. from the University of Colorado in 1970, she did graduate work in education at the University of California at Los Angeles.

Chavez then moved to Washington, D.C., and worked on Capitol Hill as a lobbyist for the National Education Association during 1974 and 1975. While the editor for the *American Federation of Teachers Journal* from 1977 to 1983, Chavez developed a passionate interest in the issue of bilingual education.

Chavez has long voiced opposition to bilingual education. She has testified before congressional subcommittees, lobbied extensively, and has been a prolific writer on the issue. She staunchly believes that bilingual education unnecessarily delays English acquisition and violates the civil rights of Hispanic students by segregating them to provide instruction. She contends that children of Latin American national origin are treated differently from non-Hispanics because, based on national origin, they get placed in Limited English Proficiency (LEP) programs when similarly situated non-Hispanics are not. Furthermore, she says that based on Spanish surnames, Hispanic children are more likely to be taken out of mainstream classes than non-Hispanics.

Her own experience with bilingual education has provided Chavez with personal evidence against it. She received a letter from her son's school that he was going to be placed in a bilingual program. However, Chavez couldn't read the letter because it was written in Spanish, which she neither speaks nor reads, and, moreover, her son knows only one language—English. He was selected for the program purely on the basis of his name. Chavez quickly rectified the situation, but it fueled her drive to abolish bilingual education in favor of alternative programs such as structured English immersion.

Chavez has never shied away from controversy. She was the director of the U.S. Commission on Civil Rights from 1983 to 1985 under President Reagan's administration. While there, she ignited turbulence by urging the removal of racial hiring quotas and other civil rights measures. She has long criticized race-based government programs. She believes that affirmative action strayed from its original mission and instead gives outright preferences based on race and gender. Chavez believes that a color-blind society is only possible if affirmative action is abolished.

Chavez became the highest-ranking woman in the Reagan administration when she was appointed Director of Public Liaison in 1985. The following year she won Maryland's Republican nomination for the U.S. Senate, but lost in the general election. From 1987 to 1988, she was the president of U.S. English, a group dedicated to promoting English as the official national language. Chavez then spent five years as a fellow at the Manhattan Institute. She also served as the U.S. expert on the United Nations Subcommission on Human Rights from 1992 to 1996. She founded the Center for Equal Opportunity in 1995.

Chavez is a prolific writer and a regular guest on national television shows such as *The McLaughlin Group, CNN & Co., To the Contrary,* and *The News Hour with Jim Lehrer.* She is a nationally syndicated columnist and writes often for a variety of publications including the *Wall Street Journal,* the *Washington Post,* the *New Republic, Commentary,* and *Reader's Digest.* Her book, *Out of the Barrio: Toward a New Politics of Hispanic Assimilation,* chronicles the untold story of Hispanic progress and achievement and addresses the implications of bilingual education, voting rights, immigration, and affirmative action. She is working on her second book, which deals with the impact of feminism on social policy.

Ellis Cose (1951–)

Ellis Cose jumped into the journalism scene as a teenager when the *Chicago Sun-Times* first hired him to write a column for the paper's school edition. Subsequently, at the age of 19, he was hired to write a column for the regular edition of the paper, making him the youngest columnist in the history of Chicago newspapers. The year was 1970, and Cose suddenly was the spokesperson for Chicago's black population in one of the country's leading newspapers during a time of great tension and turbulence. He rose to the occasion and went on to a brilliant career in journalism, working for the *Detroit Free Press,* the *New York Daily News,* and *Newsweek.*

In his 1997 book, *Color-Blind: Seeing beyond Race in a Race-Obsessed World,* Cose argues that it is impossible for the United States to move from a hellish history of race relations without a prolonged stint in purgatory, if there is any hope of a racial utopia. He states that blatant racism has yielded to more subtle discrimination and racial misunderstanding. About affirmative action, Cose says he is ambivalent: "If forced to choose a yes/no answer, am I for it or against it, I end up in the yes column. . . . But I think it's a very flawed approach to a much broader problem than it can solve. . . . The problem is that we don't seem to have come up with anything much better."

Still, Cose states, the country needs to strive for race neutrality, meaning that all persons have the same opportunities regardless of race. In *Color-Blind* Cose writes, "If [Martin Luther] King's call for 'special compensatory programs' was not exactly a demand for affirmative action as it is now known, he was clearly demanding some form of governmental activism aimed largely at blacks. Wiping out slums, eradicating poverty, ensuring access to a decent education—all these things and more, he saw as partial payment for an incalculably colossal debt." Cose believes that removing affirmative education programs from colleges and universities will have a devastating effect on society. The results, he says, of failing to educate many black and Latino students would be to mitigate the talents they have in helping move the country forward.

Cose believes that racial problems cannot be left to take care of themselves. He says that it is essential to dispel the myth that time will solve race problems. He suggests a 12-step program to create a race-neutral society that begins with taking responsibility for race problems and seeking multiple collaborative solutions. He contends that Americans have a long history of ambivalence regarding racial equality, witnessed by separate schools, churches, and neighborhoods. Cose believes that a segment of the population is ready to have a serious dialogue about race and affirmative action. He offers *Color-Blind* as a starting point to that conversation. Cose has authored five other books, including the best-seller *The Rage of a Privileged Class* (1994), dealing with the anger and race-related pain of the black middle and upper classes.

Nathan Glazer (1923–)

Nathan Glazer has been a prominent figure in the affirmative action debate from its inception. By the time he graduated from the City College of New York in 1944, he was recognized as a member of a group that was known as the New York Intellectuals. He is an eminent scholar known for his intellectual honesty. His book *Beyond the Melting Pot* (1963), written with Daniel Patrick Moynihan, was praised for its scholarship, readability, and candor. It won numerous awards and became standard reading in university sociology classes across the country. In it Glazer and Moynihan conclude that the vision of America as a melting pot has not been realized. Descendants of minority groups remain clustered and retain their ethnic identities. Each group pursues its own strategies for getting ahead in the world, but all remain tied to their ethnic identities. Yet, throughout much of his career, Glazer has been renowned for his strong optimism that assimilation will ultimately prevail.

Over time, Glazer's political views have moved steadily to the right from social democrat to neoconservative. As a sociology professor at Harvard for almost 30 years and an author of several books and innumerable essays, Glazer believed in a vision of a pluralistic culture that offered a niche to each new ethnic group while encouraging assimilation into the larger whole. Glazer was a staunch opponent of affirmative action because he felt that the notion of equality of opportunity had crumbled into a demand for equality of results. Glazer felt strongly that seeking equal results would lead to resentment and what he called "competitive victimization." By the mid-1960s he believed that racism was lessening. During the Kennedy administration, Glazer worked as an urban sociologist with the Housing and Home Finance Agency in Washington, D.C., and was a consultant to the short-lived Model Cities Program. He inaugurated many of the projects that became the core of the government's War on Poverty program. The failure of so many of these efforts led Glazer to conclude that sweeping social reforms initiated by the government were simply not possible. He believed that poverty needed to be attacked at the family level and doubted the government's ability to be successful.

Glazer attacked affirmative action in his 1976 book, *Affirmative Discrimination,* in which he insisted that affirmative action would do nothing to alleviate black poverty. Moreover, he claimed "it would undermine the values that had made America's unique experiment in pluralism possible." Glazer believed that values and behavior—not discrimination—accounted for the differing success rates of various ethnic minorities to overcome obstacles. However, Glazer routinely strove to understand the opposing viewpoint. As he did so, he realized that the historical experience of African Americans made it impossible to absorb immigrant values.

Throughout his distinguished career, Glazer has been unafraid to scrutinize his beliefs in search for answers to difficult questions. His tenure on a New York State committee to revise the social studies curriculum led him to revisit the liberal concept of multiculturalism. His 1997 book, *We Are All Multiculturists Now,* outraged conservatives. In it, he concluded that the idea of assimilation was dead and that multiculturalism, "with its emphasis on group identity and on building self-esteem through learning about the achievements of one's own group, has become the norm in public schools." Glazer believes that multiculturalism is an African American agenda based on irreparable feelings of exclusion that group has experienced.

However, like Abigail and Stephan Thernstrom (see further in this chapter), Glazer believes that economic improvement by African Americans preceded affirmative action and would have continued without it. In a March 1998 article in *Commentary* magazine Glazer wrote, "Although affirmative action has probably contributed something, one can hardly doubt that a good part of the movement by blacks into public jobs of all sorts would have occurred independently, as discrimination declined and as blacks became dominant, demographically and then politically, in so many cities."

Lani Guinier (1950–)

Lani Guinier became a household name in 1993 when President Clinton nominated her for the top civil rights post in the country. An outspoken defender of civil rights and affirmative action and a University of Pennsylvania law professor at the time, Guinier's nomination was withdrawn by Clinton in a firestorm of controversy. Right-wing politicians dubbed her the "Quota Queen"—a moniker that contributed greatly to her failed bid to become the assistant attorney general for civil rights. Also noteworthy was the White House's botched handling of the debacle. Guinier was known to be a friend of the president, yet he failed to mount a defense of her nomination until the opposition had so completely distilled Guinier's viewpoints into media sound bytes that there was no hope of salvaging it.

At the behest of the White House, Guinier remained silent throughout the controversy, and ultimately, she was never given the chance to defend herself. Never one to remain silent, Guinier finally got her say long afterward in her book, *Lift Every Voice: Turning a Civil Rights Setback into a New Vision of Social Justice* (1998). She asserts that traditional civil rights remedies may not be enough to protect the voting rights of minorities in racially hostile geographies. She is concerned that territorial districting can cause systemic losers whose viewpoints never get represented. She seeks reforms that increase the representation of minorities and suggests a system of cumulative voting whereby each voter gets a block of votes to cast for a particular seat. Voters may choose to cast their entire block of votes for a candidate or to disperse them among several candidates. According to Guinier, this does not conflict with "one person, one vote" since each person gets the same number of votes. This system would register the intensity of preferences among voters, making it easier for minorities to elect candidates whom they strongly favor.

Guinier also challenges the country to reframe the debate on affirmative action to get past a win/lose argument to a conversation aimed at a fair resolution. Guinier asks, "In the debate about affirmative action, is equality the same as equity? Is the goal to treat everyone the same, or to treat everyone fairly?" Guinier states that only half of the American work force will be American-born white males by the year 2000. In a 1995 speech at Cleveland State University, Guinier said, "We need to come up with new ways to distribute opportunity fairly. We tend to use fixed solutions to solve a range of complex problems." She added, "We must begin to think of diversity as an adaptation to a new environment. I believe," she continued, "the experience of those left out gives us the opportunity to form new criteria in the hiring process."

Guinier's passion for equality of opportunity and fairness came about in 1962 when she watched James Meredith, accompanied by civil rights lawyer Constance Baker Motley, walk through a jeering crowd to begin the racial integration of the University of Mississippi. She graduated from Radcliffe College and Yale Law School and then worked as a lawyer for the National Association for the Advancement of Colored People's (NAACP) Legal Defense and Education Fund until 1988. She spent five years teaching at the University of Pennsylvania Law School. In 1998, she became the first tenured black female professor in Harvard Law School's history. She is the author of a host of articles on civil rights issues as well as the book *The Tyranny of the Majority: Fundamental Fairness in Representative Democracy* (1994).

Irma D. Herrera (1951–)

Born to poor Mexican American parents in a segregated Texas barrio, Irma Herrera first became acquainted with affirmative action by benefiting from it. From an early age, Herrera aspired to a college education despite the enormous obstacles to achieving that dream. She says, "There were no lawyers, doctors or professors in my neighborhood. In fact, there were no college graduates. Most of our parents left school in their early teens to work on the farms and ranches of South Texas in order to support the family." In 1971, Herrera realized her dream, graduating with a B.A. from St. Mary's University in San Antonio, Texas.

Herrera next set her sights on earning a law degree. She graduated with a Juris Doctorate from the University of Notre

Dame in 1978, having also been a member of the National Moot Court Team. Since receiving her degree, Herrera has spent the past 20 years working on civil rights and women's rights issues. She has been a legal services attorney and an attorney with the Mexican American Legal Defense and Education Fund (MALDEF), where she also served as the director of education programs. In the mid-1980s, Herrera was a journalist covering legal and cultural issues for the *New York Times*, the *Washington Post, Newsday*, and *Ms.* magazine. She has also practiced law with a corporate law firm and served as a lawyer with Multicultural Education Training and Advocacy, Inc. (META). Since 1995 she has been the executive director of Equal Rights Advocates, Inc. (ERA), a public-interest law group started in 1974 whose aim is to eradicate gender discrimination. The organization uses a multifaceted approach to pursue equality for women. The ongoing support of affirmative action is deeply woven into the fiber of ERA. It routinely files litigation, provides education regarding affirmative action and equal rights protection, and forges alliances with other organizations to leverage its positions.

Herrera has been a passionate advocate of affirmative action since her own acceptance into law school under its auspices. She has championed the cause through her work, educating people about its benefits—touting it as a weapon to shatter the glass ceiling, narrow the gender and race gap in wages, and provide opportunities to women and minorities to reach their full potential.

For Herrera, the protection of civil rights, including affirmative action, and the fight to end sex discrimination and sexual harassment are her life's work. She has been active in the Bar Association of San Francisco, serving on the Conference of Delegates and Judicial Evaluation, the Equal Justice Committee, and the Minorities and the Law Committee. She has also served on the association's board of directors. Herrera was on the volunteer attorney panel of the Political Asylum Project with the San Francisco Lawyers Committee for Civil Rights and a member of San Francisco's La Raza Lawyers. She has volunteered her time to tutor minority bar candidates preparing for the California Bar examination. She has been a member of the board of directors for California Rural Legal Assistance, Inc., and Equal Rights Advocates, Inc.

Herrera unflinchingly defends the continued need for affirmative action programs. She says "discrimination and exclusion on the basis of race and gender are still facts of life in America today. Affirmative action programs seek to remedy discrimination and to create a more inclusive society. Is affirmative action the perfect solution for eliminating discrimination? Of course not. But it is a workable plan that helps make the American dream of equality of opportunity available to all."

A. Leon Higginbotham Jr. (1928–1998)

A. Leon Higginbotham, Jr. is considered by many to be one of the foremost judges and legal scholars of the twentieth century. Born in Trenton, New Jersey, Higginbotham left home at age 16 to attend Purdue University. He was barred from the dormitories there because of the color of his skin and assigned to live in an unheated attic. Thus began his lifelong dedication to abolishing racism. He ultimately left Purdue and transferred to Antioch College. Higginbotham subsequently went to Yale Law School, graduating at the top of his class. He attempted to get a job with major white city law firms but was declined, after which he and four other black lawyers formed their own firm in south Philadelphia (blacks were prohibited from renting office space downtown).

In 1962, President Kennedy appointed Higginbotham the first African American to head the Federal Trade Commission. Kennedy nominated Higginbotham to a federal court judgeship, but that appointment was held up for a year. After Kennedy's assassination, President Johnson renominated Higginbotham, who was appointed to the U.S. District Court for the Eastern District of Pennsylvania. He joined the Third Circuit Court of Appeals as chief justice in 1977, nominated by President Carter. He stepped down as chief justice in 1991 but remained with the court of appeals as a senior judge until he retired in 1993.

One of Higginbotham's greatest legacies is his writings. His landmark book, *In the Matter of Color* (1978), examines how slavery became legal in colonial America. It is widely considered a major contribution to the literature on race and law. Higginbotham is also prominent for his multivolume study of race called *Race and the American Legal Process*, which examines how the legal system perpetuated the oppression of blacks after the Civil War.

Throughout his long and storied career, Higginbotham promoted affirmative action and equal rights. After he retired, he helped the Massachusetts Institute of Technology (MIT) fight charges that the Justice Department leveled that MIT and other schools were in violation of the Sherman Antitrust Act. The Justice Department alleged that discussing and agreeing upon financial aid packages of students who had been offered admission to more than one of the schools constituted price fixing. Along with MIT's attorney, Higginbotham made a passionate argument that the public-service aspect of the case outweighed the alleged harm. MIT President Charles M. Vest said of Higginbotham, "He took on our case because he believed in need-blind admission and need-based aid was very important in providing access to the best of American higher education for talented youth of all races, regardless of financial status."

Higginbotham remained an outspoken advocate of affirmative action even as his health failed. Less than three months before suffering a fatal stroke, on September 25, 1998, in the inaugural speech of the National Underground Railroad Freedom Center Theodore Berry Lecture Series on Public Policy, Human Rights, Higginbotham spoke of the ongoing need for affirmative action to assist the disadvantaged. He said, "These people desperately need a contemporary Underground Railroad, a contemporary network of support, to give them hope and to help them realize their true potential." He made national headlines that same year when he spoke out against Supreme Court Justice Clarence Thomas's opposition to affirmative action.

Considered a towering presence in modern-day jurisprudence, Higginbotham won numerous accolades throughout his life. President Clinton awarded Higginbotham the Presidential Medal of Freedom in 1995 for his longtime dedication to civil rights and equality. Clinton also appointed Higginbotham commissioner of the U.S. Commission on Civil Rights in October of that year. He was given more than 60 honorary degrees in recognition of his scholarship and judicial service. Among his many other honors, Higginbotham was awarded the Martin Luther King Award for outstanding service in the field of human rights.

Reverend Jesse L. Jackson (1941–)

Born to an unwed teenaged mother in Greenville, South Carolina, Jesse Jackson has been a controversial, charismatic figure most of his life. A preacher without a congregation and a political force without an elected office to his credit, Jackson has been one of the most enigmatic and visionary characters in American politics this century. Despite the fact that he has lacked the formal authority of a duly elected public official, Jackson has carved out a remarkable role as an eloquent defender of the downtrodden. He has figured prominently in virtually every movement to end oppression of any kind. He has been a leader in the quest to achieve social and economic justice for minorities; a staunch advocate of civil rights, affirmative action, and gender equality; and has negotiated diplomatic solutions and the release of political prisoners and hostages in numerous conflicts around the globe.

Jackson began his life of activism as an undergraduate student at North Carolina A&T State University when he led a group of student protesters in a demonstration against a restaurant that refused to serve black patrons. That event proved to be a defining moment in Jackson's life. After graduating from A&T in 1964, Jackson enrolled in the Chicago Theological Seminary. In 1965 he went to Alabama to participate in the march on Selma. While there he met Martin Luther King, Jr. and decided to dedicate himself completely to the civil rights cause. After Jackson returned to Chicago, he dropped out of the seminary and joined King's staff on the Southern Christian Leadership Conference (SCLC). Some members of the SCLC viewed Jackson with suspicion because of his ambition and desire to be in the spotlight. Nonetheless, Jackson quickly became a member of King's inner circle and was with King the night King was assassinated in Memphis.

After King's death, Jackson searched for a new venue to forward his civil rights agenda, founding People United to Save Humanity (PUSH) in 1971. PUSH's goals were to gain economic empowerment and expand educational and employment opportunities for the disadvantaged and people of color. In its infancy, PUSH had little financial support as Jackson sought to build a coalition between the civil rights movement and the labor unions. He was successful in convening various labor and religious leaders to develop strategies to achieve the organization's goals.

The ministers banned together to promote affirmative action, initiating a number of tactics that they borrowed from the labor movement. They adopted a policy of selective patronage, supporting only black businesses. They educated their congregations about the existence of products made and distributed by black businesses, and they organized black consumers into a powerful market force who were known as "PUSH Resisters." Under Jackson's leadership, these same religious leaders also negotiated with supermarket chains to provide shelf space for products made by African Americans. They led buy-ins, eat-ins, and shop-ins at black restaurants and shops.

Jackson networked the religious and business communities into a united force to garner what he called "Our fair share of jobs and contracts." An ardent supporter of affirmative action, Jackson worked passionately to secure reasonable wages and decent working conditions for people. In 1984, Jackson started the National Rainbow Coalition, a social justice organization devoted to political empowerment, education, and public policy. The Rainbow Coalition and PUSH merged into the Rainbow/PUSH Coalition in 1996 to continue both efforts while maximizing resources.

Jackson surprised the nation in 1984 and again in 1988 when his bid for the Democratic presidential nomination energized millions of disenfranchised African Americans to participate in the political process and vote. His campaign was responsible for registering over a million new voters in 1984. He also won 3.5 million votes and helped the Democratic party regain control of the Senate in 1986.

In addition to his dedication to civil rights, Jackson has an abiding commitment to youth, encouraging and challenging them to achieve academic excellence and stay drug-free. He has also been a major force in the labor movement, working with unions to mediate disputes, walking picket lines, and speaking at rallies.

Jackson has proven himself an invaluable diplomat as well. He negotiated the release of captured navy lieutenant Robert Goodman from Syria in 1984. That same year, he secured the release of 48 Cuban and Cuban American prisoners. In 1990 he became the first American to bring hostages out of Iraq and Kuwait. In 1997, President Clinton and Secretary of State Madeleine Albright named Jackson the "Special Envoy of the President and Secretary of State for the Promotion of Democracy in Africa." In spring 1999, Jackson persuaded Yugoslavian president Slobodan Milosevic to release three American prisoners of war.

Jackson has been honored numerous times for his work in human and civil rights. He received the prestigious NAACP Springarm Award along with a host of other honors. He has also been on the Gallup List of "Ten Most Respected Americans" for the past ten years. Jackson has received more than 40 honorary doctorate degrees and is a frequent lecturer at Howard, Yale, Columbia, Harvard, Morehouse, Stanford, and Hampton Universities.

Lyndon B. Johnson (1908–1973)

The first child of Sam Ealy Johnson, Jr. and Rebekah Baines, Johnson was born in a farmhouse in Stonewall, Texas. His grandfather was correct when he predicted that Lyndon would grow up to be a United States senator. He accomplished that feat in 1948 when he defeated Republican Jack Porter after having won the

Democratic primary by a mere 87 votes. His grandfather did not realize that the boy would also go on to take the vice presidential oath of office in January 1961, after he and John F. Kennedy narrowly defeated the Nixon-Lodge Republican ticket for the White House.

Among his other duties, Johnson was installed as the chairman of the newly formed President's Committee on Equal Employment Opportunity. The committee, established by Executive Order 10925, was charged with ending discrimination in employment by the government and its contractors. It was this order that permanently emblazoned the words "affirmative action" into the history and language of the United States. The order required every federal contract to include the commitment that "the Contractor will not discriminate against any employee or applicant for employment because of race, creed, color, or national origin. The contractor will take affirmative action, to ensure that applicants are employed, and that employees are treated during their employment without regard to their race, creed, color, or national origin."

Less than two years later, Johnson was sworn in as the thirty-sixth president of the United States in the wake of Kennedy's assassination. Five days after Kennedy's death, in a speech before a joint session of Congress, Johnson promised to carry out Kennedy's legislative agenda, including a commitment to civil rights. Six months later, Johnson gave a historic speech at the University of Michigan in which he spoke of building "a Great Society." He said, "The Great Society rests on abundance and liberty for all. It demands an end to poverty and racial injustice, to which we are totally committed in our time."

In a televised ceremony on July 2, Johnson signed into law the Civil Rights Act of 1964. The law included provisions to protect the right to vote, guarantee access to public accommodations, and withhold federal funds from programs administered in a discriminatory fashion. Johnson followed this with the signing of the Economic Opportunity Act, which established the Office of Economic Opportunity to direct and coordinate a host of programs that were the cornerstone of Johnson's "War on Poverty."

In November 1964, Johnson and Hubert Humphrey won their bid for the White House in a landslide victory. After Johnson was sworn into office, he outlined his Great Society agenda that included protection of civil rights, urban renewal, and promotion of the arts. Within a year of signing the Civil Rights Act,

Johnson contended that fairness required more than impartial treatment. In his 1965 commencement address at Howard University, he said: "You do not take a person who for years has been hobbled by chains and liberate him, bring him up to the starting line of a race and then say, 'you're free to compete with all the others,' and still justly believe that you have been completely fair. Thus it is not enough just to open the gates of opportunity. All our citizens must have the ability to walk through those gates. . . . We seek not . . . just equality as a right and a theory but equality as a fact and equality as a result." Several months later President Johnson issued Executive Order 11246. It stated, "It is the policy of the Government of the United States to provide equal opportunity in federal employment for all qualified persons, to prohibit discrimination in employment because of race, creed, color or national origin, and to promote the full realization of equal employment opportunity through a positive, continuing program in each department and agency." That order was amended in 1968 to prohibit discrimination on the basis of sex. Ultimately, the amendment to Executive Order 11246 was used to win passage of Title IX legislation.

Despite Johnson's long record of civil rights and affirmative action support, he considered his greatest accomplishment to be the signing of the Voting Rights Act on August 6, 1965. The act sought to prevent racial discrimination in voting and to assist African Americans in registering to vote.

Johnson died on January 22, 1973, at his Texas ranch near his birthplace. During his retirement he wrote his memoirs in a book entitled *Vantage Point: Perspectives of the Presidency, 1963–1969* (1971).

Martin Luther King, Jr. (1929–1968)

The man whose very name is synonymous with the civil rights movement was originally christened Michael Luther King—he later had his name changed to Martin Luther King, Jr. Although gunned down in Memphis, Tennessee, before he could see his visions realized, King's impact on civil rights and affirmative action could not be more profound. Though he has become a cultural icon since his assassination, he was a fiery man with a radical message for America. He challenged the nation to repent from its racist ways, abandon materialism, and eschew violence. He spoke as a moral authority who championed peace and loathed injustice.

King attended segregated public schools in Atlanta, graduated from high school at the age of 15, and received a B.A. from Morehouse College in 1948. He received his doctorate in systematic theology from Boston University in 1955. Spurning academic offers, King returned to the South to accept the pastorate at Dexter Avenue Baptist Church in Montgomery, Alabama.

On December 5, 1955, King led the first nonviolent black demonstration in contemporary U.S. history when area blacks boycotted buses in support of Rosa Parks's refusal to comply with segregation. As the boycott wore on, King was arrested, subjected to abuse, and had his house bombed. Nonetheless, he emerged a victorious leader when, one year after the boycott began, the United States Supreme Court declared Alabama's segregation laws unconstitutional.

King became the president of the Southern Christian Leadership Conference in 1957 to provide leadership for the growing civil rights movement. King saw its ideals as Christian but took his operational tactics from Mohandas Gandhi. He spent a year touring India to learn more about nonviolent strategies for change. Over the next 11 years, until his death, King led protest after protest, spoke to audiences more than 2,500 times, traveled over six million miles, and wrote five books and many articles.

One of his most famous protests occurred in the spring of 1963 in Birmingham, Alabama, when he and his staff organized mass demonstrations to protest segregation and brutality against African Americans. King himself went to Birmingham to train protesters in nonviolent protest techniques, recruit people who were willing to go to jail, and carefully plan a strategy designed to bring down segregation. King's goal was to create a crisis so great that the government could no longer ignore discrimination. King created a crisis of the highest order.

The protest began with African Americans parading cheerfully downtown in their finest Sunday clothes. They were hauled off to jail, and yet protesters kept coming back, flooding the streets of downtown. Police commissioner Bull Connor could not contain his fury, and he finally ordered the police to use clubs, dogs, and fire hoses on the demonstrators. The police swarmed into the throngs of demonstrators, and an armored car bulldozed its way through the crowds. In all, more than 3,300 blacks were jailed, including King, and hundreds were injured at the hands of the police.

That incident inspired his now famous "Letter from a Birmingham Jail" in which King chastised religious leaders for their lack of support and served as a call to action to those who had been reluctant to become directly involved in fighting injustice. The Birmingham protest became a flash point of the civil rights movement and galvanized the conviction of minorities to overcome oppression. Suddenly, King's presence was demanded everywhere, and in the months following Birmingham, the black community marched, demonstrated, protested, and fought for civil rights in over 800 cities. Consequently, President Kennedy met with King and began to work in earnest to get a civil rights bill drafted.

As the summer drew to a close, King and other leaders led the famous March on Washington, during which some 250,000 protesters marched to the capital. King delivered the most quoted and well-known oration of his life from the steps of the Lincoln Memorial that August day in 1963. He lifted his voice in a stirring proclamation and infused hope into the hearts of weary protesters, when he said, "I have a dream. . . ."

Eleven months later the Civil Rights Act of 1964 was passed. The black community made enormous gains because of King's unwavering stance on equal rights and his unflinching commitment to win the battle, regardless of personal cost. Affirmative action brought new job opportunities in cities across the country. Despite pockets of resistance and bigotry, minorities got their first real chance to participate fully in society. King did not stop fighting with the passage of the civil rights bill. He supported Lyndon Johnson's candidacy for the White House. When Johnson was elected, King worked side by side with him to achieve the next goal—the passage of the Voting Rights Act, which was accomplished in 1965.

Early in 1968, King began a "poor people's campaign" to address economic issues that were left undone by other reforms. King did not live to see that campaign come to fruition. Later that year, on April 4, 1968, he was assassinated as he stood on a hotel balcony in Memphis, Tennessee.

King has since gained almost mythic status for his role in civil rights and affirmative action. For although there were many who fought to make all people equal, it is King's voice that most remember and his speeches that still echo. King was named by *Time* magazine as the 1963 Man of the Year, won the Nobel Peace Prize, and was awarded five honorary degrees. King is revered by many as a martyr for nonviolent civil disobedience and condemned by others for his insurgency. He remains a central figure in the affirmative action debate posthumously as people from all camps quote him to defend their own views.

Nancy B. Kreiter (1947–)

Nancy Kreiter, research director of Women Employed Institute, has spent more than 20 years overseeing the institute's research and equal employment monitoring programs. Her work was nationally honored in 1994 when Women Employed became the first recipient of the U.S. Department of Labor's Exemplary Public Interest Contribution (EPIC) Award. Kreiter and Women Employed were cited for their significant contributions to the effectiveness of the federal contract compliance program through two decades of national leadership in advocating enforcement of affirmative action, executing model training and placement programs, creating public awareness, and promoting partnerships with corporations to encourage voluntary programs to improve equal opportunity practices.

In 1995, Kreiter was instrumental in organizing the Illinois Coalition for Equal Opportunity (CEO). She is the director for this broad-based group of 60 women's, civil rights, labor, religious, and business organizations dedicated to protecting the gains that minorities and women have achieved through affirmative action. She also led the landmark discrimination case against Chicago's Harris Trust and Savings Bank, which resulted in the largest back-pay settlement ever secured by the Department of Labor under Executive Order 11246.

Kreiter holds a master's degree in economics from the London School of Economics and Political Science. She has testified numerous times before various U.S. House and Senate subcommittees on civil rights, employment opportunities, the glass ceiling, and the need for affirmative action and enforcement of equal employment opportunity. She is widely published on these same issues and regularly provides analyses regarding pay equity and job evaluations, and expert witness testimony on the same.

Judith L. Lichtman (1940–)

Judith L. Lichtman has been an influential force in the women's movement for more than 20 years. After receiving her law degree from the University of Wisconsin in 1965, Lichtman held positions at the Urban Coalition and as a legal advisor to the Commonwealth of Puerto Rico. From 1972 to 1973, she worked as a consultant on a set of hearings for the U.S. Commission on Civil Rights. For the first time she understood the intersection of race, gender, and class—poor women of color had triple burdens, making the odds against them insurmountable. This experience ignited a passion within her to work against race and gender discrimination.

In 1974 Lichtman became the first paid staff person for the Women's Legal Defense Fund when she accepted the executive director's position. She became president of that organization in 1988—a title she still holds—although the organization in 1998 changed its name to the National Partnership for Women and Families to more clearly reflect the organization's mission. The National Partnership is dedicated to promoting "fairness in the workplace, quality health care, and policies that help women and men meet the dual demands of work and family."

Lichtman built the National Partnership from a small volunteer group to a powerful national organization, exerting tremendous political influence and shaping national policy through its advocacy, lobbying, litigation, and public education. Lichtman's vision, coupled with the strength of the National Partnership, has resulted in the passage of some of the most important legal protections for American women and their families, including the Pregnancy Discrimination Act of 1978 and the Family Medical Leave Act (FMLA) of 1993. More recently, the National Partnership assisted in shaping key provisions of the Health Insurance Portability and Accountability Act (HIPAA) of 1996. The HIPAA makes it easier for women to get and keep health coverage.

Lichtman has become a leader for families while raising her own. Her daughters are grown and she lives in Washington, D.C., with her husband, Elliot Lichtman. Lichtman has been recognized by civic and legal organizations, business and labor leaders, and others for her invaluable contributions, tireless commitment to building a just society, and her remarkable abilities to build powerful and effective diverse coalitions. At the National Partnership's twenty-fifth anniversary luncheon in 1996, President Clinton called Lichtman "a remarkable national treasure." *Washingtonian* magazine has identified her as one of Washington's most powerful women. The Women's Bar Association and Foundation of the District of Columbia named her Woman Lawyer of the Year in 1989, the year in which she also received the Sara Lee Frontrunner Award. In 1993 she was honored with the Martin Luther King, Jr. Civil Rights Leadership Award, and in 1996 she was the recipient of the Washington, D.C., Bar Association's Thurgood Marshall Award.

Frederick R. Lynch (1945–)

Frederick R. Lynch was teaching sociology at California State University in the 1970s when he rattled the political sensibilities of academia by exploring the emerging phenomenon known as reverse discrimination. In an article he wrote for *Commentary* magazine in 1990, Lynch stated, "In the mid-1970s, I became interested in what I assumed were two sociologically compelling questions: (1) how did white males . . . respond to reverse discrimination and (2) how were the media portraying affirmative action?"

Lynch proceeded with his research to investigate whether white males were being injured by affirmative action and whether outright preferences were being given to women and minorities. He slowly uncovered reluctant white males who felt they had been discriminated against. Ironically, Lynch himself soon came to join that group. He writes, "while my resume continued to grow with more publications and references, I was unable to move beyond temporary faculty status to a tenure-track position. . . . There could be no doubt that reverse discrimination was a major cause of my stalled career." He offers evidence of his beliefs, citing the fact that during the hiring process at other colleges he was told that he lost positions strictly because he was male or because he was white.

In 1991 Lynch published a book that chronicled his findings in the first and only book written about this topic, entitled *Invisible Victims: White Males and the Crisis of Affirmative Action*. In it he wrote, "The ideal of merit hiring has been subverted by politicized hiring, with white men unable to defend themselves against open discrimination. But quotas bring other problems, including conflict among the 'protected classes' they benefit, and growing racial polarization, particularly as the articulate middle class begins to suffer." This effort catapulted him onto the national media scene, where he gave over 200 radio and television interviews.

He was frustrated by attempts to make him a spokesman for the white male in America. He said, "I want to maintain my status as a social scientist and not as an advocate or (to be) partisan." Lynch is passionate about how he sees his own role, stating, "I describe myself as a 'flaming moderate' who is still the consummate sociologist. I want to map the sociological terrain and find out what is out there—regardless of whether or not I like my own findings. But, in these delicate policy matters, to ask questions about 'sacred cow' politics ipso facto implies criticism."

Lynch followed *Invisible Victims* with five years of research on the related issue of diversity management in his book *The Diversity Machine: The Drive to Change the "White Male Workplace"* (1997). According to Lynch, this book "looks at the transformation of affirmative action from a backward-looking making up for past discrimination into a business-oriented effort to achieve work forces that mirrored the broader ethnic representation of customer bases or 'America' in general." He objects to "the diversity machine's" disregard for differences within groups of people and believes that such blindness about internal differences mitigates the value of generalizations about group traits. He does acknowledge that there are group-based cultural differences but believes that public policies and laws should not serve as vehicles to institutionalize those differences.

Lynch has been an associate professor of government at Claremont McKenna College since 1991. He has appeared on innumerable radio and television programs and written voluminously on these topics throughout his career as a sociologist.

Mari J. Matsuda (1956–)

In June 1963, Mari Matsuda rode with her family to participate in a Los Angeles motorcade honoring Medgar Evers, who had been assassinated that week in Jackson, Mississippi, for his efforts to end racism against blacks. Matsuda recalls how her mother turned to her three children in the back seat of the car and warned them that she might have to tell them to get down on the floor and stay down until told otherwise because of possible danger. Matsuda wondered why her parents would take them into harm's way.

In the book *We Won't Go Back: Making the Case for Affirmative Action*, coauthored with her husband, Charles L. Lawrence, III, Matsuda states, "We learned the answer in pieces. We were picket-line babies, pushed in buggies before we could walk on marches for labor rights, for civil rights, for peace." And so it was from an early age that Matsuda learned about the complexities of race and privilege. The experiences of her childhood and the commitment of her Okinawan-born father and her Hawaiian mother to seek a better world imbued in Matsuda a fundamental sense of diversity and fairness.

Matsuda was the first Asian American law professor to be granted tenure and has been a pioneer in the relatively new body of legal thought known as critical race theory. This emerging approach to jurisprudence draws upon the subjective experiences of people of color, recognizing that the ideal of neutrality has often been superceded by the reality of oppression. Critical race theory demonstrates the way in which social and legal systems have been fashioned by race, gender, socioeconomic class, and individual experience. Matsuda supports identity politics "because it is still a radical act to stand in my shoes and speak when someone who looks like me is not supposed to do what I do. This is resistance. . . . I see it as a form of resistance to stand in the front of the room on the first day of class and introduce myself as a Japanese-American, a feminist and your law professor."

A passionate believer in affirmative action, Matsuda was persuaded to cowrite *We Won't Go Back: Making the Case for Affirmative Action* (1997) in large part because the students she and her husband taught didn't know the history of affirmative action. Few knew that Asian Americans played a critical role in the civil rights movement. They argue that affirmative action is the result of demands for inclusion into a society that has been patriarchal and hierarchical at the expense of people of color, women, gays, lesbians, and all economically disadvantaged.

She believes that unconscious prejudices still prevail and block opportunity. Although strides have been made, privilege and opportunity still need to be redistributed so that all races and both genders are fairly represented in boardrooms, classrooms, executive ranks, skilled trades, and governmental positions. Matsuda and Lawrence invoke a plethora of statistics to support their position that affirmative action is still needed to redress disparities in income and opportunity.

Matsuda argues that the civil rights acts were not enough to reverse "a four-hundred-year history of racism and patriarchy." Concerned about the weakening of support for affirmative action during the 1990s, Matsuda and Lawrence write, "The attack on affirmative action is an attempt to shore up a tottering tower of privilege, and in responding with an aggressive defense of affirmative action, we hope to repeal privilege and dethrone it." Furthermore, *We Won't Go Back* suggests an expanded role for affirmative action to include all subordinated peoples.

If that ambitious goal were to be attained, Matsuda sees affirmative action as one part of "a larger claim to substantive equality." She and Lawrence note that equality is at the heart of the Constitution. And, though cost-benefit analyses show that the costs of crime, poverty, health epidemics, poor public schools, and a lack of child care are enough to support the notion of equality, there is a larger reason beyond financial self-interest to fight for equality. As human beings, we should all care what happens to other humans. When one among us is injured, abused, or debased, we all suffer. There is trauma to the individual and collective psyche of humanity—and that, they say, is the real case for affirmative action.

Matsuda is a law professor at Georgetown University. In addition to coauthoring *We Won't Go Back,* she has written numerous articles on constitutional law, hate speech, affirmative action, and feminist theory. Her other books are *Called from Within* (1992) and *Words that Wound* (1989).

Charles A. Murray (1943–)

Charles Murray has been a controversial and outspoken author, speaker, and social scientist for the better part of two decades. After receiving his B.A. from Harvard University in 1965, Murray did a stint as a Peace Corps volunteer in Thailand. He returned to the United States to work for the American Institutes for Research and pursue a Ph.D. from the Massachusetts Institute of Technology, which he completed in 1974. Since that time, Murray has been a voice of conservative and often radical views on social policy.

He splashed into the media in 1984, making waves with his first book, *Losing Ground: American Social Policy 1950–1980.* Without reservation, Murray declared that all social programs, with the exception of unemployment, should be dismantled. He cited statistics showing that African Americans have been adversely impacted—not helped— by affirmative action. He stated that the percentage of young black men gainfully employed or actively seeking employment fell while violent crime and illegitimate births for African Americans rose.

In his subsequent book, *In Pursuit of Happiness and Good Government* (1988), Murray goes on to make a case that social programs actually contribute to low self-esteem. He claims that because social programs provide what many Americans routinely provide for themselves, those that do receive aid may lose self-respect. This, in turn, interferes with the pursuit of happiness as outlined in the Constitution.

Murray's most incendiary work has been the book he coauthored with Richard J. Herrnstein in 1994 called *The Bell Curve: Intelligence and Class Structure in American Life.* The book was so controversial that Murray and his employer, the Manhattan

Institute for Policy Research, a conservative think tank, severed ties. The president of the institute felt that there was little to gain by publishing the book and a disproportionate risk of negative publicity. Murray finished his work on the book under the auspices of the American Enterprise Institute.

Murray asserted that intelligence scores vary by ethnic groups, and stated that even allowing for all other factors, including racial bias in testing instruments, intelligence is influenced by ethnicity. Murray and Herrnstein claim that intelligence is the best predictor of economic status. Furthermore, they allege that individuals of below-average IQ in all races have more babies than those with average or above average IQs. This, they say, will result in a large underclass of people who will require more governmental assistance.

Scholars do not dispute the disparities in the IQ findings. At issue are the cause of the gap and whether the gap can be reduced. Critics, politicians, media figures, and academics continue to argue over the findings. Again, in *The Bell Curve*, Murray and his coauthor submit that social programs should be abolished because they encourage "the economically disadvantaged and intellectually challenged to have more children and undervalue education and training."

Murray is currently a Bradley Fellow at the American Enterprise Institute in Washington, D.C. His coauthor, the late Richard J. Herrnstein, received his Ph.D. in psychology from Harvard and taught there from 1958 until his death in 1998.

Bernice Resnick Sandler (1928–)

In 1997, the twenty-fifth anniversary of the passage of Title IX, Bernice Resnick Sandler recounted her role in that historic legislation in the quarterly publication of the National Association for Women in Higher Education, *About Women on Campus*. She states, "The year was 1969. I had been teaching part time at the University of Maryland for several years during the time I worked on my doctorate and shortly after I finished it. There were seven openings in the department and I had just asked a faculty member, a friend of mine, why I was not considered for any of the openings. It was not my qualifications; they were excellent. 'But let's face it,' he said. 'You come on *too strong for a woman.'*"

Little did she know that that rejection would not only dramatically change the course of her own life, it would irreversibly alter the lives of women and girls across the country, coloring the landscape of education forever. While continuing her job hunt, two more incidents of sex discrimination in rapid succession fueled Sandler's curiosity. She could no longer rationalize the discrimination, and she began to investigate laws pertaining to sex discrimination.

Knowing that sex discrimination was immoral, she says, "I assumed it was illegal." Almost immediately, Sandler determined that although sex discrimination was indeed illegal in certain circumstances, "I quickly discovered that none of the laws prohibiting discrimination covered sex discrimination in education." Further research led Sandler to read a report of the U.S. Commission on Civil Rights, which looked at the impact of antidiscrimination laws on race discrimination. The report described a presidential executive order prohibiting federal contractors from discrimination in employment on the basis of race, color, religion, and national origin. She discovered a footnote stating that Executive Order 11246 had been amended by President Johnson, effective October 13, 1968, to include discrimination based on sex.

Sandler saw the implications of the executive order almost immediately. She realized that since most colleges and universities had federal contracts, they could not discriminate in employment on the basis of sex. Although few people seemed aware of it, this fact opened the door to a legal route to fight discrimination.

Subsequently, she contacted Vincent Macaluso, director of the Office of Federal Contract Compliance at the Department of Labor, to confirm that sex discrimination was covered by the executive order. He had been waiting for someone to use the order to fight sex discrimination. Together they planned the first complaint against colleges and universities.

Under the auspices of the newly formed Women's Equity Action League (WEAL), Sandler began a national campaign to end discrimination in higher education that culminated with the passage of Title IX on June 23, 1972. Sandler also successfully filed charges of sex discrimination against more than 250 colleges and universities under Executive Order 11246. This was a huge undertaking, as there was no official documentation to substantiate the claims. The evidence was painstakingly gathered by women and men at academic institutions around the country who pressured Congress and organized and acted without regard for their own careers. According to Sandler, "They are the unsung heroes of this story. They took enormous risks. Many did not have tenure and, as a result of their activities, never received it and were lost to the higher education community. Some became lawyers or found other successful careers. A few went on welfare."

Previously, Sandler directed the Project on the Status and Education of Women at the Association of American Colleges. Among her many firsts is the fact that she made the first known reports about campus sexual harassment, gang rape, campus peer harassment, and gender bias in the classroom. She was the first person ever appointed to a congressional committee staff to work specifically on women's issues and the first to testify about discrimination against women in education.

In 1975, Sandler was appointed by President Ford to chair the National Advisory Council on Women's Educational Programs. She was reappointed to the council by President Carter and served until 1982. She has also served on more than 30 boards, has nine honorary doctorates, and has received numerous other awards. In 1994 she was honored with a Woman of Achievement Award from Turner Broadcasting Systems. The Harvard University Anna Roe Award was given to her in 1988, and that same year she was named by *Ladies Home Journal* as one of the nation's 100 Most Important Women.

Dr. Sandler (she completed her doctorate in education at the University of Maryland in 1966) is currently a senior scholar in residence at the National Association for Women in Education in Washington, D.C. She consults with institutions and others about achieving equity for women and writes a quarterly newsletter, *About Women on Campus.* She is well known for her expertise on women's educational equity and sexual harassment and for her extensive knowledge of policies and programs affecting women on campus. A prominent speaker and author, Sandler has given over 2,000 campus presentations, written more than 60 articles about sex discrimination, and coauthored the book *The Chilly Classroom Climate: A Guide to Improve the Education of Women* (1993) with Lisa A. Silverberg and Roberta M. Hall.

Shelby Steele (1946–)

Shelby Steele was awarded the National Book Critic's Circle Award in 1990 for his book *The Content of Our Character: A New Vision of Race in America,* in which he decried affirmative action and called upon African Americans to stop trying to get power by claiming victim status. He believes that the Black Power movement is a failure precisely because it is predicated on the notion that blacks deserve power because they're blacks. He is firm in his belief that "any time you make race a source of power ⁄ you are going to guarantee suffering, misery, and inequity."

Steele finds that the basis of entitlement in the United States has made a fundamental shift away from the rights of citizenship that are outlined in the Declaration of Independence and the Constitution. He contends that the civil rights movement was founded on the principle that blacks deserve equal treatment because they are citizens. However, that goal has been lost as minorities "began demanding entitlement solely based on their history of oppression, their race, their gender, their ethnicity, or whatever quality that allegedly made them victims."

He argues that affirmative action does the opposite of what was intended by judging people according to the color of their skin and not the content of their character, as Martin Luther King, Jr. implored. On an issue where so few African Americans have publicly voiced opposition, Steele became something of a celebrity for his vehement stance against affirmative action. He objects to those who claim victim status to demand extra entitlements beyond what citizenship should afford. He writes, "As a black, I am said to 'deserve' this or that special entitlement. No longer is it enough just to have the right to attend a college or university on an equal basis with others or to be treated like anyone else. Schools must set aside special money and special academic departments just for me, based on my grievance." This grievance mentality further segregates the races, he believes. "They have made our differences, rather than our common bonds, sacred. Often they do so in the name of building the 'self-esteem' of minorities. But they are not going to build anyone's self-esteem by condemning our culture as the product of 'dead white males.'"

Steele is a prolific writer and regular speaker on the issue of race in America and the consequences of affirmative action on race relations. His work has appeared in *Time, Newsweek, U.S. News and World Report,* the *New York Times,* the *Washington Post,* and countless other publications. He holds a Ph.D. in English from the University of Utah and is on leave of absence from his position as an English professor at San Jose State University. He is currently a Senior Fellow at the Hoover Institution at Stanford University.

Abigail M. Thernstrom (1936–)

Abigail Thernstrom catapulted onto the national affirmative action scene with her 1987 book, *Whose Votes Count? Affirmative*

Action and Minority Voting Rights. She has remained firmly ensconced in the national dialogue on this issue since.

Since the publishing of *Whose Votes Count?*, Thernstrom has been a consistent voice of conservatism, writing voluminously and speaking regularly on issues related to equality, voting rights, and affirmative action. She has made innumerable public appearances on national television and was selected by President Clinton to participate in his first "town meeting on race" in Akron, Ohio, on December 3, 1997.

A strident and scholarly conservative, Thernstrom, and her husband, Stephen, are vociferous critics of affirmative action. They argue that African American progress toward equality is not an outcome of affirmative action at all. They claim statistics show that African Americans made much greater progress in achieving equality prior to affirmative action, and they believe that if the nation's public school system were improved, affirmative action policies would be moot. Abigail Thernstrom states, "All the preferences, all the double standards, are driven by a very simple fact. A continuing racial gap between whites and Asians on one hand, blacks and Hispanics on the other, in terms of educational attainment. There is only one solution—do something about the quality of schools that urban African-Americans and Hispanics are going to. There's just no reason to have this continuous gap in what students know."

Thernstrom is a Senior Fellow at the Manhattan Institute, an independent research and educational organization whose goal is to "develop and encourage public policies at all levels of government, which will allow individuals the greatest scope for achieving their potential, both as participants in a productive economy and as members of a functioning society." She holds a Ph.D. from the Department of Government at Harvard University and is a member of the Massachusetts State Board of Education, appointed by Governor Weld in 1995.

Thernstrom has devoted herself to the study of race relations. Ten years after publishing *Whose Votes Count?*, she and her husband coauthored the book *America in Black and White: One Nation Indivisible.* In it they describe the country as "no longer separate, much less unequal than it was, and by many measures, less hostile." They criticize affirmative action policies designed to promote racial equality, stating: "Race-conscious policies make for more race-consciousness; they carry America backward."

Stephen A. Thernstrom (1934–)

Stephen A. Thernstrom is the Winthrop Professor of History at Harvard University, where he teaches American social history. He and his wife, Abigail, are among the organizers of the Citizens' Initiative on Race and Ethnicity (CIRE), a group formed in response to President Clinton's Initiative on Race. CIRE's focus is "how to protect the civil rights for all Americans." Specifically, its mission is to "carefully examine how the realities of race affect the social problems that exist in America; engage Americans in a national dialogue on race relations and provide realistic recommendations on how race relations can be improved."

Thernstrom has given voice to conservative views on race relations and affirmative action since the inception of the civil rights movement. He has long objected to affirmative action policies, stating that those policies failed to give equal opportunity to individuals, instead seeking to provide equal outcomes between groups of people. He is a well known and outspoken critic of the 1968 Kerner Commission report, which found that the United States was moving toward two separate and unequal societies of black and white. The Kerner Commission squarely put the burden of that conclusion on white racism and recommended a massive redistribution of wealth. Thernstrom counters with statistics showing that the socioeconomic condition of African Americans had improved more than any other group between the end of World War II and the passage of the Voting Rights Act of 1965. He and his wife offer a lengthy rebuttal to the commission's finding in their book *America in Black and White: One Nation Indivisible* (1997). The book presents an abundance of statistics to support their opposition to affirmative action. The continuing use of racial standards and preferences only incites greater racial tension, according to Thernstrom.

Thernstrom is the editor of the *Harvard Encyclopedia of American Ethnic Groups* and the author of *Poverty and Progress: Social Mobility in a Nineteenth-Century City* (1964); *Poverty, Politics and Planning in the New Boston: The Origins of ABCD* (1969); *The Other Bostonians: Poverty and Progress in the American Metropolis, 1880–1970* (1973); and a two-volume survey, *A History of the American People* (1989). He has been awarded the Bancroft Prize in American History, the Harvard University Press Faculty Prize, the Waldo G. Leland Prize of the American Historical Association, and the R. R. Hawkins Award of the Association of American Publishers. He has written over 50 other articles, chapters, and reviews.

Stephen Thernstrom received his Ph.D. in the history of American civilization from Harvard University in 1962. He is a Senior Fellow at the Manhattan Institute, a New York think tank. Previously he was a John S. Guggenheim Fellow, a Samuel S. Stouffer Fellow, and a Woodrow Wilson Fellow. Thernstrom is a frequent speaker, lecturing on racial issues around the country. He has also served as an expert witness in 18 federal court cases involving civil rights issues—predominantly in conflicts over minority voting rights and racial preferences in public education.

R. Roosevelt Thomas Jr.

R. Roosevelt Thomas is an expert on diversity leadership and training. He is the founder and chief executive officer of the American Institute for Managing Diversity, Inc., a think tank on organizational diversity issues. Thomas also manages his own consulting business on diversity issues. He has written two books dealing with diversity management in the wake of affirmative action. *Beyond Race and Gender: Unleashing the Power of Your Total Work Force by Managing Diversity* (1992) contends that successfully managing diversity is essential to corporate survival. The book gives action plans and case studies, prodding readers to address diversity issues that encumber their organizations and hinder the potential of their work forces.

Thomas states that the job of affirmative action is to get a fair representation of women and minorities on the job. The job of diversity management is to eliminate hurdles and capitalize on diversity by harnessing the unique contributions and talents they bring with their different backgrounds and experiences. According to Thomas, the workplace needs to be more flexible because the same strategies employed by white males to garner success may backfire if used by a female or minority manager. Instead of trying to get others to conform to a traditional "white male approach" to management, the organization needs to be fluid and allow many different styles to flourish.

In his second book, *Redefining Diversity* (1996), Thomas takes the premise of his first book to its next evolution. He outlines his new model for diversity management called the "diversity paradigm." He details a diversity management process and eight action options to give business managers a working framework for clarifying goals, reducing bias and conflict, and increasing the effectiveness of individuals and operating units within organizations.

Thomas isn't certain that prejudice can be eradicated with diversity training. He acknowledges that the diversity critics might be right. Prejudice is still here. However, Thomas states, "People can have racist thoughts and still effectively manage a diverse work force." He argues that though attitudes of bias may exist, the behavior of people can still be changed so that they are required to assist women and minorities with their careers, promote them, and retain them. The new movement afoot is to tie compensation to the success of diversity programs. The thinking is that when managers have a financial stake in the outcome, they are more likely to be invested in the program's success.

Thomas believes that people need to expand their understanding of the term *diversity*. He says, "because we are so accustomed to thinking of diversity in terms of workforce demographics, and equating it with the minority constituencies in that workforce, we tend to think diversity means the qualities that are different. . . . But the definition that is put forth here includes not only differences, but also similarities."

According to Thomas, it is essential to think about differences and similarities simultaneously. He offers this example: "Visualize a jar of red jellybeans; now imagine adding some green and purple jellybeans. Many would believe that the green and purple jellybeans represent diversity. I suggest that the diversity instead is represented by the resultant mixture of red, green, and purple jellybeans."

Cornel West (1953–)

Scholar Cornel West has long involved himself in the national discourse on affirmative action and race. A respected intellectual thinker and author, he finds that the pressing problem of black poverty is largely due to inequities in the distribution of wealth and power that were unaddressed prior to affirmative action. In his 1993 book, *Race Matters,* he states, "recent efforts to broaden access to America's prosperity have been based upon preferential policies. Unfortunately, these policies always benefit middle-class Americans disproportionately. The political power of big business in big government circumscribes redistributive measures and thereby tilts these measures away from the have-nots and the have-too-littles."

Although in principle West favors class-based affirmative action, he believes that given the political climate of the 1960s and the rampant discrimination against people of color and women, race- and gender-based affirmative action was the best possible compromise. Still, West sees another flaw in affirmative action: "The problem is that affirmative action could never really get at the issue of corporate power in the workplace, and so you ended up with the downsizing; you ended up with de-industrializing. You ended up with the marginalizing of working people even while affirmative action was taking place and a new black middle class was expanding."

West also contends that the assassination of Martin Luther King, Jr. created overwhelming barriers to progress on racial issues. The Black Power movement and the white backlash were two sides to the same coin—identity politics. From West's vantage point, while they were clashing, "King was trying to talk about a multiracial alliance that talked about class and economic inequality . . . if brother Martin had lived, it still would have been very difficult." King, West asserts, had the credibility and legitimacy to hold a multiracial alliance together.

West finds affirmative action a strategically weak but necessary part of the American landscape. It offers limited benefits, but nonetheless, those benefits provide some measure of insurance against regression to an even more untenable situation.

Cornel West is a professor of Afro-American studies and philosophy of religion at Harvard University. He received his master's degree in 1975 and his Ph.D. in philosophy from Princeton University in 1980.

Steven Yates (1957–)

Steven Yates jumped into the affirmative action fray with his book, *Civil Wrongs: What Went Wrong with Affirmative Action* (1994). He claims with conviction that the goals of affirmative action were undermined from the beginning. Affirmative action degenerated into a quota system that, according to Yates, instigated hatred and violence among minority groups. He claims that incompetent teachers were hired routinely at colleges and universities across the country in the name of affirmative action quotas. Yates states, "several generations of black public school students have now had many black teachers and administrators, yet academic performance indicators remain low and dropout rates remain high. . . . Asian and Asian American students have excelled in public schools with virtually no role models at all."

In *Civil Wrongs*, he writes, "Affirmative action is one of several policies in contemporary American society that are pursued zealously in the face of growing evidence of many negative, and few positive, results." He states that affirmative action was never actually defined in the executive orders or the Civil Rights Act that birthed it. Yates laments, "I discovered that 'affirmative action' basically meant whatever the federal courts and government bureaucrats wanted it to mean, which meant that its actual meaning shifted from case to case. It was clearly more than 'equal opportunity.'"

According to Yates, affirmative action will never solve the issues of racial, ethnic, class, and gender discrimination that pervade society. The flaw, he says, is that affirmative action "assumes that racial/gender harmony, justice, etc., can be created by superimposing informal ratios on institutions and entire occupations." Affirmative action pits minority against minority, causing divisiveness instead of healing. Ruefully, Yates says, "I was always amused by the belligerent denial that quotas existed. . . . But the way the policies were written and because of the threat of lawsuits, organizations were forced to adopt informal, behind the scenes quotas and then deny that they were doing anything of the sort."

He sees the only plausible solution to be one in which the government withdraws from affirmative action and allows minorities and women the opportunity to succeed on their own merits. The destruction of overt discrimination has facilitated this possibility, and if other economic hurdles are lowered—such as occupational licensure fees—minorities and women can attain their goals sans affirmative action.

Civil Wrongs was initially just a lengthy essay that eventually became a book, almost by accident. Yates's interest in affirmative action came about as a result of his observations that many women with substantially fewer credentials than he had were getting hired at universities. Despite a Ph.D. in philosophy from the University of Georgia and numerous publishing credits in academic journals, he was unable to obtain a tenured position. Yates believes that his views on affirmative action made him an outcast in the academic community despite his popularity as a professor. He has since left academia to pursue a master's degree in public health from the University of South Carolina Health Sciences program.

Carl Robert Zelnick (1940–)

Longtime journalist Bob Zelnick is noted for his stinging criticism of affirmative action in his 1996 book, *Backfire: A Reporter's*

Look at Affirmative Action. His tenet is that affirmative action is discriminatory and harmful. From the beginning of the book, Zelnick delivers potent statistics and facts to support his conclusions. He states, "When the University of California at Berkeley routinely admits African-American students with lower grades and SAT scores 200 points lower than Chinese Americans who are rejected, there is nothing fancy or esoteric about what the university is doing: It is discriminating against Chinese Americans on the basis of race."

According to Zelnick, affirmative action was originally designed to bring greater awareness to employers regarding the existence of qualified minority job applicants. He believes that affirmative action's lofty goal was derailed when it was transformed into a series of quotas, preferences, and entitlements. In his estimation, those programs actually hinder equal opportunity instead of providing it. He staunchly believes that it is hypocritical to counter discrimination with reverse discrimination. Furthermore, the hiring and promotion of less-qualified individuals on the basis of race reduces the overall competency and efficiency of businesses and public services. He also claims that the use of affirmative action endangers public safety as it relates to medical care, crime prevention, and emergency services.

A hefty 400 pages of anecdotes, statistics, and charts left critics with vastly different viewpoints on Zelnick's book. It was trumpeted by some as a major new exploration of the real workings of affirmative action, whereas others claimed it offered just another "angry white male" perspective that brought little new information to the debate. Like the larger dialogue on affirmative action, discussion about this book has ranged over the full political spectrum.

Zelnick's book offers limited alternatives to affirmative action to achieve the same goals in a nondiscriminatory manner. In lieu of minority set-asides in contracting, Zelnick proposes that additional training in business practices and financial strategies be offered to support contractors. With respect to leveling the playing field in assessing mortgage applications, Zelnick suggests that possible loan officer bias be mitigated through a more mechanical scoring of loan applications.

Zelnick was a 21-year veteran journalist with ABC News when, in 1998, the network forced him to choose between his job and writing a biography about Vice President Al Gore. Zelnick chose the latter and then wrote a scathing article about that experience in the *Wall Street Journal*. In the article he stated, "My original sin may have been my earlier book, *Backfire.*" The firing of Zelnick was widely condemned by journalists of varying political viewpoints and evoked outrage among reporters on the national scene. Zelnick continues his work on the Gore biography and is a Media Fellow at the Hoover Institution.

Facts and Statistics

4

This chapter provides general facts and statistics relating to affirmative action law, policies, and studies so that readers can evaluate what they see and hear about affirmative action from other sources. Because the laws, government orders and policies, and court decisions on affirmative action are evolving and changing at a rapid rate, these facts and statistics may soon be outdated. The significance or meaning of any particular fact or statistic will vary depending upon the individual point of view. Because the presentation of facts is necessarily brief, suggestions for additional reading are included where appropriate as well as in the reference section. This chapter includes an overview of the law, including statutes and important cases, government policies, and statistics and surveys relating to affirmative action and related discrimination issues.

Overview of the Laws on Affirmative Action

Legal Justifications for and against Affirmative Action

Affirmative action law is governed by Title VII of the Civil Rights Act of 1964, the Equal Protection Clauses of the Fifth and Fourteenth Amendments to the U.S. Constitution, and U.S. Presidential Executive Order 11246. The purpose of employment discrimination law is to eliminate discrimination in employment decisions made after the passage of the Civil Rights Act of 1964.

Affirmative action advocates argue that these programs are a means of remedying the present effects of past discrimination in the employment setting. They decrease the likelihood that an employer will be found liable in a discrimination suit because such programs rectify the statistical disparity between the utilization of a marginalized class and the availability of a protected class in the qualified labor market (here and below, see Estreicher and Harper 1992: 207–208). Affirmative action programs are also a means of eliminating the chilling effect on minority participation in traditionally segregated occupations. They are used as compensation for discrimination imposed in the past or present in employment, education, housing, or other areas that have created a cycle of poverty and low education levels. Affirmative action provides incentives to minorities to make the necessary investments in education and training to enable them to compete for jobs in occupations that were traditionally filled through discriminatory practices. Affirmative action accelerates the undoing of the effects of past societal discrimination.

Contrary to these justifications for affirmative action, many arguments are made against the adoption of affirmative action policies: (1) If the law should be color-blind, then any consideration—whether against or in favor of minorities—should not be accepted under the law. (2) The disadvantages attributable to minority status vary by individual experience. Therefore, a single standard of preference for all minorities provides benefits to those who do not need them. (3) Discrimination may be more closely linked to economic status than minority status. If this is the case, preferences could be given on that basis rather than on a race-conscious basis. (4) Preferential hiring also imposes social costs by encouraging race- and status-conscious decisionmaking that leads to animosity between those that benefit and those that do not benefit from the program. This animosity is magnified by the historical feelings of prejudice toward those who benefit from affirmative action programs. (5) Preferential treatment can also stigmatize both the people receiving benefits and people who are aware of the existence of benefits. People who receive affirmative action benefits may feel as though their accomplishments are un-earned, while others may discount the value of any achievement made with the aid of affirmative action. (6) The final—but most widely used—argument against affirmative action programs is that they result in the hiring and promotion of unqualified work-ers who cause all of society to lose.

The legislature and courts have thus far ruled that the justi-fications of affirmative action outweigh the potential harms from it, but the courts have instituted a very high standard for evalu-ating affirmative action programs. Following is an analysis of the significant affirmative action case law.

Classifications of Affirmative Action Cases in Employment

The legality of an affirmative action program comes into question in employment discrimination suits when an employee has made a prima facie case for discrimination, and the burden of produc-tion has shifted to the employer to show the reason it used a racial or status classification in its direction. Affirmative action is a valid reason for using race or status considerations in only a limited number of situations.

There are four types of affirmative action programs: (1) pub-lic and involuntary, (2) public and voluntary, (3) private and in-voluntary, and (4) private and voluntary. Public affirmative action programs are engaged in by a governmental entity or are judicially mandated. Private programs are engaged in by a pri-vate business entity. The difference between voluntary and in-voluntary is blurred because judicially mandated affirmative action programs engaged in by private entities are considered public programs. Due to these definitions, the first three types can be classified as constitutional cases governed by the Equal Protection Clause of the Fifth and Fourteenth Amendments. The fourth type is classified as Title VII suits brought under the Civil Rights Act of 1964.

Affirmative Action: Equal Protection of Review in Employment, Education, and Contracting Cases

The standard of review for challenges of affirmative action plans made under the Equal Protection Clause has been a subject of debate since the Supreme Court decided the first affirmative action claim in 1978. In *Regents of the University of California v. Bakke,* the Supreme Court held, by a plurality, that constitutional claims of racial discrimination in education must be evaluated under strict scrutiny. Allan Bakke, a white student denied admission, alleged that he was more qualified than blacks who had been admitted. The court determined that to pass this rigorous examination, the racial classification must be "precisely tailored to serve a compelling government interest." The *Bakke* opinion was by plurality vote, which left open the possibility that different standards of review could be applied. The dissent in *Bakke* by Justices Brennan, White, and Marshall asserted that a lower degree of scrutiny should be applied to racial classifications that burden nonminorities.

In decisions since that time, the U.S. Supreme Court has examined the standards for review of affirmative action in education, employment, and government contracting, concluding that the standards should be similar.

In 1980 the Court in *Fullilove v. Klutznick* opted to apply the "objectives and means" test when evaluating affirmative action mandated by congressional act. The objectives and means test requires that Congress have the power to legislate with respect to its objective. If this first part is true, then the court will decide if the means used to achieve the objective is permissible under the Constitution. A program can distribute the burden of remedying the effects of prior discrimination over innocent parties. But the program can only confer benefits if the recipient is roughly qualified for the position and the employer can identify the present effects of past discrimination. Finally, the program must be "limited in extent and duration." The *Fullilove* plurality chose not to apply a specific level of scrutiny, but felt that the objectives and means test would survive constitutional review by strict scrutiny.

In 1985, a plurality once again held that strict scrutiny is the appropriate standard to apply when evaluating the constitutionality of an affirmative action program in education. In *Wygant v. Jackson Board of Education,* the Court reiterated the two tests applied in the strict scrutiny analysis. "First, any racial classification 'must be justified by a compelling government interest.' Second, the means chosen by the State to effectuate its purpose must be 'narrowly tailored to the achievement of that goal'" (see *Wygant v. Jackson Board of Education*, 476 U.S. 274, citing *Palmore v. Sidoti*, 466 U.S. 429 [1984], and *Fullilove*, 448 U.S. 480). Two years later, in *United States v. Paradise*, the Court held by plurality opinion that some elevated level of scrutiny should be used when analyzing racial classifications, but it did not explicitly hold in favor of strict scrutiny (see *United States v. Paradise*, 480 U.S. 149, 166 [1987]). The Court evaluated the program in *Paradise* by a heightened standard and felt that the affirmative action programs would survive strict scrutiny.

Until this point in the history of affirmative action law, no court had held by majority decision in favor of strict scrutiny. Finally, two years after *Paradise*, in *City of Richmond v. J. A. Croson Co.*—a case involving city government contracting—a majority of the Supreme Court held in favor of strict scrutiny. This case clarified that strict scrutiny should be applied to all state-level affirmative action plans but could not require federal plans to be evaluated by this rigorous standard.

The *City of Richmond* case involved an affirmative action plan adopted by a city government, and therefore some debate remained regarding the standard applied to federal as opposed to state (or one of its political subdivisions) affirmative action programs.

The debate was fueled by the holding in *Metro Broadcasting, Inc., v. F.C.C.* (1990)—a case involving a congressional mandate requiring that a certain number of Federal Communications Commission radio licenses be granted to minority owners. The Court held in *Metro Broadcasting* that federal affirmative action programs are mandated by Congress and that the Supreme Court must give proper deference to the legislative branch; therefore, strict scrutiny is not applicable. In the case of affirmative action programs mandated by Congress, the Court chose to apply intermediate scrutiny. This evaluation finds affirmative action programs "constitutionally permissible to the extent that they serve important governmental objectives within the power of Congress and are substantially related to the achievement of those objectives" (*Metro Broadcasting, Inc., v. F.C.C.*, 497 U.S. 565).

The debate over the application of strict scrutiny to all constitutional claims regarding affirmative action programs was resolved in 1995. The Supreme Court in *Adarand Constructors, Inc.*, *v. Pena*—a city contracting case—held that the evaluation of all public affirmative action programs, both state and federal, are subject to strict judicial scrutiny. This standard states that racial "classifications are constitutional only if they are narrowly tailored measures that further compelling governmental interests" (*Adarand Constructors, Inc. v. Pena*, 515 U.S. 227).

Compelling State Interests under Strict Scrutiny

Adarand requires all public affirmative action programs to be strictly scrutinized. This evaluation ensures that state or federally mandated racial classifications are justified by a compelling state interest. The Supreme Court has provided explicit examples of state interests that are sufficient and those that are not. Insufficient government interests include racial and status classification for the purpose of remedying societal discrimination, achieving diversity based exclusively on ethnicity, and providing minority teachers as role models for students.

A racial classification made for the purpose of remedying societal discrimination is insufficient because it imposes disadvantages on persons who are not responsible for the burdens placed on minorities (see *University of California v. Bakke*, 438 U.S. 310). Racial classifications made for the purpose of diversity in education based purely on ethnicity are prohibited because ethnicity is only one of many factors that creates true educational diversity. The role-model theory of providing teachers who closely reflect the makeup of the student body is forbidden by the Supreme Court because it is not related to any remedial purpose (see *Wygant v. Jackson Board of Education*, 476 U.S. 275). This theory was rejected because it could also be used as an excuse not to engage in legitimate remedial action "by justifying a small percentage of black teachers by reference to the small percentage of black students" (*Wygant v. Jackson*, 276).

The only purpose for racial or status discrimination that is considered a compelling government interest is remedying the present effects of past discrimination. Public employers must provide "sufficient evidence to justify the conclusion that there has been prior discrimination" in order to make such classifications (*Wygant v. Jackson*, 277). There is debate over the existence of other sufficient compelling government interests that would justify racial classifications. The cases that did not apply strict scrutiny indicate that something less than prior discrimination would constitute a sufficient justification, but in the wake of *Adarand*, it is likely that these interpretations of sufficient government interests will no longer be applicable.

Narrowly Tailored under Strict Scrutiny

The *Wygant, Croson,* and *Adarand* cases applied and discussed the narrowly tailored means of strict scrutiny analysis. "Narrowly tailored" is the standard applied under strict scrutiny "to test the validity of the means chosen by a state to accomplish its race-conscious purpose" (*Wygant v. Jackson,* 279). Layoff provisions in an affirmative action plan is an example of specific action that is not narrowly tailored. The Court reasoned that layoff provisions are too intrusive because they place the entire remedial burden on one individual. This is contrasted with hiring goals, which spread the remedial burden over the entire qualified applicant pool. Layoff provisions is the only policy that has been explicitly rejected by the Court. All other discussions of the "narrowly tailored" test consist of guidelines regarding how the plan will be evaluated.

An affirmative action plan may survive strict scrutiny analysis if the means employed to achieve the state interest are the least intrusive. It may also survive if the employer considers all possible methods that do not take race into account (see *City of Richmond v. J. A. Croson Co.,* 507). A successful program should be limited in its scope and duration so it will expire no later than when the effects of the prior discrimination cease (see *Adarand Constructors, Inc., v. Pena,* 238). The Court in *City of Richmond v. Croson* also suggested that quotas will not be considered narrowly tailored because they imply racial balancing rather than an effort to achieve a numerical goal. Programs may be considered narrowly tailored even if innocent parties must "bear some of the burden of the remedy" (*Wygant v. Jackson Board of Education,* 281).

Affirmative Action under Title VII

Title VII of the Civil Rights Act of 1964 is designed to "break down old patterns of racial segregation and hierarchy" (*United Steelworkers of America v. Weber,* 443 U.S. 193, 208 [1979]). In furtherance of this goal, the Supreme Court held that Title VII allows private, voluntary affirmative action plans that "eliminate conspicuous racial imbalance in traditionally segregated job categories" (*United Steelworkers of America v. Weber,* 209). The Supreme Court does not impose as stringent a standard of review of plans under Title VII as it does when applying strict scrutiny to constitutional claims (see *Johnson v. Transportation Agency, Santa Clara County, California,* 480 U.S. 616, 632 [1987]). A Title VII analysis determines if a voluntary affirmative action plan takes steps to "eliminate manifest racial imbalances in traditionally segregated job categories" (*United Steelworkers of America v. Weber*, 197). If this is true, the analysis will then determine if the plan unnecessarily trammels the rights of nonminority employees.

An affirmative action program is justified if the employer can show that a manifest imbalance exists in a job category that has traditionally been segregated. The employer does not have the burden of proving that it discriminated in the past; it need only show a substantial imbalance in the makeup of a particular job category relative to the makeup of the qualified labor market. The employer is not required to provide evidence so extensive as to make a prima facie case of discrimination against themselves. This requirement of something less than prior discrimination may allow for remedial action based on societal discrimination. The "manifest imbalance" requirement applies to both racial and gender classification. Affirmative action plans that hire minorities based solely on the calculated imbalance of the work force relative to the labor market may be struck down because hiring decisions must take the qualifications of the applicant into account.

An affirmative action program under Title VII unnecessarily trammels the rights of nonminority employees if the discharge of nonminorities is required or the plan creates an absolute bar to nonminorities. The plan must have a logical stopping point, and it must not be intended to maintain a racial balance rather than eliminate a racial imbalance. It is arguable that a program unnecessarily trammels nonminorities' rights when it provides for set-asides or quotas. *United Steelworkers of America v. Weber* created a 50 percent set-aside for African Americans, but the Court in *Johnson v. Transportation Agency, Santa Clara County, California,* found the lack of set-asides to be a positive aspect of the program. The Court seems to prefer a plan that considers minority status a plus factor rather than eligibility for a set-aside. If set-asides are utilized, the plan may be required to contain a specific ending date (see *Local Number 93 v. City of Cleveland,* 478 U.S. 501, 510 [1986]). Minority status may be taken into account in the hiring decision in conjunction with other qualifying factors. Furthermore, the numerical goals specified in any affirmative action plan should be flexible. The flexibility of the goal plan indicates the use of numbers as a benchmark by which progress can be measured rather than as a method of racial balancing (see *Local 28 of Sheet Metal Workers v. E.E.O.C.,* 478 U.S. 421, 478 [1986]).

Affirmative Action Circuit Court Cases

Circuit courts are federal courts spread throughout the United States that are below the U.S. Supreme Court. The trend in recent circuit court decisions has been to limit the ability of employers to maintain affirmative action programs. These decisions have done so by restricting the interpretation of "manifest imbalance" and "compelling state interest." The court in *Taxman v. Board of Education of the Township of Piscataway* held that the purpose of Title VII is to "remedy the segregation and under-representation of minorities that discrimination has caused in our Nation's work force" (*Taxman v. Board of Education of the Township of Piscataway*, 91 F.3d 1547, 1557 [3d Cir. 1996]). The court interpreted this purpose to mean that affirmative action plans may only be used for a remedial purpose. Affirmative action programs are not valid without evidence of past discrimination or the present effects of past discrimination. The court held that Title VII is limited to remedial purposes and, therefore, rejected the assertion that the purpose of an affirmative action plan could be to increase cultural diversity. The Third Circuit also held in *Taxman* that the plan unnecessarily trammeled the interests of nonminorities because it did not set goals, was very discretionary, and was unlimited in duration. This case was settled after certiorari was granted, but the Supreme Court heard the case. In fact, a coalition of civil rights groups raised the money to settle the case because they were concerned that the decision would create an unfavorable precedent. The *Bakke* case had earlier held that educational diversity was a compelling state interest in constitutional affirmative action claims. Such claims are evaluated under strict scrutiny, which is a more stringent analysis than that imposed on Title VII claims. Therefore, it would seem that the purpose of educational diversity would be sufficient in a Title VII claim.

Other circuit court cases have held for limited interpretations of the compelling state interest element of a constitutional affirmative action claim. The Fifth Circuit created the same restriction as the *Taxman* case, but there it was under the Equal Protection analysis. The *Hopwood* case held that an affirmative action program engaged in for the purpose of achieving diversity in education did not rise to the level of a compelling state interest and, therefore, was unconstitutional. This holding expressly deviates from the plurality holding in *Bakke*, but certiorari was denied.

These cases are examples of the recent trend in circuit court decisions to restrict the circumstances in which affirmative action programs—either public or private—may be used. Each circuit has made its own choices regarding the interpretation of the tests that determine the validity of affirmative action programs, but the general trend has been toward restricting the applicability of such programs or, in the case of California, disposing of them entirely.

Statutes and Policies to End Affirmative Action

A number of states, cities, and other government entities have passed laws or resolutions aimed at eliminating affirmative action. The most well known and argued of these is the Proposition 209 ballot initiative in California. This proposition was passed in November 1996 by nearly 55 percent of California's voters. As argued by *Newsweek* reporter Ellis Cose, "No one ever expected affirmative action to succumb without a whimper. And if the Proposition 209 battle is any indication, death will be fought every inch of the way" (Cose, 1997 p. 123).

Cose's prediction turned out to be correct. In the first battle, within a few weeks of the election, a federal judge temporarily blocked enforcement, saying that the groups that filed the lawsuit (including the American Civil Liberties Union, the National Organization for Women, and the National Association for the Advancement of Colored People) had "demonstrated a strong probability" of proving the proposition to be unconstitutional. Experts predict that a final ruling on Proposition 209—which will probably be appealed all the way to the U.S. Supreme Court—will not be made for years.

Other government entities around the country have passed—or attempted to pass—propositions, statutes, and ordinances similar to Proposition 209. All of these, as of this writing, are still tied up in court, political, or other entanglements so that no final statements about the effectiveness or consequences of these actions can be made at this time.

Some Historical Perspective

In Lyndon B. Johnson's commencement address at Howard University in 1965 (see Chapter 3), when he delivered his famous analogy to a race between a man who has just been freed from hobbles and a man who has been coached and fed all along for the race, he also quoted a number of facts regarding the status of blacks compared to whites:

- In 1930, the unemployment rate for blacks and whites was about the same, but 35 years later the black rate of unemployment was twice as high.
- In 1948, the 8 percent unemployment rate for black teenage boys was actually less than that of whites, but by 1964 the rate had grown to 23 percent for blacks versus 13 percent for whites.
- From 1952 to 1963, the median income of black families compared to white families dropped from 57 percent to 53 percent.
- Between 1955 and 1957, 22 percent of experienced black workers were out of a job at some point; for the period 1961 through 1963, that proportion rose to 29 percent.
- Since 1947, the number of white families living in poverty decreased 27 percent while the number of poorer nonwhite families decreased only 3 percent. In 1963, a fifth of the white population had incomes below the poverty line, compared to half of the black population.
- The infant mortality rate of nonwhites in 1940 was 70 percent greater than whites. Twenty-two years later it was 90 percent greater.

Although strides have been made by women into the ranks of middle management, males, who constitute about 43 percent of the work force, make up 95 to 97 percent of senior management positions in *Fortune 2000* industrial and service, *Fortune 1000* industrial, and *Fortune 500* companies. Only 0.6 percent of those male senior management positions are African American; 0.3 percent are Asian American; and 0.4 percent are Hispanic. The black unemployment rate remains over twice the white unemployment rate (Federal Glass Ceiling Commission 1995). The Urban Institute testing study and many other studies based on census data show that blacks and whites with similar qualifications are not treated equally by employers (Bergmann 1996). In 1992, 33.3 percent of blacks and 29.3 percent of Hispanics lived in poverty compared to 11.6 percent of whites (Bureau of the Census 1993). In

1995, the poverty rate was 11.2 percent for whites, 14.6 percent for Asians/Pacific Islanders, 29.3 percent for blacks, and 30.3 percent for Hispanics, although the majority of poor people (67.1 percent) were white (Bureau of the Census 1998). Census data from 1990 showed that the average woman with a master's degree earns the same amount as the average man with an associate's degree. The Federal Glass Ceiling Commission (FGCC) report of 1995 found that across the board, men advance more rapidly than women.

Statistics and Studies about Equal Employment Opportunity

For several years, the Equal Employment Opportunity Commission (EEOC) has supervised those agencies and companies bound not to discriminate on the basis of race, sex, or national origin by Title VII of the Civil Rights Act of 1964, and made great progress in eliminating discrimination in the workplace. Before the Civil Rights Act of 1964, the average black male earned 60 percent as much as his white male colleague, yet by 1993 the same black male earned 74 percent as much as the white male—a 14-point improvement.

The same narrowing occurred during that time in the male/female wage gap as female earnings rose from about 60 percent of male earnings to 72 percent of male earnings. In the federal agencies advised by the EEOC, minorities comprise a relatively large proportion of the work force—about 30 percent—compared to the nation's overall work force, of which minorities make up 22 percent. White women and Hispanics are the only groups whose employment in the overall federal work force remains below their availability. Women and minorities are employed at a disproportionate rate in clerical jobs and in the lower grade levels of other occupational fields. In fiscal year 1993, 86 percent of clerical jobs were held by women and 39 percent by minorities, while their employment in the professional workforce was 35 percent and 18 percent, respectively (Stephanopoulos and Edley 1995).

In 1994, the Federal government received over 90,000 complaints of employment discrimination while state and local Fair Employment Practices Commissions received 64,423 complaints, bringing the total to over 154,000. Thousands of other accusations alleging racially motivated violence and discrimination in housing, voting, and public accommodations were filed (Stephanopoulos and Edley 1995). The EEOC receives on average 63,000 complaints of employment discrimination a year, but with limited resources it is able to bring suit in fewer than 500 cases (Bergmann 1996).

An American Bar Association survey found that between 1972 and 1987, only 19 percent of the employment discrimination lawsuits focused on hiring, whereas 59 percent alleged discrimination in termination and 22 percent in pay, promotion, or employee benefits, indicating that people are more likely to accept being passed up for a job initially or are, in fact, offered a job more often than when it comes to promotion or termination (Zelnick 1996). The Fair Employment Council of Greater Washington, Inc., conducted a series of tests between 1990 and 1992 to isolate the prevalence of discrimination in employment practices. Their tests revealed that blacks were treated significantly worse than equally qualified whites 24 percent of the time, and Hispanics were treated worse 22 percent of the time. Hispanic testers received 25 percent fewer job interviews and 34 percent fewer job offers than other testers (U.S. General Accounting Office 1990).

In 1993, less than 3 percent of college graduates were unemployed, yet 22.6 percent of whites had college degrees, whereas only 12.2 percent of blacks and 9 percent of Hispanics held college degrees (Stephanopoulos and Edley 1995). Many people argue that these inequalities are created by scores on achievement tests, education, family structure, drug use, involvement in crime, language facility, and many women's attempts to accommodate both home and careers rather than to discrimination (Zelnick 1996).

Yet, others claim that the lasting numerical imbalances aren't fully accounted for by this list when of the 17 percent of women and 5 percent of men who work in state and local government law, 63 percent of the women make less than $40,000 compared with 10 percent of the men. Outside of the confines of government work, over half of the women lawyers (53.1 percent) make under $40,000, compared to just 20.6 percent of their male counterparts. Nearly 85 percent of the women make $59,999 or less, in contrast to 50 percent of the men. For graduates in the period 1985 to 1989 there is a difference of approximately 10 percentage points in favor of men in compensation levels up to $50,000 to $60,000—the level where women tend to peak in their income, whereas males over time soar well above that mark even after controlling for experience. When asked, these women confirmed what the numbers have pointed to, with 48 percent reporting inadequate compensation as an obstacle to their success as a lawyer compared with 27.6 percent of their male counterparts (Gellis 1991). Tables 4.1, 4.2, and 4.3 show further breakdowns related to this study.

Office of Federal Contract Compliance Programs (OFCCP)

According to five academic studies, government contractors moderately increased their hiring of minority workers due to the active enforcement by the OFCCP during the 1970s (Ashenfelter and Heckman 1976; Goldstein and Smith 1976; Heckman and Woplin 1976; Leonard 1984a, 1984b). Studies also find that con-

Table 4.1
Salary Levels, Controlling for Experience

Years Experience	Up to $40,000		$40–60,000		$60–80,000		Over $80,000	
	F	M	F	M	F	M	F	M
Less than 5	70%	46%	29%	43%	2%	9%	0%	3%
5–9	38%	33%	43%	37%	11%	18%	7%	11%
Over 10	27%	8%	28%	22%	19%	20%	27%	50%

Source: Adapted from Ann Gellis, "Women in the Legal Profession," *Indiana Law Journal* 66:948. 1991. Reprinted by permission.

Table 4.2
Non-Partners' Salary Levels, Controlling for Experience

Years Experience	Up to $40,000		$40–60,000		$60–80,000		Over $80,000	
	F	M	F	M	F	M	F	M
Less than 5	74%	47%	25%	44%	0.6%	9%	0.3%	0%
5–9	52%	40%	38%	47%	7%	12%	2%	1%
Over 10	45%	17%	33%	32%	14%	18%	9%	34%

Source: Adapted from Ann Gellis, "Women in the Legal Profession," *Indiana Law Journal* 66:948. 1991. Reprinted by permission.

Table 4.3
Partners' Salary Levels, Controlling for Experience

Years Experience	Up to $40,000		$40–60,000		$60–80,000		Over $80,000	
	F	M	F	M	F	M	F	M
Less than 5	44%	11%	44%	56%	11%	0%	0%	33%
5–9	28%	11%	30%	30%	19%	33%	23%	26%
Over 10	15%	5%	15%	14%	20%	19%	49%	63%

Source: Adapted from Ann Gellis, "Women in the Legal Profession," *Indiana Law Journal* 66:948. 1991. Reprinted by permission.

tractor establishments that underwent OFCCP review in the 1970s had a faster rate of white female and black employment growth than contracting firms that did not have a review (Stephanopoulos and Edley 1995). The employment share of black males in contractor firms (those with an affirmative action plan) increased from 5.8 percent in 1974 to 6.7 percent in 1980, whereas the black male share in noncontractor firms only increased slightly from 5.3 percent to 5.9 percent. Because no systematic qualitative evidence that productivity is lower in contracting firms has been found, this suggests that the OFCCP's existence has not caused firms to hire or promote less qualified workers (Leonard 1984a). Although enforcement and thus effectiveness of the programs was scaled back in the 1980s, the programs continue to perform on average more than 4,000 reviews in a fiscal year. By 1996, the OFCCP was supervising nearly 200,000 government contractors and subcontractors hiring about 26 million people—just under 24 percent of the total labor force (Zelnick 1996). From a random customer satisfaction survey conducted by the OFCCP (with an 80 percent response rate), the agency received mostly satisfied (70 to 80 percent) feedback, with only 10 construction (of 278) and four nonconstruction (of 363) firms addressing the issue of quotas or reverse discrimination (Stephanopoulos and Edley 1995).

Other researchers insist that affirmative action has done little to increase minority employment and has instead caused black men and women to migrate from smaller noncontracted firms to larger government contractors where they have less to fear. In 1966, black men were 10 percent less likely than white men to work in firms required to file EEO-1 reports. Yet, by 1980, black men were 25 percent more likely—and black women were 50 percent more likely—to work in such firms. Table 4.4, constructed by Farrell Bloch in *Antidiscrimination Law and Minority Employment* (1994), uses EEO-1 reports, OFCC filings, and data from the 1990 census to show rather small differences in the positions achieved by minority employees of covered and uncovered establishments, finding those uncovered establishments in the technical, sales, professional, and managerial positions to actually have higher percentages (Zelnick 1996).

Although the U.S. Bureau of Labor Statistics reported in 1994 that of the nation's skilled jobs available, only 2 percent were held by women, 6.5 percent by blacks, and 11.4 percent by Hispanics, there remains concern that OFCC remedies have adverse effects on long-term goals. For example, during a 1990 to 1992

Table 4.4
Minority Employment among Federal Contractor Firms,
Those Firms Filing EEO-1 Reports, and the Experienced Labor Force

Occupational Category	Federal Contractors	Firms Filing EEO-1 Reports	Experienced Labor Force*
		Minorities (%)	
Officials and Managers	10.1	10.1	13.1
Professionals	13.5	13.0	15.6
Technicians	18.8	19.0	19.6
Sales Workers	18.6	18.8	17.5
Office and Clerical Workers	24.2	23.1	21.7
Craft Workers	17.0	17.5	18.5
Operatives	28.8	28.9	30.3
Laborers	36.1	37.2	31.8
Service Workers	40.5	39.4	32.5
Total	**23.1**	**23.0**	**22.3**
		Women (%)	
Officials and Managers	25.0	28.1	36.0
Professionals	37.8	48.0	53.4
Technicians	35.4	44.8	44.1
Sales Workers	52.5	57.2	53.9
Office and Clerical Workers	82.5	83.4	77.2
Craft Workers	8.8	10.6	7.5
Operatives	32.5	33.4	31.5
Laborers	33.4	34.4	16.4
Service Workers	51.0	55.5	58.2
Total	**39.9**	**43.9**	**42.0**

*Experienced Labor Force includes all workers currently employed plus those who have worked within the past five years and are actively seeking employment.
Source: Farrell Bloch, 1994. *Antidiscrimination Law and Minority Employment* (Chicago: University of Chicago Press, 1994). Reprinted by permission.

economic downturn, blacks employed at the nation's largest companies lost their jobs at the following disproportionate rate: According to the congressional testimony of former Transportation Secretary William T. Coleman Jr., a study of 35,000 companies employing more than 40 million workers concluded that blacks lost 59,479 jobs during the period in question while Asian Americans gained a net of 55,104, Hispanics a net of 60,040, and whites a net of 71,144. Economists James P. Smith and Finnis Welch offer an account for this inconsistency by going back to the initial rampant hiring of young educated black males to satisfy OFCCP numerical analysis that then backfired during a recession when those less-skilled workers hired to make the numbers look right became vulnerable to cutbacks (Zelnick 1996).

Evidence of Discrimination in Contracting

Several programs outside of the EEOC and the Office of Federal Contract Compliance Programs (OFCCP) work within the Department of Defense, Department of Transportation, and Small Business Administration to increase buying and contracting with minority- and women-owned businesses, but still 93 percent of procurements are with nonminority firms. These numbers have shifted only slightly over time from 1 percent of all federal procurement concluding with minority businesses in fiscal year 1976 to 2.7 percent in 1986 (Stephanopoulos and Edley 1995). In 1990, blacks accounted for 12.1 percent of the population, but they owned just 3.1 percent of the total businesses and 1.0 percent of receipts of all U.S. firms. In the same year, Hispanics accounted for 9 percent of the population, but owned 3.1 percent of U.S. businesses and 1.2 percent of all receipts. It is also interesting to note that in 1987 the average payroll among white-owned firms with employees was $85,786, yet for minority-owned firms the average payroll was $38,318 (Stephanopoulos and Edley 1995). The 1990 census reflected that of the nation's 2.4 percent businesses owned by blacks, almost 85 percent of them had no employees (Hacker 1992). Women have faced similar challenges, evidenced by data from 1990 when women-owned businesses averaged $19,876 per year in annual receipts, only 45 percent of the overall average. Women's share of federal procurement dollars has also been limited but showed progress from 1985, when just 0.6 percent of all Department of Defense prime contracts went to women-owned businesses, to 1994, when that number had climbed to 1.7 percent (Stephanopoulos and Edley 1995).

Statistics and Studies about Equal Education Opportunity

In 1955, only 4.9 percent of college students ages 18 to 24 were black. Not until the late 1960s and early 1970s did that number start to climb steadily. In 1970, 7.8 percent of college students were black; in 1980, 9.1 percent; and in 1990, 11.3 percent (Stephanopoulos and Edley 1995). However, since 1977, when the college-going rates for blacks and whites were about equal, the proportion of black 18- to 24-year-old high school graduates enrolled in college has not kept pace with that of white students. The portion of black students attending college in 1995 had dropped to 25 percent below that of white students (Stephanopoulos and Edley 1995). Hispanics have a similar story of enrollment rates. The college-going rate for 18- to 24-year-old Hispanics who had recently graduated from high school (53 percent) exceeded the rate for whites (49 percent), but by 1994, the white college-going rate had risen to 64 percent while the Hispanic rate had fallen to 49 percent (National Center for Education Statistics 1994).

Admissions, Graduation, and Attrition Rates and Measures of Performance

The following is a list of factors influencing admissions at most institutions of higher education, but specifically where race-neutral admissions policies have been adopted. The information was compiled from a 1997 *Admission Trends* survey conducted by the National College Admissions Council.

- Grades in college preparatory classes
- Admissions test scores
- Grades in all subjects
- Class rank
- Counselor recommendation
- Teacher recommendation
- Essay/writing sample
- Interview
- Extracurricular activities
- Personal recognition programs
- Ability to pay

Elaine Woo reports in a 1995 *Los Angeles Times* article that the Office of Civil Rights, after calculating average Scholastic Achievement Test (SAT) scores over a 10-year period, found the mean score for Harvard's legacy (alumni) students was 35 points lower than that of nonalumni students who were not athletes. Recruited athletes had the lowest mean scores—about 130 points lower than the nonalumni group (although still in the top percentiles of SAT test takers nationally). However, the gap seen between most minority test scores and white test scores is just as wide, if not wider, in many of the admission practices of the approximately 120 elite institutions of higher education across the nation. In fall 1995, the *Journal of Blacks in Higher Education (JBHE)* presented data from the College Board comparing the SAT credentials of blacks and whites

Table 4.5
Percentage of 1995 Blacks and Whites Who Scored in Each Range

SAT Score	VERBAL SAT		MATH SAT	
	White (%)	Black (%)	White (%)	Black (%)
750–800	0.1	0.0	1.4	0.1
700–749	1.2	0.2	4.4	0.5
650–699	2.9	0.4	7.6	1.4
600–649	5.4	1.1	10.3	2.6
550–599	9.1	2.5	11.5	3.8
500–549	12.3	4.5	14.3	6.8
450–499	17.5	8.8	14.3	10.2
400–449	19.4	14.5	14.1	15.1
350–399	15.4	18.6	11.1	19.0
300–349	10.1	20.8	7.8	23.9
250–299	4.9	16.2	2.8	13.1
200–249	1.9	12.3	0.5	3.5

Source: Adapted from College Board data comparisons in the Autumn 1995 edition of the *Journal of Blacks in Higher Education*. Reprinted by permission.

based on scores that might be required by one of the most selective schools conducting color-blind admissions policy. For that year, 649 black students, or 0.6 percent, scored 650 or higher on the verbal SAT, and 28,000 white students, or 4.2 percent, broke the 650 verbal line. Thus, whites were seven times as likely as blacks to score above 650 on the verbal SAT. On the math portion, 2,050 blacks (1 percent) scored above 650 compared to 90,000 whites (13 percent). See Table 4.5 for a further breakdown.

According to a 1995 *JBHE* analysis based on the number of blacks who share the top SAT scores, of the 45,000 places for entering freshmen at the nation's highest-ranked universities, 3,000 of which are now held by blacks, only 2 percent (900 seats) will eventually be filled by blacks if those institutions adopt race-neutral admission policies. (See Table 4.6 for overall and black acceptance rates at 25 of the nation's top schools in 1995.) The universal standard remains that race and ethnicity are considered in admissions policies, although these practices are currently being challenged and abolished by organizations at institutional, state, and district levels (Zelnick 1996).

A study published in the November 1992 issue of *Academic Medicine* shows that minorities with low grade point averages (GPAs) and low Medical College Admissions Test (MCAT) scores will in most years find a medical school that will accept them about 30 percent of the time, whereas whites with the same credentials will get in about 15 percent of the time. The spring 1995 issue of the *JBHE* stated that the average GPA for blacks admitted

Table 4.6
Percentage of Overall and Black Acceptance Rates in Fall 1995

	All Applicants	Total Students Accepted	Overall % Acceptance Rate	Black Applicants	Blacks Accepted	Black Acceptance Rate	Black % Freshman Class
Harvard	17,847	2,106	11.8	*	215	*	9.3
Princeton	14,311	2,010	14.0	*	*	*	9.0
Yale	12,617	2,397	19.0	*	*	*	7.4
MIT	7,888	2,133	26.8	322	138	39.8	6.1
Stanford	15,390	2,907	18.8	*	278	*	8.3
Duke	14,437	4,124	28.6	*	*	*	7.7
CalTech	1,893	511	27.0	29	10	34.5	0.0
Dartmouth	10,006	2,370	23.7	*	177	*	6.4
Columbia	8,714	2,042	23.4	*	*	*	8.9
U. of Chicago	5,846	3,177	54.3	358	138	38.5	2.8
Brown	13,898	2,792	20.1	730	253	34.7	7.3
Rice	6,780	1,730	25.5	288	149	51.7	10.0
U. of Pennsylvania	15,073	4,960	32.9	938	*	*	6.7
Northwestern	12,926	5,200	40.2	568	*	*	6.1
Cornell	20,599	7,004	34.0	950	371	39.1	4.3
Emory	9,504	4,420	46.5	1,054	562	53.3	9.0
U. of Virginia	17,895	6,546	36.6	1,490	807	54.2	12.5
Vanderbilt	8,879	5,152	58.0	448	179	39.9	4.0
Notre Dame	9,999	3,700	37.0	295	187	63.4	3.8
Washington	9,379	5,285	56.3	714	346	48.5	3.8
U. of Michigan	19,208	12,984	67.6	1,498	1,103	73.6	11.2
Johns Hopkins	7,875	3,383	42.9	513	*	*	5.6
U. of Ca., Berkeley	22,780	8,767	38.4	1,204	614	50.9	6.5
Carnegie Mellon	10,310	5,634	54.6	484	310	64.0	4.7
Georgetown	12,835	2,849	22.2	986	285	28.9	7.2

* Declined to provide statistics
Source: *Journal of Blacks in Higher Education* survey of college and university admissions offices. Reprinted by permission.

to medical school in 1994 was 3.05 compared to 3.50 for whites. The *JBHE* also reported that on the 1988 National Board exam, pass rates were 88 for whites, 84 for Asian Americans, 66 for Hispanics, and 49 for blacks. The mean score was 369 for black females, 392 for black males, 467 for white females, and 499 for white males.

Michael Lynch of the Pacific Research Institute in *Choosing by Color: Affirmative Action at the University of California* (1994) cites the record of some of the state's graduate schools on admission:

- UC Berkeley School of Law admitted every black applicant with a GPA of 3.5 and Law School Admission Test (LSAT) of 90.0 or above, when only 42 percent of similarly qualified whites were admitted.

- UC Davis School of Law admitted all three black applicants with GPAs between 2.75 and 2.99 and LSATs in the 70.0 to 74.9 range, yet none of the 23 whites or Asians with similar ranges.
- UCLA School of Law admitted 61 percent of black applicants but only 1 percent of whites and 7 percent of Asians all having a GPA between 2.5 and 3.49 and an LSAT score between 60.0 and 89.0.
- UCLA School of Medicine admitted 27 blacks, but no whites or Asians, with GPAs of 3.24 or below and MCAT biology and chemistry percentile scores of 93.4 and below.

Most minorities, with the exception of Asian Americans, score lower on SATs than whites—refer to Tables 4.7 and 4.8 for 1998 averages based on race, ethnicity, and gender. Empirical and statistical evidence suggests, however, that many of those who are excluded based on test scores could perform comparably to those admitted. For example, a calibration scoring error of the Armed Services Vocational Aptitude Battery of 1976 resulted in the admission of over 300,000 recruits who actually failed the screening test used by the armed services. Studies of this group compared to control groups found that the performance differentials were not large, and in several cases, those otherwise "potentially ineligibles" ("PIs") performed as well if not better than the controls. The "PIs" completed training without unusually high attrition rates, and they typically reenlisted (Guinier and Sturm 1996).

Some critics of affirmative action have argued that the practice of admitting minorities with lower average test scores and

Table 4.7
1998 Mathematical SAT Scores by Race, Ethnicity, and Gender

	Men	Women
Asian American	579	546
White	547	512
Other	538	497
American Indian	499	468
Other Hispanic	489	449
Mexican American	481	445
Puerto Rican	465	434
Black	436	419

Table 4.8
1998 Verbal SAT Scores by Race, Ethnicity, and Gender

	Men	Women
Asian American	500	496
White	531	523
Other	514	508
American Indian	484	477
Other Hispanic	470	454
Mexican American	461	447
Puerto Rican	456	448
Black	432	435

Source: Adapted from College Board data, 1998. Reprinted with permission. Copyright © 1998 by College Entrance Examination Board. All rights reserved.

GPAs will result in lower overall school performance and higher attrition rates (Zelnick 1996). Although many factors go into accounting for a group's dropout rate—for example, class size (need for personal attention), economic situation, academic preparation (prior schooling and training), and peer support—blacks and Hispanics have on average lower graduation rates nationwide. In fact, the average attrition rate for black students at all NCAA Division schools is 60 percent, and nationally, the black student dropout rate is often 50 percent higher than it is for whites. However, that rate decreases dramatically among the more selective schools, averaging just over 25 percent for "College and Beyond" schools (see below) (Bowen and Bok 1998).

In contrast to the continued emphasis placed on test scores for performance measurement, a recent study at Bell Laboratories, a high-tech "think tank," found that the most valued and productive engineers "were not those with the highest IQs, the highest academic credentials or the best scores on achievement tests," but those who "excelled in rapport, empathy, cooperation, persuasion, and the ability to build consensus among people" (Goleman 1995, p. 6). Various studies show that "experts often fail on 'formal' measures of their calculating or reasoning capacities, but can be shown to exhibit precisely those same skills in the course of their ordinary work" (Gardner 1993, p. 172).

The enduring unevenness between race and ethnicity groups tends to show up more measurably after schooling, where studies have looked at family incomes compared to SAT scores. These statistical studies have suggested that test scores most accurately reflect income and socioeconomic status, both before and after college (Zelnick 1996). At over 25 percent of the colleges participating in a 1984 validity study by the Educational Testing Service, the correlation between SAT scores and family income was larger

Table 4.9
1995 Profiles of SAT Scores by Income and Race

Income	Latin American SAT-V	SAT-M	Puerto Rican SAT-V	SAT-M	Mexican SAT-V	SAT-M	White SAT-V	SAT-M	Asian SAT-V	SAT-M	Black SAT-V	SAT-M	NATIONAL SAT-V	SAT-M
Less than $10,000	332	380	320	358	330	386	409	460	343	482	320	355	354	415
$10–20,000	356	402	346	383	349	403	418	459	363	500	337	369	380	433
$20–30,000	379	424	371	406	369	420	428	471	397	518	352	382	405	454
$30–40,000	397	442	382	420	384	431	433	478	415	528	362	393	420	468
$40–50,000	415	460	395	434	399	446	439	488	432	537	375	405	431	482
$50–60,000	421	473	408	449	409	456	446	498	444	549	382	414	440	493
$60–70,000	431	482	412	454	415	458	453	506	453	558	385	415	448	502
$70,000 or more	454	514	424	475	430	478	475	533	476	595	407	442	471	533

Source: Adapted from Lani Guinier and Susan Sturm, "The Future of Affirmative Action." Copyright © 1996 *California Law Review.* Reprinted from *California Law Review* 84: 989 by permission.

than the correlation between SAT scores and freshman grades (Guinier and Sturm 1996). A recent study of the University of Pennsylvania Law School found that LSAT scores were weak predictors of performance in law school—14 percent of the differences in first-year grades, 15 percent in second-year grades, and 21 percent in third-year grades (Guinier and Sturm 1996; see Table 4.9).

It is widely recognized, even by authors of the SAT, that high school grades are more predictive of college freshmen-year grades than is the SAT (Guinier and Sturm 1996). Although high school grades tend to be a better predictor of college performance, college performance seems to be a stronger predictor of income. Refer to Figure 4.1, which presents data from a group of highly selective, race-sensitive institutes, to see the difference in wage earnings among male and female blacks and whites from the bottom, middle, and top third of their classes.

The managing partner at a large New York law firm confirmed this in a study he did to assess which hires eventually became partners over a 30-year period. He found that those who tended to excel in law school, especially those in the top 1 percent, were more likely to be outstanding lawyers and were often the top 1 percent of the firm's lawyers. (The correlation did not hold beyond the top 1 percent, however.)

A study at the University of Pennsylvania Law School showed how men and women were admitted with virtually identical entry-level criteria, but by the end of the first year the men were three times as likely to be in the top 10 percent and 1.5 times as likely to be in the top 50 percent (Guinier and Sturm 1996). There is evidence that training programs to prepare incoming minority freshmen can drastically reduce the performance gap. For example, the

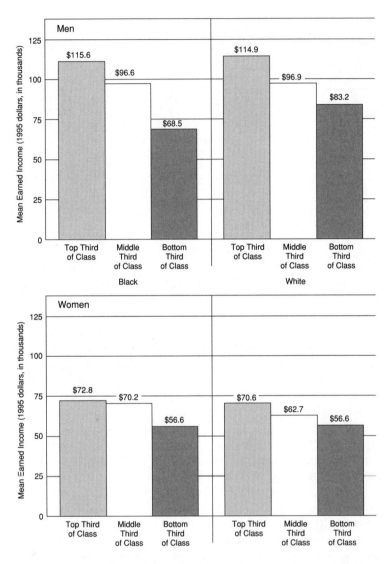

Figure 4.1. Mean Earned Income in 1995 by Class Rank, Gender, and Race (*Source:* William G. Bowen and Derek Bok. *The Shape of the River* (Princeton: Princeton University Press, 1998). Reprinted by permission.)

GPA of black and Hispanic freshmen who preenrolled in an intensive five-week summer course exceeded the overall average in the Georgia Tech engineering program (Smothers 1994).

College and Beyond Study (C and B)

In *The Shape of the River,* authors William Bowen and Derek Bok describe their study, a "College and Beyond" universe of 28 selective institutes of higher education to examine the long-term consequences of considering race in college and university admissions. The schools were broken down into selective categories based on the average test score of their matriculants:

- SEL-1: Average combined SAT score for entering class in 1989 was at least 1300 (Bryn Mawr, Duke, Princeton, Rice, Stanford, Swarthmore, Williams, Yale)
- SEL-2: Average SAT score for entering class in 1989 was between 1151 and 1300 (Barnard, Columbia, Emory, Hamilton, Kenyon, Northwestern, Oberlin, Pennsylvania, Smith, Tufts, Vanderbilt, Washington University, Wellesley, Wesleyan)
- SEL-3: Average SAT score for entering class in 1989 of 1150 or below (Denison, Miami [Ohio], University of Michigan [Ann Arbor], University of North Carolina [Chapel Hill], Penn State, Tulane)

As shown in Figure 4.2, black applicants across the board have a greater chance than whites of being admitted to institutions that have a commitment to enrolling a diverse student population. Conversely, Bowen and Bok then ask the question: What would happen to these admittance rates if race-neutral policies were sanctioned? They found their hypothesis that black admissions would drop from 41.9 percent to 13 percent to be remarkably close to the actual decrease the University of California at Berkeley experienced when their admission rate of 48.5 percent for blacks and 29.9 percent for whites—just prior to the installation of race-neutral policies—dropped to 15.6 percent for blacks and rose slightly to 30.3 percent for whites.

In the College and Beyond universe, SATs serve somewhat consistently to predict overall graduation rates and the likelihood of students to attain advanced degrees, both of which were much higher in these selective schools than they were nationwide, although the data in Figure 4.3 indicate a similar pattern in C and

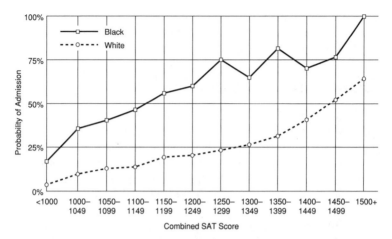

Figure 4.2. Probability of Admission to Five Selective Institutions, by Combined SAT Score and Race, 1989 (*Source:* William G. Bowen and Derek Bok, *The Shape of the River* [Princeton: Princeton University Press, 1998]. Reprinted by permission.)

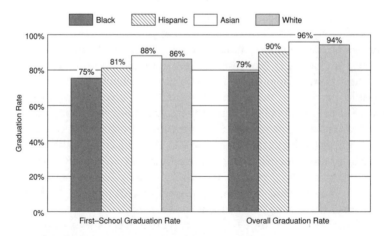

Figure 4.3. First-School and Overall Graduation Rates, by Race, 1989 Entering Cohort (*Source:* William G. Bowen and Derek Bok, *The Shape of the River* [Princeton: Princeton University Press, 1998]. Reprinted by permission.)

B graduation rates according to race in comparison with national patterns. In Figure 4.4, College and Beyond data show a comparison of whites and blacks based on their SAT scores and the percentage of whom go on to obtain advanced degrees. Consistently, blacks were more likely to continue beyond an undergraduate degree even though, according to Bowen and Bok, they generally lack information about certain kinds of advanced study and related career options when they enter college.

Bowen and Bok examined black and white worker satisfaction levels regarding their college or university experience, and their propensities toward leadership roles after college, a focus many institutes have stressed in preparing their students to do more than just participate. Differences in earnings, sectors of employment, family circumstances, treatment of women and minorities, and personal expectations, of course, account for a wide range of satisfaction levels among male and female blacks and whites in their jobs. Overall, however, whites were appreciably more likely than black respondents to be satisfied with their jobs. In contrast, the number of black men and women filling leadership roles compared to whites is noteworthy (see Figure 4.5). Also notable was the percentage of black matriculants (both men and women) with multiple leadership responsibilities—25 percent were leaders in three or more areas, whereas the corresponding percentage for whites was 19 percent.

Legacy and Donor Programs

Ivy League and other elite schools give a "tip" to children of alumni through legacy programs. From 1984 to 1994, Harvard University admitted on average 35 to 40 percent of the children of alumni, commonly known as "legacies," who applied compared to their overall admission rate of 14 percent. Stanford University has admitted legacies at twice the rate of other applicants, and the University of Virginia has admitted 57 percent of the legacies who applied, compared to their general 36 percent admission rate. In 1994, legacies accounted for about 12 percent of Yale University, 25 percent of the University of Notre Dame, and 16 to 20 percent of Harvard students (according to former Harvard Dean Henry Rosovsky). In contrast, 9 percent of the freshman class at Harvard was black; and overall, according to a 1991 report by Berkeley's Institute for the Study of Social Change, far more whites have entered the gates of the ten most elite institutions through alumni preference than the combined numbers of all the blacks and Hispanics entering through affirmative action programs.

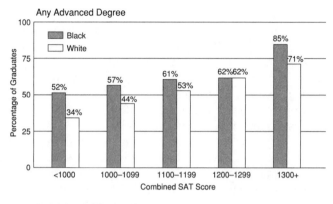

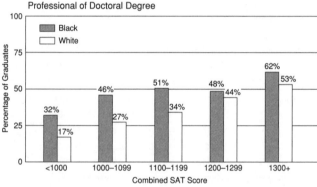

Figure 4.4. Percentage of Graduates Attaining Advanced Degrees, by Combined SAT Score and Race, 1976 Entering Cohort (*Source:* William G. Bowen and Derek Bok, *The Shape of the River* [Princeton: Princeton University Press, 1998]. Reprinted by permission.)

Many critics of legacy programs ask why this protected class of students has not attracted the scrutiny other classes receive under affirmative action guidelines. A U.S. Department of Education Office of Civil Rights investigation of Harvard University found that legacy preferences disproportionately help white applicants because 96 percent of all living Ivy League alumni are white (Guinier and Sturm 1996). A Bryn Mawr College sociology professor calculated that if Harvard's 1988 legacies had been admitted at the same rate as applicants without alumni connections, the number of alumni offspring would have fallen by nearly 200, a number that exceeded the total number of blacks, Mexican Americans, Puerto Ricans, and Native Americans admitted that year (Woo 1995).

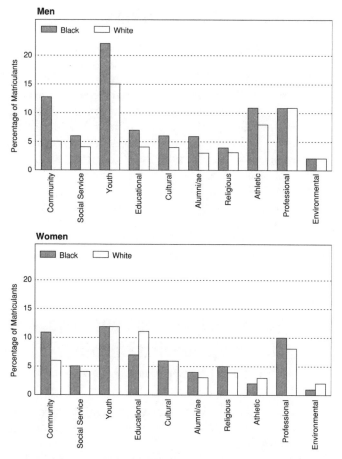

Figure 4.5. Percentage of Matriculants Leading Civic Activities in 1995, by Type of Activity, Race, and Gender, 1976 Entering Cohort (*Source:* William G. Bowen and Derek Bok, *The Shape of the River* [Princeton: Princeton University Press, 1998]. Reprinted by permission.)

Similar preferential treatment was discovered in a 1994 University of Minnesota study of poor youths in Boston, which found blacks had more schooling but were earning lower wages because whites had commonly been hired into better jobs. In the sample, whites who found jobs through relatives earned 38 percent more than the blacks who did, but for those who got jobs without contacts, the wage earning gap decreased considerably, to only 5 percent (Tilove 1995).

Minority-Targeted Scholarships

The General Accounting Office found in a 1994 study that at the undergraduate level, scholarships from all funding sources for which minority status is the only requirement for eligibility are rare (less than 0.25 percent); scholarships where minority status is one of several requirements represent 3 percent of all scholarship monies; and scholarships for which minority status is one factor among many considered are somewhat more common. The Department of Education estimates that only 40 cents of every $1,000 in federal educational assistance funding is devoted to these targeted programs. Numbers indicate that minorities need financial assistance on a greater level— 86.7 percent of blacks, 67.9 percent of Hispanics, 73.1 percent of Native Americans, 44.4 percent of Asian Americans, and 34 percent of white students require some financial assistance (Zelnick 1996).

Additional Surveys and Studies Relating to Discrimination and Affirmative Action

- The typical survey, as reported by Jennifer Hochschild in *Black Issues in Higher Education* in summer 1995, finds that only one-tenth of black faculty think affirmative action "perpetuates the myth of minority and female inferiority."
- In 1970, fewer than 1 percent of 10,000 lawyers in the state of New Jersey were nonwhite, but by 1990, 2,000 blacks, Hispanics, and Asian Americans were practicing law in the state. Forty percent of those 2,000 had come through the Rutgers University minority admissions program (Lawrence and Matsuda 1997).
- *Fortune Magazine* conducted a poll of chief executive officers and found that in 1989, 68 percent of the CEOs believed that affirmative action produced "good" or "very good" results, but in 1995 only 52 percent of the CEOs endorsed this view, and 78 percent supported the elimination of "racial and gender preferences" (*Fortune*, November 13, 1995).

- A *Time*/CNN poll conducted in 1995 reported that 77 percent of whites believe that affirmative action often discriminates against whites; 66 percent of blacks agreed with that conclusion (*Time*, February 20, 1995).
- A 1995 *Wall Street Journal*/NBC News poll found that two out of three Americans opposed affirmative action (Guernsey 1997).
- Most whites surveyed in a poll published by the *New York Times* on July 31, 1995, thought that when minority members are given "preferential treatment" in hiring, an unqualified black is given a job that a qualified white man deserves.

Housing Discrimination Study

A synthesis of a 1991 Housing Discrimination Study (HDS) that looked at the incidence of unfavorable treatment experienced by black and Hispanic homeseekers found that in a composite index both groups were treated unfavorably nearly half the time. This study may show additional evidence of continued discrimination (see Table 4.10).

With regard to the Housing Discrimination Study, most of those who experienced unfavorable treatment in "contributions to transaction" (stage one) also experienced it with "housing availability" (stage two), but for both blacks and Hispanics, the index of such treatment at stage two is about ten percentage points higher than at stage one. By using some of this data in comparison to a 1977 Housing Market Practices Survey (HMPS), analysis shows the HDS information to yield lower measures of discrimination than the HMPS. In the rental market, whites were

Table 4.10

Composite Index of Unfavorable Treatment in a Housing Discrimination Study*

Share of Audits with Unfavorable Treatment in:	RENTALS		SALES	
	Blacks	Hispanics	Blacks	Hispanics
Stage One—Housing Availability	39.0%	35.5%	35.7%	38.0%
Stage Two—Contributions to Transaction	44.5%	42.1%	45.9%	46.7%
Stage Three—Steering	—	—	20.9%	21.3%
Overall Index of Unfavorable Treatment	45.7%	42.7%	50.4%	44.6%

*All values reflect the gross incidence of unfavorable treatment, using weighted data. All reported estimates are statistically significant at a 95 percent confidence level.
Source: Margery Turner, Michael Fix, and Raymond Struyk, *Housing Discrimination Study Synthesis* (Washington, D.C.: The Urban Institute Press, 1991). Reprinted by permission.

shown or recommended more units than their black partners in 35 percent of the HDS audits, compared to 42 percent in HMPS. In the sales market, whites were shown or recommended more units than blacks in 42 percent of HDS audits, in contrast to 54 percent of the HMPS audits. However, in the overall composite indices of renters' information requested or volunteered, it is clear that differential treatment was considerably higher in the HDS (1991) than in the HMPS (1977). Unfortunately, these results present a mixed picture and don't delineate whether incidence of unfavorable treatment experienced by black and Hispanic home-seekers has increased or declined since the 1970s.

In synthesizing the HDS data, a formal model of agent choice was developed and statistically estimated to alleviate the random component of differential treatment. Again, the results were similar to the previous findings, with an overall probability of discrimination for minorities seeking housing more than half the time. In evaluating the various characteristics of the study, these patterns emerged: First, discrimination in some types of agent behavior is lower for higher-priced housing units, thus for higher income homeseekers as well. Corresponding to this is the overall index of discrimination being the highest in the sales market for low-cost housing. Also related was that most blacks and Hispanics seeking to rent or buy have incomes below the average white homeseeker, and HDS measures applied to the average advertised housing unit, not the average minority homeseeker. According to a Census Bureau Current Population survey, about 81 percent of white married-couple family renters could not afford a modestly priced house in 1993, compared with 92 percent of black married-couple families. Skin color appeared to be related to variations of treatment; the dark-skinned Hispanics encountered more discrimination overall on housing availability in the sales market.

College Students Look at Affirmative Action in the Workplace

One of the few studies that deals specifically with affirmative action asked a group of college students various questions regarding scenarios involving the antidiscrimination policies. Part of the study, conducted by author Barbara Bergmann and Sandra Tangri in *In Defense of Affirmative Action* (Bergmann 1996), sets up two situations to look at the opinion of 52 black students concerning the effects of affirmative action on black job incumbents and then on black job applicants (see Tables 4.11 and 4.12).

Seventy-five percent of the students (all black) were in favor of an affirmative action plan even though some (19 percent) were concerned that they would be considered not competent because of such a plan. Although 27 percent would be worried about the plan's effect on them, when asked specifically, 64 percent to 72 percent thought that affirmative action did more good than harm (24 percent said it made no difference). And although more than 80 percent thought that its abolition would make it harder for African Americans to get jobs, only one student claimed to have personal knowledge of anybody who had been hurt through affirmative action, whereas 46 percent said they knew of people it had helped.

In another part of the study, Bergmann asked a mostly white group of 173 undergraduate students at American University to respond to a scenario in a fictitious company, Acme, that is looking to hire a machine operator. Blacks and women have been excluded until now, which concerns the Acme manager, who wants to treat them fairly. Tables 4.13 and 4.14 show people responding in various ways to exclusion by sex and race.

Table 4.11
Opinions of Black Students Regarding Effects
of Affirmative Action on Black Job Incumbents

Situation I: In this case, you have a job in a company that has never had an affirmative action plan. You got your job because you were clearly the best applicant. There are very few blacks at your level or above—only you and one other person. You have been doing very well and seem to be well liked. The company wants to increase the numbers of black employees and has decided to start an affirmative action plan. What would you think about that?

	Disagree	Agree	Undecided
1. I would be worried about the plan's effect on me.	58%	27%	15%
2. I think they could probably find quite a few really good black applicants.	8%	79%	13%
3. I would be glad that there will be more blacks around.	0%	92%	8%
4. I would be worried that they might hire blacks who wouldn't work out.	60%	17%	23%
5. Since there are plenty of mediocre whites on the payroll, I wouldn't be worried about a few mediocre blacks.	42%	33%	25%
6. I would fear that some white coworkers would think I had been hired through affirmative action and couldn't do the job. My chances for respect would go down.	60%	19%	21%
7. If even one mediocre black were hired, my future would be threatened.	83%	6%	11%
8. I'd be glad to help the company find promising blacks to hire.	4%	88%	8%
9. On the whole, I would favor establishing the affirmative action plan.	4%	75%	21%

Source: Barbara Bergmann, *In Defense of Affirmative Action* (New York: Basic Books, 1996). Reprinted by permission.

Table 4.12
Opinions of Black Students Regarding Effects of
Affirmative Action on Black Job Applicants

Situation II: In this case, you are looking for a job. You answer an advertisement and are told about a job that sounds quite good. You feel confident that you could do well at it. You are offered the job. You find out the company has very few black employees and has recently instituted an affirmative action plan. You guess that the plan might have played a part in your being offered the job. What would your reaction be to this offer?

	Disagree	Agree	Undecided
1. I would welcome the chance for such a job, to show what I could do.	0%	89%	11%
2. I would rather be considered only on merit, even if that lowered my chance for an offer.	46%	21%	33%
3. I would accept the job, if it was the best offer I could expect.	6%	71%	23%
4. I would take the job, but I would worry that my white coworkers would think I was unqualified.	56%	21%	23%
5. The people doing the hiring have not judged black applicants fairly in the past, and that's why the company has so few of them.	11%	56%	33%
6. I would expect that most of the white employees would treat me fairly and accept me if I do good work.	35%	42%	23%
7. If even a few of my white coworkers doubted my abilities, that would make things very hard for me on the job.	52%	27%	21%
8. If I had another offer in a company where affirmative action wasn't an issue, I would take the other offer, even if it weren't quite as good as the one I could get through affirmative action.	61%	12%	27%
9. I would probably pass up any job offered because of affirmative action, no matter how good.	83%	11%	6%

Source: Barbara Bergmann, *In Defense of Affirmative Action* (New York: Basic Books, 1996). Reprinted by permission.

Table 4.13
Responses to Statements about the Exclusion of Blacks in the Workplace

	Disagree	Agree	Undecided
1. The Acme interviewers would probably have felt uncomfortable hiring a black as a machine operator.	28%	41%	30%
2. Very few blacks would really be willing to do those kinds of jobs, and that's why you don't see blacks holding them.	82%	6%	12%
3. Things would be a lot better in this country if blacks had more of the well-paying jobs like the ones at Acme.	24%	38%	38%
4. The Acme interviewers probably tried to give the black candidates a fair shake.	44%	30%	25%
5. Putting blacks on a job of this kind might be disruptive, and the company has a right to be concerned about that.	84%	9%	7%
6. The Acme jobs are not the type that a lot of blacks would do well at, and that's why blacks don't have them.	94%	2%	4%
7. Lots of people could perform the machine operator job well.	9%	81%	10%
8. Despite the complete lack of blacks, Acme should not hire even a well-qualified black if it has a white candidate whom the interviewer thinks is better.	53%	30%	17%

Source: Barbara Bergmann, *In Defense of Affirmative Action* (New York: Basic Books, 1996). Reprinted by permission.

Table 4.14

Responses to Statements about the Exclusion of Women in the Workplace

	Disagree	Agree	Undecided
1. The Acme interviewers would probably have felt uncomfortable hiring a woman as a machine operator.	19%	70%	11%
2. Very few women would really be willing to do those kinds of jobs, and that's why you don't see women holding them.	51%	37%	12%
3. Things would be a lot better in this country if women had more of the well-paying jobs like the ones at Acme.	34%	37%	29%
4. The Acme interviewers probably tried to give the women candidates a fair shake.	40%	25%	36%
5. Putting women on a job of this kind might be disruptive, and the company has a right to be concerned about that.	63%	30%	7%
6. The Acme jobs are not the type that a lot of women would do well at, and that's why women don't have them.	71%	15%	14%
7. Lots of people could perform the machine operator job well.	5%	82%	12%
8. Despite the complete lack of women, Acme should not hire even a well-qualified woman if it has a male candidate whom the interviewer thinks is better.	36%	53%	10%

Source: Barbara Bergmann, *In Defense of Affirmative Action* (New York: Basic Books, 1996). Reprinted by permission.

Class-Based Affirmative Action

Although class-based affirmative action is suggested by many as a viable alternative to race- and gender-sensitive policies, opponents insist that this substitution doesn't produce the same results, and they suggest that the two categories are separate issues to be met accordingly. Based on the analysis of Thomas Kane of Harvard's Kennedy School of Government, a college limiting itself to those who score 1100 or above on the Scholastic Aptitude Test—the common threshold for applicants to leading colleges where affirmative action is concentrated—would have to admit 16 students through a low-income preference to get one Hispanic or black (Caplan 1997). Basing admissions on GPAs, test scores, class rank, and other academic factors unquestionably limits the pool of blacks, who are only half as likely as whites to finish in the top 10 percent of their high school class and less than 40 percent as likely to earn an A average. Some data also show that overall, students with low socioeconomic backgrounds are less likely than students of equivalent ability from high socioeconomic backgrounds to complete their studies, attain professional or doctoral degrees, and earn high incomes (Bowen and Bok 1998).

Discrimination in the Military

Despite the goal of the U.S. Navy and Marine Corps to commission a group of officers by the year 2000 to reflect the overall population—12 percent African American and Hispanic, and 5 percent Asian American—both services continue to lag behind the others, and all services report little success in integrating minorities into the ranks of technical specialties and certain "technical" career tracks. Overall, the military has increased opportunities for minorities since 1975. The Department of Defense reports that minorities constitute 24 percent of Air Force general enlisted personnel, but less than 2 percent of the enlisted missile maintenance personnel; in the Army, in contrast, 17 percent of the enlisted electronic warfare/intercept maintenance personnel and more than 41 percent of their general enlisted personnel are minorities. Although minorities are generally overrepresented in the enlisted ranks, they are typically underrepresented as officers. For example, only 6 percent of the Navy's physical scientists and 7 percent of the Marine Corps' electronic maintenance officers are minorities. A congressional task force interviewed 2,000 military personnel and found reports of continuing perceived discrimination as well as some perceptions of reverse discrimination and an overall need to strengthen equal opportunity training. When minority enlisted personnel were asked to rate the equal opportunity climate on a scale of 1 to 5 (1 = poor, 5 = excellent), the average was 1.9 compared to the majority's enlisted personnel rate of 4.1 (Stephanopoulos and Edley 1995).

Discrimination in the Marketplace

Researchers looked specifically at automobile dealers' treatment of women and blacks and found that these two groups end up paying significantly higher prices for cars than are paid by white men. At first, the researchers suspected that blacks and women might bargain less aggressively or less skillfully than white men might. Therefore, they took a diverse group of people, taught them all to bargain in the same style, and sent them out to visit car dealerships. Again, blacks and women were still offered markedly worse deals than the white men were (Bergmann 1996).

Cost of Urban Rebellion

In the span of three months during 1963, the Department of Justice recorded 1,412 civil rights demonstrations. The combined human and property costs of urban rebellion from 1964 to 1972 were over 250 deaths, 10,000 serious injuries, 60,000 protests, and a cost in police, troops, and losses to business in the billions of dollars (Lawrence and Matsuda 1997, p. 18).

The Federal Glass Ceiling Commission Fact-Finding Report of 1995

The Federal Glass Ceiling Commission, a 21-member bipartisan body appointed by former President George Bush and Congressional leaders, chaired by the Secretary of Labor, was created by the Civil Rights Act of 1991. The commission was mandated to identify the "glass ceiling" barriers that have blocked the advancement of minorities and women as well as the successful programs that have led to their advancement, but it was disbanded once that objective was complete. The commissioners conducted their study based on public hearings, research papers, surveys of chief executive officers, focus groups, and statistics from census data. They compiled these findings and identified three levels of barriers in their investigation:

- Societal barriers that may be outside the direct control of business
- Internal structure barriers within the direct control of business
- Governmental barriers

The results are organized in a 243-page report that offers first a summary of all the FGCC's research, including certain industry comparisons, and then the characteristics of the identified barriers, with possible solutions to overcome them. This is followed by an environmental scan of the five groups of people who are most directly affected by a glass ceiling and, finally, an extensive classification of terms, tables, and methodologies.

In general, the FGCC found that African Americans, American Indians, Asian and Pacific Islander Americans (APIs), and Hispanic Americans resist the use of the term minority, which they feel implies inferiority. One focus group participant said, "'Minority' means 'lower' or 'less,' and I don't see myself any lower or less than anybody else." Another participant illustrated that minority women often experience the double hardship of being a minority and a woman: "[Black women] are only 3 percent of all women managers, and women managers are estimated to be less than 2 to 3 percent [of all managers]. So, we have a nonexistence. We don't even have a wall—no ceiling, no glass to look through. There is nothing."

Even so, the American population and work force are becoming increasingly diverse (see Tables 4.15 and 4.16). Minority representation (not including Hispanics of a white race) has nearly doubled between 1950 and 1990 to 15.2 percent, and white women increased their presence in the labor force during the same period from 24.2 percent to 35.3 percent. As Hispanics and Asians/Pacific Islanders (APIs) continue to be the fastest growing populations in the country, their representation in the work force has grown equally. Hispanic men had a 78.2 percent participation rate in the labor force (the highest of any race/ethnicity), compared to non-Hispanic men at 74 percent. Although Hispanics remain below the rest of the population in educational attainment, the API population sets unusual records in this category as the third largest minority after Hispanics and African Americans. Only 20.3 percent of the general population had graduated from college with a bachelor's degree or higher in 1990, whereas almost twice that proportion—38 percent—of APIs had earned at least a bachelor's degree.

Although the five groups (African Americans, American Indians, APIs, Hispanics, and women) included in the environmental scan of the Federal Glass Ceiling Commission report are examined later in this chapter, it is important to note here some of the highlights of the report, which included a collection of basic facts to compare to common perceptions and stereotypes. For example, the commission's look at African Americans' preparedness to participate in business revealed that the proportion of blacks ages 20 to 44 with four or more years of college increased by 36.2 percent between 1982 and 1991. In the same period, the proportion of blacks 35 to 44 years of age completing college increased to 52 percent. Although these increases are significant, in 1989, black men still earned only 4.6 percent of the bachelor's degrees awarded to men that year, compared to 84.5 percent earned by white men. A similar disproportionate rate exists among black and white women as well as between blacks and whites at the master's degree level. Unfortunately, equal educational attainment does not guarantee that black men and women are getting through the barriers or are being fairly compensated (see Table 4.17).

The FGCC reported extensive results from the focus group surveys regarding minority stereotypes. One participant in the

Table 4.15
Population of the United States by Percent (1980, 1990, 2000)

Ethnicity	1980	Year 1990	2000*
White	79.7	75.3	71.2
African American	11.7	12.0	12.6
American Indian	0.6	0.8	0.8
API American	1.5	2.9	4.3
Hispanic American	6.5	9.0	11.1

*Year 2000 numbers are a projection by the Bureau of the Census—Population Branch.
Source: Bureau of the Census.

Table 4.16
Total Workforce Population by Sex and Race in 1990

Race	% of Total Workforce	Male	Female
Non-Hispanic White	78.8	43.2	35.6
African American	10.1	4.1	5.3
American Indian/ Eskimo/Aleut	0.6	0.3	0.3
Asian & Pacific Islander	2.8	1.4	1.3
Hispanic (of "White" & "Other" races)	7.8	4.6	3.2
Non-Hispanic Other	0.0	0.0	0.0
	100.0	54.3	45.7

Source: Federal Glass Ceiling Commission, 1995.

Table 4.17
Executive, Administrative, and Managerial Income by Education Attainment, Race, and Gender (Private Sector Only*)

Education	Black Female	Black Male	White Female	White Male
Doctoral	$44,230	$54,741	$47,876	$70,414
Professional	$54,171	$71,114	$61,995	$90,610
Master's	$34,006	$47,234	$38,391	$57,371
Bachelor's	$30,584	$32,001	$31,338	$47,181
4 or more years of college	$32,452	$40,939	$32,332	$50,052
1 to 3 years of college	$24,262	$26,027	$25,195	$38,588
4 years of high school	$22,732	$25,534	$22,015	$33,074
Less than high school	$18,629	$7,203	$20,876	$30,275
Less than Bachelor's	$23,291	$23,947	$23,230	$34,862

*Private sector refers to business services, communications, construction, entertainment, manufacturing, public administration, and utilities industries.
Source: Federal Glass Ceiling Commission, 1995, and census data.

American Indian focus group said, "I hate to repeat them . . . alcoholism, the jokes about Indian time, lack of education. . . .
There's just a whole series of negative tags that have been perpetuated in movies and in the media about native peoples in
general."

The fact is the American Indian population suffers from the
highest incidence of alcoholism, tuberculosis, and suicide of any
ethnic group in the United States, and they continue to stay well
below the rest of the U.S. population in educational attainment
(see the section on American Indians later in this chapter for
more statistics).

Some of the stereotypes affecting Asians/Pacific Islanders
are that they are excellent workers but are not equipped to fill positions that require communications skills, thus keeping them out
of the top executive, administrative, and management levels.
APIs as a whole are above the national average in terms of educational achievement at both the high school and college levels.
Within the API category, Asian Indians are the most educated,
with 21 percent holding master's or professional degrees; and
Hawaiians are the least educated, with only 7 percent having
completed a bachelor's degree. Widespread acceptance of the
stereotypes that APIs aren't affected by the glass ceiling and that
they aren't management material presents obvious barriers to
their advancement. Women within this racial category seem to
suffer substantially more discrimination than their male colleagues. Although statistics can be deceiving and the comparison
between male and female APIs was not analyzed at great length
in this report, census data show males in most ethnic divisions of
APIs are educated in consistently greater numbers and are being
compensated at considerably higher rates than their female
peers. For example, Japanese males with doctorates earned a
mean income of $85,371 for 1989, whereas Japanese women with
doctorates, although much fewer in count, earned a mean income of $13,268. This discrepancy in earnings lessens when deal-
ing with APIs in sum by median income using different control
methods (see Table 4.18).

Hispanic Americans seem to be working their way into corporate America around the edges, but they continue to face barriers to their development as well. The corporate executive
officers (CEOs) interviewed by the FGCC claim the availability of
capable Hispanics is hampered, yet CEOs of Hispanic-owned
businesses report that they can find highly qualified Hispanics
with any required credential to fill top jobs. These CEOs agree

Table 4.18
1995 Median Earnings of Year-round, Full-time Workers 25 years and Over,
by Educational Attainment, Gender, and Race

| | High School Graduate Only | | Bachelor's Degree or More | |
	Male	Female	Male	Female
Asian Pacific Islander	$25,010	$18,220	$41,370	$32,450
White, non-Hispanic	$30,540	$20,170	$50,240	$34,250

Source: Bureau of the Census, 1998.

with the mainstream CEOs that "the mainstream guys just don't know where to look." In 1990, 370,000 Hispanic men and women 18 years of age or older had earned the advanced degrees commonly considered a prerequisite for climbing the corporate ladder (see the section on Hispanic Americans later in this chapter for more statistics).

Although Hispanic women, like most minority women, experience the double burden of racist and sexist attitudes, women in general are slowly closing the gap between the sexes. In 1990, women made up 45.7 percent of the total work force populace; between 1982 and 1992 they increased their presence at the senior vice-president level from 13 to 23 percent, but they still fill only 3 to 5 percent of top senior positions. The National Center for Education Statistics reported in 1990 that 6.5 percent of all women and 8.6 percent of all men in the total civilian work force aged 25 years and older held bachelor's degrees; similar results were found in regard to postgraduate degrees. A 1990 study by *Business Week* of 3,664 business school graduates found that women with a master's degree in business administration from one of the top 20 business schools earned an average of $54,749 in her first year after graduation, while a comparable man earned $61,400, or 12 percent more. One of the misconceptions found in the 1992 Korn/Ferry Survey cited by the FGCC to perpetuate these inequities was that women lack quantitative skills, although 23 percent of women and 27 percent of men have spent most of their corporate careers in finance. Furthermore, 26 percent of women as opposed to 16 percent of men were in the commercial banking or diversified financial sectors in 1990. Other fallacies discovered were that women are not as committed to their careers as men are, women won't work long hours, and women can't or won't relocate. However, only one-third of the women surveyed had ever taken a leave of absence (82 percent of which were for maternity or family reasons), women worked on average the same number of hours as their male counter-parts, and only 14.1 percent of the women refused relocation, whereas 20 percent of males reported refusing relocation in a similar survey.

Surveys and Studies on Racism

USA Weekend surveyed almost 250,000 students in grades 6 to 12 from all over the country and found, to their surprise, that 84 percent of them felt people their age carry some form of racial prejudice. Even more (86 percent) thought these racial tensions would always exist. One 15-year-old in the survey said, "I feel accepted by my peers, but some people tell me it's because I 'act white.'" A 1993 Louis Harris poll of high school students found that 75 percent had witnessed confrontations motivated by race or religion (Guernsey 1996).

Two dozen young whites (college students or high school graduates) were surveyed by a professional pollster on behalf of People for the American Way to look at what they term a "perception gap" between whites and blacks. Among the sentiments expressed were that blacks are fundamentally different, they have too much attitude and seem angry, and they don't take advantage of opportunities or don't seem to want to work. The group complained about the existence of black-only organizations, saying that whites would be condemned for having the same one-race associations. They felt that blacks had worked so hard to be able to ride the bus with everybody else, and now they just want to separate themselves. A 23-year-old waitress said, "How long can (they) hold that grudge against something that we're not even responsible for?" Many in the group praised the few blacks they knew personally but criticized and ridiculed blacks in general. They portrayed themselves as victims, but they only rarely said that blacks had been victims. A few challenged the stereotypes being offered, and others struggled with their beliefs, unaware that they might have their own racial prejudices (Duke 1991b).

These young people's views were shared by a majority of the nation's whites surveyed by the National Opinion Research Center at the University of Chicago. Of the 1,372 participants randomly selected from 300 communities, about 170 were black, 50 were Hispanic, 30 were Jewish, fewer than ten were Asian American, and the rest were white (including 330 southern whites). The minority opinions were so few that they weren't considered statistically significant. Of the whites questioned, 78 percent said blacks are more likely than whites to "prefer to live off welfare" and less likely to "prefer to be self-supporting." Further, 62 percent said blacks are more likely to be lazy, 56 percent said they are violence-prone, 53 percent said they are less intelligent, and 51 percent said they thought blacks are less patriotic. Hispanics were rated at equally negative levels. Asians were rated less critically—34 percent of whites said they were more likely to be lazy, 30 percent said more violence-prone, 36 percent said less intelligent, 46 percent said they'd prefer to live off welfare, and 55 percent said they are less patriotic. Overall, each group rated itself significantly more positive than whites had rated it (Duke 1991a).

Evidence of Continuing Discrimination against Particular Groups

Women

Barriers Still Exist

In 1972, women were officially incorporated into affirmative action policies involving education—eight years after the initial civil rights legislation that protected them against discrimination in employment—yet still plenty of statistics indicate continuing discrimination against them in these areas. One of the more well-known inequalities women face is the wage gap: in 1996, each full-time year-round working woman made 74 cents for each dollar that a man made. College-educated women earn on average $11,900 less per year than college-educated men (Federal Glass Ceiling Commission 1995). For every dollar earned by white male managers, white women managers earn 59 cents, and minority women earn 57 cents (Equal Rights Advocates 1997). In 1995, 65 percent of the 62 million working women in the United States earned less than $20,000 a year, and 38 percent earned less than $10,000 annually (Greenberger 1995). In the FGCC report, it was found that women in senior management work the same number of hours and have the same credentials as their male counterparts, but they still earn less in these and most other areas and hold only 6.9 percent of the seats on corporate boards.

Experts have also documented discrimination in the preparation of women to enter higher-level and higher-paying positions. In 1992, girls were enrolled in only 6.5 percent of the

Table 4.19
Advances Lost from 1984 to 1994 by Women, Select Fields

	Crane Operators	Plumber/Pipe Fitters	Carpenters	Precision Woodworkers
1984	1.1%	2.4%	1.3%	15.8%
1994	0.7%	1.7%	1.0%	10.8%

Source: Adapted from data from Chicago Women in Trades survey and U.S. Department of Labor (reprinted in *Ms.*, January/February 1996).

apprenticeships available within the nation, and 90 percent of them were working toward jobs like lab technician or cosmetologist, with an average weekly wage of $247. Less than 1 percent were training for jobs like auto mechanic, with an average weekly wage of $523 (Cantrell 1996). In 1991, one in four working women had an administrative support job, and 82 percent of administrative workers in all industries were women (Greenberger 1995; Equal Employment Opportunity Commission 1993). Although the number of women in the compiled construction, machine, electrical, and repair-shop trades nearly doubled (from 5.4 percent to 9.3 percent) between 1974 and 1994, advances were lost in some areas from 1984 to 1994 (see Table 4.19).

A 1995 study by professor Alfred Blumrosen at Rutgers University Law School made reference to the *Johnson v. Transportation Agency of Santa Clara County* case, stating, in essence, that a subjective two-point difference on an aptitude test between Paul Johnson and Diane Joyce wasn't as important as a 238-job difference between men and women (Guernsey 1997). Experts face a challenge in analyzing the use of test scores as an accurate measure of performance because any particular test score is theoretically only indicative of an individual's "scoring range." In the case of Johnson and Joyce, assessment shows that while Joyce would likely score between 63 and 83 on subsequent tests, and Johnson between 65 and 85, there is little evidence to predict accurately who would perform better on any particular examination (Guinier and Sturm 1996).

Making Strides

The Equal Rights Advocates of San Francisco present in "Keeping the Door Open" the following statistics to illustrate the enormous gains women have made in the job market since affirmative action was implemented:

• Women managers in executive, administrative, and

managerial positions rose from 17.6 percent in 1972 to 43.8 percent in 1996.

- Women architects have increased in number from 3 percent in 1972 to 16.7 percent in 1996.
- The number of women in construction has grown slightly from 1 percent in 1972 to 2.6 percent in 1996. More specifically, the advances made between 1984 and 1994 were for construction-vehicle operators from 5.3 percent to 6.9 percent, electricians from 1.2 percent to 2.1 percent, precision metal workers from 6 percent to 6.5 percent, and motor-vehicle operators from 9.6 percent to 11 percent.
- The percentage of women physicians rose from 10 percent in 1972 to 26.4 percent in 1996.
- The amount of women business owners has exploded since the beginning of affirmative action programs. In 1972 there were 402,205, but by 1996 that number had grown to 7,950,000.
- Women contractors (women-owned businesses) were awarded more than twice as many federal contracts over $25,000 in 1996 as they were in 1983.
- A doubling of women in public safety occurred from 1983 to 1996, with the percentage of women in U.S. police forces jumping from 9.4 to 17.2, and women firefighters increasing from 1 percent to 2.1 percent.
- The number of women in law has also erupted, according to the American Bar Association, from 3 percent in 1971 to 25 percent in 1997.
- Probably some of the greatest gains are by women in education. In 1973, women earned 7 percent of first professional degrees and 17 percent of Ph.D.s, but by 1996 that number had risen to 41 percent and 39 percent respectively. Three percent of law students in 1968 were women, yet by 1997, 47 percent of all first-year law students were women. In 1969, 8.9 percent of first-year medical students were women, though 43 percent of the incoming medical students in 1995–1996 were women.

Other achievements were made in specific industries and companies, such as IBM, where the number of women more than tripled in less than ten years after the company set up an affirmative action plan. In five of Cleveland's largest banks, the percentage of women and managers rose more than 20 percent in the three years after an initial review by the OFCCP. In 1973, when the OFCCP first looked at the coal mining industry, there were no women miners, but by 1980, 8.7 percent were women (Citizen's Commission on Civil Rights 1984).

Studies of Sexism and Personal Testimony

In 1993, 11,908 sex discrimination and sexual harassment charges were filed with the EEOC. That number rose to 14,420 in 1994. Almost 93 percent of the 439 senior women executives surveyed by Korn/Ferry International in 1992 felt that a glass ceiling for women still exists (Federal Glass Ceiling Commission 1995). In a report issued by the U.S. Merit Systems Protection Board (USM-SPB), nearly half of the 8,000 federal workers questioned in 1994 said they had experienced unwanted, uninvited sexual attention on the job in the previous two years (U.S. Merit Systems Protection Board 1995). In a 1994 Labor Department survey, 61 percent of the women surveyed said they had little or no likelihood of advancement. In that same group, 14 percent of white women and 26 percent of minority women reported losing a job or promotion because of sex or race. At the University of Michigan Law School, although women earned 93.5 percent of male salaries during the first year (between 1972 and 1975) after they graduated, that number dropped to 61 percent after 15 years of practice (Wood, Corcoran, and Courant 1993). In a study of women in the legal profession, ten times as many women as men said their opportunities to advance were less than those of lawyers of the opposite sex in the same job setting. Forty-five percent of the women surveyed thought inadequate compensation would continue to be an obstacle (Gellis 1991). In a Chicago Women in Trades survey, nearly 70 percent of black women and more than half of white women said they had been on jobs where men refused to work with them (Cantrell 1996).

To look at some specific attitudes of mostly white college students regarding the segregation of women from a job requiring the expertise of a skilled driver, refer back to the Bergmann study in the Additional Surveys and Studies section of this chapter.

Women of Color

Of the 3 to 5 percent of senior management positions held by women, 95 percent of them are white, 2.3 percent are African

American, 1.8 percent are Asian American, and only 0.2 percent are Hispanic. Although 23 percent of the female workforce is made up of women of color, only 15 percent of female managers are members of a minority group. Minority women do not see much progress and feel that significant barriers to their advancement still exist (Federal Glass Ceiling Commission 1995). Although college educated white women earn only $1,800 more per year than white men who have only a high school diploma, equally educated black women earn $400 less per year than the same white men (Equal Rights Advocates 1997). Black women with professional degrees earn only 60 percent of what white males earn (Federal Glass Ceiling Commission 1995).

When the FGCC looked at African American women's perceptions of the glass ceiling, they found many to be laboring under the double burden of racism and sexism:

- Compared to white women, black women felt that they received less organizational support.
- Black women did not perceive their work to be as significant as did the white female respondents.
- Black women felt they were in positions where they had less control and authority than did their peers who were white women, and they believed that their jobs were less likely to allow them to use their skills and knowledge.
- Black women's perceptions of their relationships with their bosses were less positive than those of white women.
- Compared to white women, black women were more conscious of their racial identity at work, felt less accepted by their colleagues, perceived less collegial support, and perceived a higher level of sex discrimination.
- Black women were less satisfied with their salaries and how their companies managed race and gender relations, but equally satisfied with their career progress as white women were.

African Americans

In the April 1996 volume of the *New Yorker*, Hendrik Hertzberg and Henry Louis Gates, Jr. cited the successes of integration and affirmative action to have created a substantial black middle class with four times as many black families with incomes above

$50,000 a year as there were in 1964. However, according to the Urban Institute, 53 percent of black men aged 25 to 34 are either unemployed or earn too little to lift a family of four out of poverty (Guernsey 1997). In a study commissioned by the Office of Personnel Management, the researchers reported that black federal employees were fired at nearly twice the rate of their white, Hispanic, or Asian counterparts, controlling for a score based on other factors, including performance ratings, seniority, and education (Guinier and Sturm 1996). In the beginning of 1990, blacks constituted 12.41 percent of the overall American population and 14.59 percent of the American college-aged population. Yet, in October of 1988, blacks made up only 9.85 percent of those actually enrolled in college (Posner 1990). In 1996, blacks aged 25 to 29 were about half as likely as whites (14.6 percent compared to 28.1 percent) to have completed four or more years of college, although their respective high school graduation rates were statistically the same (Bureau of the Census 1998).

In a nationwide telephone survey conducted in 1989 by Chilton Research Services for an ABC News-*Washington Post* poll, 376 blacks and 1,315 whites responded to questions about attitudes and effects of interracial contact. Their analysis revealed that in several instances such contact is associated with positive racial attitudes, especially among whites, and that some effects are appreciable. However, when asked specifically about their perceptions on racial hostility and importance of racial integration, it seems the researchers reported a wide racial gap (see Table 4.20).

Refer back to the Bergmann study (p. 109) for the opinions from a survey of mostly white college students about the integration of blacks into a company looking to fill a machine operator job where the workplace had been exclusively white.

Hispanic Americans

Between 1987 and 1992, Hispanic-owned businesses rose by 83 percent (from 422,373 to 771,706), and Hispanic women-owned businesses increased by 114 percent. For that same five-year period, total Hispanic-owned business receipts grew by 295 percent, from $24.7 billion to nearly $72.8 billion. Between 1980 and 1990, the number of Hispanic men and women 25 years of age and older with four or more years of college increased from 7.7 percent to 10 percent (Federal Glass Ceiling Commission 1995).

Table 4.20

Blacks' and Whites' Perceptions and Expressions of Racial Hostility

How many whites personally share the attitudes of groups like the Ku Klux Klan?

	Only a few	About 10%	Less than 25%	Less than 50%	Over 50%
Blacks	10%	28%	12%	25%	26%
Whites	32%	33%	18%	12%	5%

Nationwide, do you think there is more, less, or about the same amount of antiblack feeling among whites as compared to four or five years ago?

	More	Less	About the same
Blacks	45%	21%	34%
Whites	24%	38%	38%

What about antiblack feeling among whites in your neighborhood?

	More	Less	About the same
Blacks	23%	31%	46%
Whites	12%	39%	49%

How many blacks personally have racist attitudes toward whites?

	Only a few	About 10%	Less than 25%	Less than 50%	Over 50%
Blacks	8%	27%	15%	26%	24%
Whites	14%	23%	25%	22%	17%

How important is it that people send their children to racially mixed schools, attend racially mixed churches, live in racially mixed neighborhoods, socialize with persons of the opposite race outside of work, and have close friends of the opposite race?

Mean on 0–15 scale   Blacks—10   Whites—8.5*

*N varies from 283 to 296 for blacks, and from 970 to 1031 for whites. Black-white response differences are statistically significant at p<.05 on all items except the fourth one.
Source: Reprinted from *Social Forces* 71 (3), March 1993. "The Contact Hypothesis Revisited" by Lee Sigelman and Susan Welch. Copyright © The University of North Carolina Press.

Although these numbers indicate progress, the Hispanic pool is still significantly limited compared to the rest of the population in qualifying for senior management positions. In 1993, Hispanic men were half as likely as white men to be managers or professionals, and they earned 81 percent of the wages earned by white men at the same education level (Equal Employment Opportunity Commission 1995). Hispanic women earned 57 cents for each dollar an equally educated white man earned in 1996 (Equal Rights Advocates 1997). The average income for Hispanic women with college degrees is less than the average for white men with high school degrees (Equal Employment Opportunity Commission 1995). See Table 4.21 for national mean incomes by race.

Table 4.21
Median Household Income by Race and Hispanic Origin

Ethnicity	Year			
	1988	1989	1994	1995
All Races	$35,073	$35,526	$33,178	$34,076
White	$37,077	$37,370	$34,992	$35,766
Black	$21,136	$22,225	$21,623	$22,393
Hispanic Origin (of any race)	$26,227	$26,942	$24,085	$22,860

Source: Bureau of the Census, 1998.

Asian Americans/Native Pacific Islanders

Asian Americans, or Native Pacific Islanders (sometimes called Asian Pacific Islanders, or APIs), as a general category typically, but not exclusively, encompass Americans of Asian Indian, Cambodian, Chinese, Filipino, Hawaiian, Hmong, Japanese, Korean, Laotian, Taiwanese, Thai, and Vietnamese descent. APIs are the fastest growing minority group in the United States; between 1980 and 1990, APIs increased by 95 percent, whites grew by 6 percent, blacks by 13.2 percent, and Hispanics by 53 percent (Dong 1995). In 1980, Japanese Americans had incomes more than 32 percent above the national average income, and Chinese Americans were more than 12 percent above the national average (Posner 1990). Also in 1980, 17.8 percent of the white population aged 25 and over had completed four or more years of college, compared to 32.9 percent of the Asian American population (Statistical Abstract of the U.S. 1990). In 1990, Asian Americans constituted only 2.9 percent of the national population but represented 20 percent, 15 percent, and 24 percent of the first-year classes entering Harvard, Yale, and Stanford, respectively, and for the first time outnumbered whites at the Berkeley and Los Angeles campuses of the University of California. These outstanding representations have led many to make claims that there are too many Asians in education to justify them as a protected race (Dong 1995). APIs tend to be an anomaly where educational affirmative action programs are concerned.

San Francisco Unified School District's Lowell High School is one of the few traditional public schools that acts more like an institution of higher education in its competitive admissions process. Lowell High School, one of the city's most prestigious public schools, limits the number of enrollees from any given racial or ethnic group to 45 percent under a desegregation con-

Table 4.22
SFUSD Student Population: Racial/Ethnic Composition, Fall 1983 and Fall 1991

	African American	American Indian	Chinese	Filipino	Japanese	Korean	Other Nonwhite	Other White	Spanish Surname
1983	13,808	368	12,212	5339	675	675	7303	10,433	10,617
1991	11,931	383	15,505	5168	638	702	7784	9124	12,506
% Change	-15.7	+3.9	+21.2	-3.3	-5.8	+3.8	+6.2	-14.3	+15.1
% Total	19	.6	24	8	1	1	12	14	20

Source: Republished with permission of the *Stanford Law Review,* 559 Nathan Abbott Way, Palo Alto, CA 94305. *Too Many Asians: The Challenge of Fighting Discrimination Against Asian-Americans and Preserving Affirmative Action* (Chart), Selena Dong, May 1995, Vol. 47, No. 1. Reproduced by permission of the publisher via Copyright Clearance Center, Inc.

sent decree. A group of Chinese Americans sparked a racial discrimination suit against the school for its racial cap and exclusively higher admission standards for Chinese students compared to the other racial categories. To be admitted for the 1992–1993 academic year, Chinese students had to score at least 66 points out of a 69-point admissions index, whereas white, Japanese, Korean, Filipino, American Indian, and "other nonwhite" students needed a 59, and black or Spanish-surnamed students needed only a 56 (Dong 1995). See Table 4.22 for the racial and ethnic composition of the school district.

American Indians

According to the Bureau of the Census, the term "American Indian" refers to those who classify themselves as American Indian, Eskimo, or Aleut. The Bureau of the Census compiled the following information from 1990 census data of the 25 largest American Indian Tribes:

- Only 2.1 percent of American Indians 18 to 24 years of age had earned a bachelor's degree, compared to the national rate of 7.6 percent, and only 9.4 percent of American Indians in the workforce aged 25 years or older had completed four or more years of college. American Indians have the highest high school dropout rate (36 percent) of any ethnic or racial group. Of approximately 1.4 million American Indians aged 18 years and older, only 3,277 held postgraduate degrees.
- Census data also reports that only 7,862 (8.6 percent) of the total American Indian population (1,937,391) held executive, administrative, or managerial positions at any

level (very little in the private sector), compared to the 12.3 percent of non-American Indian people in such positions. American Indians are more highly represented in the service, farming, forestry, craft, repair, and equipment/machine handling trades. The American Indian participation rate in the labor force increased significantly from 49 percent in 1970 to 62.1 percent in 1990. The overall number of American Indians in the labor force increased nearly fourfold from 221,733 in 1970 to 865,703 in 1990.

- The median family income in 1990 for the total U.S. population was $35,225, $13,606 higher than the total American Indian population's family median income of $21,619. On the ten largest reservations, per capita income ranged from $3,113 to $4,718; 56 percent of American Indian households earned less than $15,000 per year. The percentage of families living in poverty nationwide was only 10 percent, in contrast to 27.2 percent of American Indian families. Individual rates of poverty were even higher, at 31.2 percent for American Indians versus 13.1 percent for non-American Indians.

- Unemployment is generally substantially higher in reservation areas than anywhere else; nationally, the 1990 unemployment rate for American Indian workers was 14.1 percent, weighed against the 25 percent of American Indian workers unemployed within the boundaries of federal reservation and trust land areas.

References

Ashenfelter, Orley, and James Heckman. 1976. "Measuring the Effect of an Anti-discrimination Program." Pp. 46–89 in *Estimating the Labor Market Effects of Social Programs*. Princeton: Princeton University Press.

Bergmann, Barbara R. 1996. *In Defense of Affirmative Action*. New York: Basic Books.

Bloch, Farrell. 1994. *Antidiscrimination Law and Minority Employment*. Chicago: University of Chicago Press.

Bowen, William G., and Derek Bok. 1998. *The Shape of the River: Long-term Consequences of Considering Race in College and University Admissions*. Princeton: Princeton University Press.

Bureau of the Census, Current Population Survey. 1998. *Population Profile of the United States, 1997*. Washington, D.C.: Government Printing Office.

Bureau of the Census, Current Population Survey. 1993. *Income, Poverty and Valuation of Noncash Benefits 1993*. Washington, D.C.: Government Printing Office.

Cantrell, Patty. 1996. "Blue-Collar Workers: Breaking through the Brick Ceiling." *Ms.* (January/February), pp. 34–38.

Caplan, Lincoln. 1997. *Up against the Law: Affirmative Action and the Supreme Court*. New York: The Twentieth Century Fund Press.

College Board Data. 1998. www.collegeboard.org.

Cose, Ellis. 1997. *Color-Blind: Seeing Beyond Race in a Race-Obsessed World*. New York: HarperCollins.

Dong, Selena. 1995. "Too Many Asians: The Challenge of Fighting Discrimination against Asian-Americans and Preserving Affirmative Action." *Stanford Law Review* 47 (May): 1027.

Duke, Lynne. 1991a."Whites' Racial Stereotypes Persist: Most Retain Negative Beliefs about Minorities, Survey Finds." *Washington Post*, 9 January.

———. 1991b."Racial 'Perception Gap' Emerges as Young Whites Discuss Blacks." *Washington Post*, 24 December.

Estreicher, Samuel, and Michael C. Harper. 1990. *The Law Governing the Employment Relationship*. St. Paul: West Publishing Co.

Equal Employment Opportunity Commission. 1993. *Job Patterns for Minorities and Women in Private Industry*, table 1, pp. 1–36. Washington, D.C.: Government Printing Office.

Equal Employment Opportunity Commission, Office of Communication. 1995. *The Status of Equal Opportunity in the American Workforce*. Washington, D.C.: Government Printing Office.

Equal Rights Advocates. 1997. *Keeping the Door Open*. San Francisco: Equal Rights Advocates.

Federal Glass Ceiling Commission. 1995. *Good for Business: Making Full Use of the Nation's Human Capital*. Washington, D.C.: Government Printing Office.

Gardner, Howard. 1993. *Frames of Mind: The Theory of Multiple Intelligences*. New York: Basic Books.

Gellis, Ann. 1991. "Women in the Legal Profession." *Indiana Law Journal* 66: 948.

Goldstein, Morris, and Robert Smith. 1976. "The Estimated Impact of Anti-discrimination Laws Aimed at Federal Contractors." *Industrial and Labor Relations Review* 29: 219.

Goleman, Daniel. 1995. "The Decline of the Nice-Guy Quotient." *New York Times*, 10 September.

Guernsey, Joann Bren. 1997. *Affirmative Action: A Problem or a Remedy?* Minneapolis: Lerner Publications Company.

Guinier, Lani, and Susan Sturm. 1996. "The Future of Affirmative Action: Reclaiming the Innovative Ideal." *California Law Review* 84: 953–989.

Hacker, Andrew. 1992. *Two Nations: Black and White, Separate, Hostile, Unequal.* New York: Scribners.

Heckman, James, and Kenneth Wolpin. 1976. "Does the Contract Compliance Program Work? An Analysis of Chicago Data." *Industrial and Labor Relations Review* 29: 544–564.

Lawrence, Charles R. III, and Mari J. Matsuda. 1997. *We Won't Go Back: Making the Case for Affirmative Action.* New York: Houghton-Mifflin Company.

Leonard, Jonathan. 1984a. "The Impact of Affirmative Action on Employment." *Journal of Labor Economics* 2: 439–463.

———. 1984b. "Employment and Occupational Advance under Affirmative Action." *Review of Economics and Statistics* 42:134.

Lynch, Michael. 1994. *Choosing by Color: Affirmative Action at the University of California.* San Francisco: Pacific Research Institute for Public Policy.

National Center for Education Statistics. 1994. *Digest of Education Statistics 1994*, NCES 94–115, table 179. Washington, D.C.: Government Printing Office.

Posner, Richard A. 1990. "Comment: Duncan Kennedy on Affirmative Action." *Duke Law Journal* 1990: 1157–1162.

Public Papers of the Presidents of the United States. *Lyndon B. Johnson, 1965,* Book II. Washington, D.C: U.S. Government Printing Office.

Sigelman, Lee, and Susan Welch. 1993. "The Contact Hypothesis Revisited: Black-White Interaction and Positive Racial Attitudes." *Social Forces* 71, 3 (March): 781–795.

Smothers, Ronald. 1994. "To Raise the Performance of Minorities, a College Increased Its Standards." *New York Times,* 29 June.

Statistical Abstract of the United States. 1990. Washington, D.C.: Government Printing Office.

Stephanopoulos, George, and Christopher Edley Jr. 1995. *Report to the President: Review of Federal Affirmative Action Programs.* Washington, D.C: U.S. Government Printing Office.

Tilove, Jonathan. 1995. "Here's a Tip: Get Yourself Born to the Right Folks, Affirmative Action or Not, Lineage Means Plenty at Nation's Top Schools." *San Francisco Examiner,* 6 April.

Turner, Margery, Michael Fix, and Raymond J. Struyk. 1991. *Housing Discrimination Study Synthesis*. Washington, D.C.: The Urban Institute Press.

U.S. Bureau of the Census. 1992. *Current Population Reports, Money Income of Households, Families, and Pensions in the United States*. Series P-60, no. 184, Table 31. Washington, D.C.: U.S. Government Printing Office.

U.S. General Accounting Office. 1990. *Immigration Reform: Employer Sanctions and the Question of Discrimination*. Report to Congress GAO/GGD-990–62 (March): 48.

U.S. Merit Systems Protection Board. 1995. "Sexual Harassment in the Federal Workplace: Trends, Progress, Continuing Challenges." Report to the President and the Congress of the United States (October).

Woo, Elaine. 1995. "Belief in Meritocracy an Equal-Opportunity Myth." *Los Angeles Times*, 30 April.

Wood, Robert, Mary Corcoran, and Paul Couvant. 1993. "Pay Differentials among the Highly Paid: The Male-Female Earnings Gap in Lawyers' Salaries." *Journal of Labor Economics* (July).

Zelnick, Bob. 1996. *Backlash*. Washington: Regnery Publishing, Inc.

Directory of Organizations

5

Alexander Hamilton Institute
70 Hilltop Road
Ramsey, NJ 07456
201-825-3377
800-879-2441
Fax: 201-825-8696
E-mail: custsvc@ahipubs.com
Web site: www.ahipubs.com

The Alexander Hamilton Institute is a private company that has been helping executives manage their companies and careers since 1909. It specializes in human resource management issues and serves primarily as a publishing company, producing a wide variety of personnel topics with a legal emphasis.

Publications: The institute publishes booklets, loose-leaf manuals, and newsletters on employment law targeted to top management, human resource directors, personnel managers, front-line managers, and supervisors in small- to medium-sized firms. The publications deal with all aspects of employment law and are specifically designed to keep managers and executives from violating employment law regulations and potential lawsuits and fines. Various loose-leaf manuals, booklets, executive strategy briefings, and newsletters are available on myriad topics,

133

including age discrimination, disability accommodation, race harassment, compliance record keeping, and employment law.

American Association for Affirmative Action (AAAA)
3905 Vincennes Road #304
Indianapolis, IN 46268-3026
800-252-8952
Web site: www.affirmativeaction.org/mission.html

Founded in 1974, the mission of the American Association for Affirmative Action is to promote understanding and advocacy of affirmative action to enhance access and equity in economic, educational, and employment opportunities. The AAAA is dedicated to the advancement of affirmative action, equal opportunity, and the elimination of discrimination on the basis of race, gender, ethnic background, or any other criterion that deprives people of opportunities to live and work. The organization works to help Equal Employment Opportunity/affirmative action professionals be more successful and productive in their careers. Among the AAAA's goals: to communicate relevant and timely information concerning pending legislation and regulations related to Equal Employment Opportunity/affirmative action; to provide an advocacy role in the protection and promotion of EEO/AA legal issues; and to provide ongoing and enhanced education opportunities, including a comprehensive certification training program.

American Association of University Women (AAUW)
111 16th Street NW
Washington, DC 20036-4873
202-785-7793
800-608-5286
Fax: 202-466-7618
E-mail: infor@aauw.org
Web site: www.aauw.org

For well over a century, the American Association of University Women, an organization of 150,000 members, has been a catalyst for the advancement of women and their transformations of American society. In more than 1,500 communities across the country, AAUW members work to promote education and equity for women and girls, lifelong learning, and positive societal change. The AAUW plays a major role in activating advocates nationwide on priority issues, including gender equity in education, reproductive choice, and workplace and civil rights issues. The AAUW is active in advocating retention of affirmative action policies. As cochair of the Leadership Conference on Civil Rights (LCCR), it is a leader in advocating civil rights issues. The association holds workshops on affirmative action at the AAUW Convention and Conference of State Presidents.

Publications: Up to ten copies of an AAUW brochure are available free of charge from the AAUW Member Helpline, 800-821-4364, ext. 8. For a history of the AAUW's policy, principles, and positions, see *AAUW Historic Principles, 1881–1989,* available from the AAUW. The association publishes a monthly public policy newsletter called *Action Alert.*

American Bar Association Commission on Women in the Profession
750 North Lakeshore Drive
Chicago, IL 60611
312-988-5522
Fax: 312-988-5688

The ABA Commission on Women's goal is to secure the full and equal participation of women in the American Bar Association, the legal profession, and the justice system. The commission was created in August 1987 to assess the status of women in the legal profession, identify barriers to advancement, and make recommendations to the ABA for action to address the problems identified. The commission recently reevaluated its objectives and has identified new goals to accomplish its mission: to serve as a voice for the concerns of women lawyers, address impediments that prevent full and equal participation of women lawyers, serve as a catalyst for change, enhance the visibility and influence of the commission, develop opportunities for participation in the work of the commission, focus attention on the concerns of multicultural women, and forge coalitions with other groups to advance shared objectives. To meet these goals the commission engages in numerous ongoing projects, publishes regular reports, and presents programs at ABA meetings.

Publications: Unfinished Business: Overcoming the Sisyphus Factor documents the overt and subtle barriers that impede the full integration and equal participation of women in the law. *Elusive Equality: The Experiences of Women in Legal Education* distills findings from national hearings at which students, administrators, faculty members, and deans have provided their perspectives on gender influences in law schools. *Women in the Law: A Look at the Numbers* is a survey report of statistics currently available that documents women's roles in all sectors of the legal profession. *Directory of Associations of Women Lawyers* is a comprehensive directory that contains over 170 listings for national, state, and local as well as multicultural women's bar associations. *Lawyers and Balanced Lives: A Guide to Drafting and Implementing Workplace Policies for Lawyers* describes ways to make law firms "family friendly" for men and women.

American Civil Liberties Union (ACLU)
125 Broad Street, 18th Floor
New York, NY 10004-2400
Fax: 212-549-2646
Web site: www.aclu.org/library/pbp1.html

Founded in 1920, the American Civil Liberties Union is the nation's foremost advocate of individual rights—litigating, legislating, and educating the public on a broad array of issues affecting individual freedom in the United States. The organization describes itself as neither liberal nor conservative, Republican or Democratic. The ACLU is a nonprofit, nonpartisan, 275,000-member public interest organization devoted exclusively to protecting the basic civil liberties of all Americans and extending civil rights to groups that have traditionally been denied them. The mission of the ACLU is to assure that the Bill of Rights is preserved for each new generation.

Publications: The Year in Civil Liberties, published annually, and *ACLU Briefing Papers.* For a complete list of publications, search the library on the ACLU's Web site.

American Civil Rights Institute (ACRI)
P. O. Box 188350
Sacramento, CA 95842
916-444-2278
Fax: 916-444-2279
Web site: www.acri.org

The American Civil Rights Institute is a national, not-for-profit civil rights organization created to educate the public about racial and gender preferences. The ACRI's initial focus is on three areas: assisting organizations in other states with their efforts to educate the public about racial and gender preferences; assisting federal representatives with public education on the issue; and monitoring implementation and legal action on California's Proposition 209. The ACRI also seeks to effect a cultural change by challenging the "race matters" mentality it believes is embraced by many of today's so-called "civil rights leaders." ACRI members believe that civil rights are individual rights and that government policies should not advocate group rights over individual rights.

In order to achieve ACRI's mission of federal and state reform, the organization has undertaken the following activities and projects: conducting research on the evidence and effects of racial and gender preferences; conducting public opinion polling on racial and gender preferences; educating the public and media about racial and gender preferences by actively working with national, state, and local media; serving as a watch dog organization to monitor state and local efforts to implement Proposition 209, California's Civil Rights Initiative; and sponsoring conferences, meetings, and debates about racial and gender preferences.

Publications: The Egalitarian, a free bimonthly newsletter.

**American Federation of Labor–Congress
of Industrial Organizations (AFL-CIO)**
Civil and Human Rights Department
815 16th Street NW
Washington, DC 20006
202-637-5000
Fax: 202-508-6902
Web site: www.aflcio.org

The AFL-CIO is a voluntary federation of 72 national and international labor unions representing 13 million working men and women. Their mission statement: "to improve the lives of working families and to bring economic justice to the workplace and social justice to the nation. To accomplish this mission we will *build* and *change* the American labor movement; we will build a broad movement of American workers by organizing workers into unions; we will build a strong political voice for workers in our nation; we will change our unions to provide a new voice to workers in a changing economy; we will change our labor movement by creating a new voice for workers in our communities." The civil rights department assists members who have civil rights issues, including those related to affirmative action.

Publications: Brochures and technical assistance for labor unions and related groups.

**American Federation of Labor-Congress
of Industrial Organizations (AFL-CIO)**
Working Women's Department
815 16th Street NW
Washington, DC 20006
202-637-5390
Fax: 202-508-6902
Web site: www.aflcio.org

The Working Women's Department was created in 1996 as a new department of the AFL-CIO. The department's charge is to be an activist voice for *all* working women and to inject the concerns of working women into the labor movement. Through political programs, policy, and outreach work at the local, state, and national levels, the department promotes the issues and concerns of working women. The department also runs a clearinghouse of resources for women; convenes coalition meetings of labor, civil rights, women's, and religious groups; and plans conferences related to its program activities.

American Federation of Teachers (AFT)
555 New Jersey Avenue NW
Washington, DC 20001
202-879-4400
Fax: 202-393-8648
Web site: www.aft.org

The AFT has supported the concept of affirmative action since 1975 and continues to support the freedom of both public and private higher education institutions to make admission decisions based on the benefits of their students, their particular institution, and the larger society using a genuine rule of merit that considers a broad spectrum of qualifications and talents, including strong academic achievement as measured by a variety of solid indicators. The AFT promotes programs of affirmative opportunity such as investing in minority recruitment programs, easing the financial burden of higher education for qualified but poor students, investing in second-chance and college-preparatory programs, and guaranteeing access for all to high-quality public education from early childhood to higher education. The AFT is an affiliate of the AFL-CIO international union. Organized into local chapters, the union holds a national conference each year to consider educational, civil, human, and women's issues.

Publications: A variety of materials on various educational, civil, human, and women's issues are available, including *Resolutions on Affirmative Action, Sexual Harassment: Unprofessional, Unacceptable and Unlawful* (pamphlet), and *AFT Resource Guide on Sexual Harassment.*

Americans United for Affirmative Action (AUAA)
400 Colony Square, Suite 200
1201 Peachtree Street NE
Atlanta, GA 30361
619-274-1791
Web site: www.auaa.org

Americans United for Affirmative Action is a national nonprofit organization established to defend affirmative action programs and uphold the principles of equal opportunity and diversity championed by the civil rights movement. The organization is committed to educating the public on the importance of maintaining affirmative action programs and the principles of equal opportunity in employment and education. Its goal is to carry on the social justice work begun by civil rights leaders more than 30 years ago. It is the organization's belief that affirmative action programs remain vital safeguards and the nation's best tools for removing the roadblocks of race and gender discrimination.

The AUAA assists grassroots organizations, coalitions, and local leaders with the resources and guidance they need to guard against political attacks on affirmative action. Staff members meet with local political leaders and members of the business, educational, and social justice communities to help maintain national and statewide commitment to affirmative action programs. The AUAA organizes speaking engagements and works with the media to alert the public to attacks on civil rights laws. AUAA supports litigants in defense of affirmative action in the courts.

Asian American Legal Defense
and Educational Fund (AALDEF)
99 Hudson Street, 12th Floor
New York, NY 10013
212-966-5982
Fax: 212-966-4303
E-mail: AALDEF@worldnet.att.net

AALDEF was the first organization on the East Coast to protect and promote the legal rights of Asian Americans through litigation, legal advocacy, and community education. Founded in

1974, the fund focuses on the critical issues facing Asian Americans, including economic justice for workers and affirmative action. The AALDEF provides legal advice and attorney referrals for Asians and Asian Americans on employment and a wide variety of other issues. It also conducts legal rights workshops and provides information on any new legal developments that concern the Asian American community. The fund has worked for improvements in the areas of immigration, labor, Japanese American redress, anti-Asian violence, and voting rights as well as discrimination in employment.

Publications: A newsletter, *Outlook,* may occasionally include articles on employment discrimination relating to the Asian American community.

Association for Union Democracy (AUD)
Women's Project
500 State Street, 2nd Floor
Brooklyn, NY 11217
718-855-6650

Open to members of any union for dues of $15 per year, the Association for Union Democracy provides nationwide attorney referrals, legal advice, counseling, and organizational assistance for women in unions. The AUD is a prounion civil liberties group that helps all union members develop democracy within their unions. The Women's Project helps women with problems on the job and within their unions and offers training, workshops, and educational programs for members and nonmembers.

Publications: Union Democracy Review and *50+ Club News,* two newsletters that contain occasional articles on discrimination issues.

BNA Communications, Inc.
9439 Key West Avenue
Rockville, MD 20850
301-948-0540
800-233-6067
Fax: 301-948-0540
Web site: www.bna.com/bnac

For the past 50 years, BNA Communications, Inc., has been a source for employee training solutions with consulting and customized on-site training services, supported by training programs in the areas of affirmative action, diversity, sexual harassment prevention, and equal employment opportunity.

Publications: Videos—*Respect vs. Harassment* (1997), *Diversity: The Competitive Advantage* (1996), *A Winning Balance* (1993), *Connections: Managing Today's Workforce* (1993), *Synergy: EEO, Diversity and Management* (1993), *BRIDGES: Skills for Managing a Diverse Workforce* (1990), *CHOICES: Management Training in Equal Employment Opportunity* (1988), *A Costly Proposition, Invent vs. Impact, Myth vs. Facts* and *Preventing Sexual Harassment;* Booklets—*Diversity Works Resource Series* (1988).

Business and Legal Reports, Inc. (BLR)
39 Academy Street
Madison, CT 06443-1513
203-318-0000
Fax: 203-245-2901
E-mail: service@blr.com
Web site: www.safetyonline.net/blr
On-line subscriptions: www.blr.com

Business and Legal Reports, Inc., is a legal publishing house specializing in legal compliance materials for professionals in the human resources, environmental, and health and safety markets. BLR publishes hundreds of problem-solving publications in the form of CD-ROMs, newsletters, posters, booklets, pocket guides, and videos. The goal of each publication is to interpret, in plain English, the many complex federal and state laws that pertain to the operation of U.S. businesses. The company's mission is "to help companies to problem solve in a proactive, rather than reactive, fashion."

Publications: Call 800-727-5257, write, or E-mail for free catalog/listing of over 200 publications, including *HR Training Repros;* the book *How to Hire and Fire Legally and Fairly;* and the training guidebook *What Every Employer Should Be Doing about Sexual Harassment. What to Do about Personnel Problems (in your state)* is a comprehensive offering of two-volume sets available for every state. The publisher details requirements and rules for human resource professionals in all 50 states, including sections pertaining to affirmative action (available in print or CD-ROM.)

Business and Professional Women/USA (BPW)
2012 Massachusetts Avenue NW
Washington, DC 20036
202-293-1100
Fax: 202-861-0298
Web site: www.bpw/usa.org

Founded in 1919, BPW promotes equity for all women in the workplace through advocacy, education, and information. With 70,000 members in more than 2,000 local organizations represented in every congressional district in the country, BPW includes among its members women and men of every age, race, religion, political party, and socioeconomic background. The organization monitors federal legislation that affects working women and educates its members to become involved in public policy development in their own workplaces, and at the local, state, and federal government levels. Among the first of the women's organizations to endorse the Equal Rights Amendment in 1937, BPW has been a leader in passing key legislation affecting working women, including the Women's Business Ownership Act, the Violence Against Women Act of 1994, the Civil Rights Act of 1964, the Equal Pay Act of 1963, and the Family and Medical Leave Act of 1993.

BPW/USA annually releases its national legislation platform, which includes planks that call for economic equity (ensure pay equity, equal educational and economic opportunities at all stages of life, and promote affordable, quality dependent care to help ensure economic self-sufficiency for women); and civil rights (ensure equal rights and remedies for women in all phases of their lives, support affirmative action, and eliminate sexual harassment and violence against women).

The BPW Foundation collects, conducts, and analyzes research on issues affecting women in the workplace while providing financial assistance for women to further their education. The foundation, which has awarded over $5 million in scholarships, loans, and grants to almost 8,000 women, raises money to educate women who need additional skills to advance in their careers or reenter the workforce.

Publications: A Crime of Power, Not Passion: Sexual Harassment in the Workplace, a position paper on sexual harassment; a national magazine, *National Business Women,* which may include articles on discrimination against women; and a number of other publications and reports related to women and work, including *You Can't Get There From Here: Working Women and the Glass Ceiling.*

CCH Incorporated
4025 West Peterson Avenue
Chicago, IL 60646
312-583-8500

CCH Incorporated is a private publishing company offering materials on many legal issues. It publishes a training manual on equal employment opportunity for managers and supervisors as well as other publications on related personnel issues.

Publications: Call or write for a current catalog. *Sexual Harassment Manual for Managers and Supervisors,* a training manual; *Equal Employment Opportunity Manual for Managers and Supervisors,* a guide to EEO concepts and procedures; *Explanation of Civil Rights Act of 1991,* a guide to the new law; and several other titles on legal issues in employment.

Center for Individual Rights (CIR)
1233 20th Street NW, #260
Washington, DC 20036
202-833-8400
Fax: 202-833-8400
Web site: www.wdn.com/cir/index.html

The purpose of the Center for Individual Rights is to defend individual rights, with particular emphasis on civil rights, freedom of speech, the free exercise of religion, and sexual harassment law. The center provides free legal representation to deserving clients who cannot otherwise obtain or afford legal counsel and whose individual rights are threatened.

CIR's litigation addresses not only the content of the antidiscrimination norm but also its scope. Although the government, in light of its coercive powers, must remain strictly race neutral, there are good reasons—for example, freedom of association and freedom of contract—why private individuals should not be held to the same standard. Accordingly, CIR advocates a limited application of civil rights laws that would preserve private citizens' right to deal with other private citizens without government scrutiny.

Publications: CIR's Web site contains a complete listing and links to various publications.

Center for Women Policy Studies (CWPS)
1211 Connecticut Avenue NW, Suite 312
Washington, DC 20036

202-872-1770
Fax: 202-296-8962
E-mail: HN4066@Handsnet.org

The Center for Women Policy Studies, founded in 1972, is a national nonprofit, multiethnic, and multicultural feminist policy research and advocacy institution that addresses cutting-edge issues that have significant future implications for women. The center seeks to incorporate the perspectives of women, in all their diversity, into the formulation of public policy that ensures just and equitable treatment of women. The center's work is grounded in the belief that all issues affecting women are interrelated and that policy research, analysis, and proposals must reflect women's diversity—by race and ethnicity, by economic status, by disability, by sexual orientation, and by age.

The center believes that community leaders, philanthropy, business, and government share responsibility for ensuring women's rights and justice. It provides its research, analysis, and strategies for action to policy makers and advocates to influence policy in government, business, community, and nonprofit sectors; bring women's voices into public policy debates; help share the debate around women's roles and status; and empower women to create positive change.

Publications: An extensive list is available; call or write for current catalog. *New Frontiers for Worker-Friendly Companies: Report of the Corporate Symposium on Linking Work/Family and Workplace Diversity* (1996); *Workplace Cultures: A Reality Check—Listening to the Voices of Women of Colorado* (1995); *Reforming our Thinking on Welfare: Strategies for State Action* (1996); *More Than Survival: Higher Education for Low Income Women* (1991); *Women, Welfare and Higher Education: A Selected Annotated Bibliography* (1992).

Coalition of Labor Union Women (CLUW)
1126 16th Street NW
Washington, DC 20036
202-466-4610
Fax: 202-776-0537
E-mail: CLUW@pressroom.com

The Coalition of Labor Union Women is a national organization representing unionized women in many diverse industries and professions across the country. Since its founding in 1974, CLUW has advocated for fair and equitable working conditions, benefits, and employment policies in the nation's work forces on behalf of all working women and people of color. At its founding conference, CLUW adopted four goals of action: organizing unorganized women; political action and legislation; affirmative action in the workplace; and participation of women within their unions. These goals continue to be the cornerstone of CLUW's activities.

CLUW members in more than 75 chapters work to implement CLUW's agenda through education, training programs, negotiations, legislation, advocacy, research, and public events. CLUW has been in the forefront of the struggle for child care benefits, pay equity, family and medical leave, national health care, reproductive freedom, and equal educational and economic opportunity. CLUW provides working women with the authority and support necessary to create positive change in their workplaces as well as in the larger political process.

CLUW has sponsored numerous conferences and educational programs featuring workplace equality issues, including the efforts to end discrimination against women and minorities in the workplace and the importance of affirmative action to correct past discriminatory policies and practices. CLUW members testify before Congress, state legislatures, and regulatory agencies on issues important to working women. CLUW participates as a "friend of the court" in briefs in legal cases involving employment discrimination issues. CLUW's programs are also aimed at assisting women in obtaining jobs traditionally held by men, and in educating and training women to play leadership roles within their unions and their communities. CLUW has an active Affirmative Action Committee that develops program and policy initiatives on this topic.

Publications: Affirmative Action: Dispelling the Myths (booklet, 1995); and *CLUW News,* a newsletter that sometimes includes articles on discrimination issues.

Equal Employment Advisory Council (EEAC)
1015 15th Street NW, Suite 1220
Washington, DC 20005
202-789-8650
Fax: 202-789-2291
E-mail: info@eeac.org
Web site: www.eeac.org

The Equal Employment Advisory Council is a nonprofit organization made up of more than 315 major companies that are committed to the principle of equal employment opportunity.

Founded in 1976, EEAC provides a wide variety of services and benefits to its member companies (some are also available to non-members), including training programs and seminars as well as off-the-shelf courses that any company can use for its internal training. EEAC also offers a variety of "special services" at a modest charge, including EEO-related software packages, pamphlets, and agency opinion letters.

Publications: Available EEAC publications, which can be ordered via the Web site, include *EEO Resource Manual, Developing Effective Affirmative Action Plans, Managing OFCCP Compliance Reviews, Investigating and Responding to Discrimination Charges, Representing Your Employer in Mediation of Employment Disrupts, Statistics for Non-statisticians, Equity at Work: A Manager's Guide to Fair Employment Laws and Practices,* and *Alternative Dispute Resolution Techniques.*

Equal Employment Opportunity Commission (EEOC)
303 East 17th Avenue, Suite 510
Denver, CO 80203
303-866-1300
800-669-4000
Fax: 303-866-1085
Web site: www.eeoc.gov

The mission of the EEOC, as set forth in its strategic plan, is to promote equal opportunity in employment by enforcing the federal civil rights employment laws through administrative and judicial actions as well as education and technical assistance. The Equal Employment Opportunity Commission enforces the federal civil rights statutes that prohibit employment discrimination based on race, color, national origin, sex, religion, age, and disability. The commission investigates alleged violations and litigates when a violation is found. The EEOC also provides technical assistance and outreach education to the public regarding the exercise of EEO rights and how to prevent discrimination in the workplace. The commission's role in affirmative action is limited to monitoring federal agencies and their plans.

Publications: The commission's regulations are published annually in Title 29 of the *Code of Federal Regulations,* available on-line through the U.S. Government Printing Office.

Equal Rights Advocates (ERA)
1663 Mission Street, Suite 550
San Francisco, CA 94103

415-621-0672
Fax: 415-621-6744
E-mail: info@equalrights.org
Web site: www.equalrights.org

Equal Rights Advocates is a public interest women's law center that works to achieve social, political, and economic equality for all women and girls. ERA employs a multistrategic approach that includes impact litigation, public education, legislative work, and grassroots organizing to protect and expand women's rights. The center operates a free advice and counseling line through which it offers legal information and advice to women who face sex discrimination in employment. ERA is currently working to defend affirmation action programs in California and achieve equal opportunities for all.

Publications: Various pamphlets on women's issues as well as *The Equal Rights Advocate,* a newsletter that sometimes addresses discrimination issues; *The Affirmative Action Handbook: How to Start and Defend Affirmative Action* Programs, a joint publication of Equal Rights Advocates and the San Francisco Lawyers' Committee for Urban Affairs; a booklet and video, *Keeping the Door Open: Why Affirmative Action is Still Necessary* (14 min. video and booklet); *Reaching for the Dream: Profiles in Affirmative Action; The Impact of Proposition 209 on Education, Employment and Contracting Opportunities for Women in California;* and a number of fact sheets about affirmative action.

Executive Office of the President
1600 Pennsylvania Avenue NW
Washington, DC 20500
Fax: 202-395-5608
E-mail: president@whitehouse.gov
Web site: www.whitehouse.gov or, for government agency information, www.information.gov

This office distributes information concerning President Clinton's views on affirmative action as well as the review of affirmative action in federal agencies that the president directs. On the issue of affirmative action, Clinton states: "This Administration will continue to support affirmative measures that promote opportunities in employment, education, and government contracting for Americans subject to discrimination or its continuing effects. In every instance, we will seek reasonable ways to achieve the objectives of inclusion and antidiscrimination without specific reliance on group membership." Also, as quoted on the executive office Web site, Clinton says, "The policy principles are that any program must be eliminated or reformed if it: (a) creates a quota; (b) creates preferences for unqualified individuals; (c) creates reverse discrimination; or (d) continues even after its equal opportunity purposes have been achieved. . . . [Existing programs] must actually work to effectuate the goals of fighting discrimination and encouraging inclusion; and they must be fair; that is, no unqualified person can be preferred over another qualified person in the name of affirmative action, decisions will not be made on the basis of race or gender except when there is a special justification for doing so, and these measures will be transitional."

Federally Employed Women (FEW)
1400 Eye Street NW, Suite 425
Washington, DC 20005-2252
202-898-0994
Fax: 202-898-0998
E-mail: execdir@few.org
Web site: www.few.org

Federally Employed Women, Inc. (FEW), is a private nonprofit organization founded in 1969 that works as a constructive pressure group to improve the status of women employed by the federal government and by the District of Columbia government. FEW strives to eliminate sex discrimination in the federal government; enhances opportunities for career advancement of women; establishes and maintains with federal agencies working relationships that advocate the fair application of EEO and personnel laws, policies, procedures, and practices; improves the quality of life for women by influencing congressional and presidential administration actions; and works to achieve a unified and diverse membership that values and capitalizes on similarities and differences at all levels of the organization.

Through its diversity program, FEW develops strategies to identify and eliminate barriers and increase diversity within the federal government. FEW examines the demographics of the workforce according to age, race, sex, ethnic background, religious affiliation, disability, and sexual orientation. FEW also seeks to expand the notion of culture groups beyond the categories protected by law and regulation to include socioeconomic status, body-size diversity, and family composition. Diversity training is offered annually at FEW's national training program and at all regional training programs. A section of FEW's Web site is devoted to affirmative action.

Publications: The national office publishes a newsletter, *FEW's News and Views,* sometimes containing articles about discrimination.

Fund for the Feminist Majority

1600 Wilson Boulevard, #801
Arlington, VA 22209
703-522-2214
Fax: 703-522-2219
E-mail: femmaj@feminist.org
Web site: www.feminist.org

The Feminist Majority was founded by former National Organization for Women president Eleanor Smeal with the goal of involving more women in "areas of power," including politics, business, and government. A nonprofit women's rights organization, the Feminist Majority works for social, political, and economic equality for women. A section of their Web site is devoted to affirmative action.

Publications: Feminist Majority newsletter, published quarterly.

Haimes Associates, Inc.

437 West Chestnut Hill Avenue
Philadelphia, PA 19118
215-248-4920
Fax: 215-248-4331

Haimes Associates is a private firm that provides training aids on equal employment and discrimination issues. Its handbooks are brief and written for lower-level managers and supervisors as well as laypersons.

Independent Women's Forum (IWF)

1319 18th Street NW
Washington, DC 20036
202-833-4553
800-224-6000
Fax: 202-833-4543
E-mail: information@iwf.org
Web site: www.iwf.org

The Independent Women's Forum is a nonprofit, nonpartisan organization dedicated to research and public education on policy issues concerning women. The IWF seeks to broaden the debate on women's issues through its conferences, speakers, and publications. It believes it is the voice of reasonable women with important ideas who embrace common sense over divisive ideology.

Publications: A magazine, *The Women's Quarterly,* and a newsletter, *Ex Femina.* Also, the *Media Directory of Women Experts.*

Leadership Conference on Civil Rights (LCCR)
1629 K Street NW, #1010
Washington, DC 20006
202-466-3111
Fax: 202-466-3435
E-mail: komar@civilrights.org
Web site: www.civilrights.org

Founded in 1950, the Leadership Conference on Civil Rights is the nation's oldest, largest, and most diverse coalition of organizations committed to the protection of civil and human rights in the United States. Founded on the eve of historic victories in the struggle against racial discrimination, the Leadership Conference has become a nerve center for the struggle against discrimination in all its forms. Beginning with 30 organizations, mostly civil rights and labor groups, the Leadership Conference has grown in numbers, scope, and effectiveness. The LCCR now consists of over 185 national organizations that work together in solving the significant civil rights problems of the day. These organizations include groups representing people of color, women, labor unions, persons with disabilities, major religious groups, gays and lesbians, and civil liberties and human rights groups. Together, over 50 million Americans belong to the organizations that comprise the Leadership Conference on Civil Rights.

The LCCR continues to work to pass the Employment Non-Discrimination Act, prohibiting employment bias on the basis of sexual orientation, and to monitor welfare reform to make sure it is fair to those without work and those who already labor for low wages.

The LCCR Web site lists background materials on affirmative action and includes links to a variety of publications pertaining to affirmative action.

Maryland Association of Affirmative Action Officers (MAAAO)
Fax: 443-778-6123
Web site: www.jhuapl.edu/maaao/officer.tm

The Maryland Association of Affirmative Action Officers was established in March 1975 to provide a mechanism for the advancement of equal opportunity throughout the State of Maryland. Dedicated to the promotion of affirmative action in both the public and private sectors, MAAAO attempts to foster growth and understanding through sponsorship of educational programs and seminars, and volunteers' efforts designed to enlist community support for its goals. The association provides members with professional development opportunities through monthly membership meetings and the sharing and dissemination of information to assist in implementing affirmative action goals and resolving issues of conflict.

**Mexican American Legal Defense
and Educational Fund (MALDEF)**
1518 K Street NW, Suite 410
Washington, DC 20005
202-628-4074
202-393-4206
E-mail: maldefdc@aol.com
Web site: www.maldef.org

The Mexican American Legal Defense and Educational Fund is a national nonprofit organization whose mission is to protect and promote the civil rights of the over 29 million Latinos living in the United States. Dedicated to securing rights in employment, education, immigration, political access, and language, the organization achieves its objectives through litigation, advocacy, community education, and collaboration with other groups and individuals. MALDEF has been at the forefront of precedent-setting civil rights litigation and has also worked extensively on the issues of redistricting and census adjustment. Through its leadership programs, MALDEF empowers and trains Latinos to serve on community commissions and parents to become advocates for their children's education.

Mountain States Legal Foundation (MSLF)
707 17th Street, Suite 3030
Denver, CO 80202
303-292-2021
Fax: 303-292-1980
E-mail: mslf@mslf.net
Web site: www.mslf.net

The Mountain States Legal Foundation is a nonprofit, public interest legal center dedicated to individual liberty, the right to own and use property, limited government, and the free enterprise system. MSLF was founded in 1977 by Western business leaders in response to what they viewed to be judicial activism (judges who wanted to write, rather than interpret, the law) and the lack of representation of property rights and the public interest in a strong and vibrant economy.

The MSLF is active in the area of race-based decision making (affirmative action). At MSLF's Web site, under the heading Civil Rights, there is a discussion of the cases in which MSLF is involved in this area. Under "Active Cases," one may read a detailed description of each case as well as its current status.

Publications: Contributors receive Mountain States Legal Foundation's newsletter, *The Litigator,* three times annually.

**National Advancing Women
in Higher Education (NAWE)**
1325 18th Street NW, Suite 210
Washington, DC 20036-6511
202-659-9330
Fax: 202-457-0946
E-mail: lgangone@nawe.org
Web site: www.aawe.org

NAWE was the first professional association for women working in higher education. Founded in 1916 as the National Association of Deans of Women, today NAWE membership includes administrators, faculty, staff, and students from all sectors, plus women working in associations, businesses, and government agencies related to education. NAWE's mission is to address issues in higher education, with particular attention to the interests, scholarship, and advancement of women educators and students. NAWE sponsors an institute for emerging women leaders, a professional conference, a conference for women in higher education, and a national conference for college women student leaders.

Publications: Initiatives: The Journal of NAWE, a journal available from NAWE for $50/yr.; *About Women on Campus,* NAWE's fact-filled newsletter on equity issues for women and girls in education, $30/year; *The Chilly Classroom Climate: A Guide to Improve the Education of Women,* which reports on how girls and women are treated in classrooms and institutions of higher education; and *NAWE News,* a quarterly newsletter for members only.

**National Association for the Advancement
of Colored People (NAACP)**
1025 Vermont Avenue NW, Suite 1120
Washington, DC 20005
202-638-2269
Web site: www.naacp.org

Formed in 1909 in New York City by a group of black and white citizens committed to helping to right social injustices, the NAACP is the oldest, largest, and strongest civil rights organization in the United States. The principal objective of the NAACP is to ensure the political, educational, social, and economic equality of minority-group citizens in the United States. The NAACP is committed to achievement through nonviolence and relies upon the press, the petition, the ballot, and the courts to effect change. The organization also uses marches, demonstrations, and effective lobbying to voice its opinions. The NAACP has focused on educational issues and has directed its energy toward ensuring quality-integrated education. It seeks to promote educational excellence among African Americans and other minorities.

Publications: Crisis Magazine explores the full spectrum of black thoughts and concerns and supports the principles of the NAACP Charter. It is included with some NAACP membership levels.

NAACP Legal Defense and Education Fund, Inc.
99 Hudson Street
New York, NY 10013
212-965-2200
800-221-7822
Fax: 212-226-7592
Web site: www.naacp.org

The NAACP Legal Defense and Education Fund works to advance the rights of African Americans. It brings and defends litigation involving discrimination based on race. In that capacity, the fund has defended affirmative action programs and has sought appropriate affirmative action relief to correct discrimination.

Publications: Briefs of various lengths and a quarterly newsletter.

**National Council of Educational
Opportunity Associations (NCEOA)**
1025 Vermont Avenue NW, Suite 900

Washington, DC 20005
202-347-7430
Fax: 202-347-0786
E-mail: link from Web site
Web site: www.trioprograms.org

The Council for Opportunity in Education is a nonprofit organization that represents institutions of higher education, administrators, counselors, and teachers who are committed to advancing equal educational opportunity and to promoting diversity in America's colleges and universities. The council's principal concern is sustaining and improving educational opportunity program services. The majority of educational opportunity programs are the federally funded TRIO programs, which currently operate in over 1,200 postsecondary institutions and more than 100 community agencies.

The NCEOA's mission is to advance and defend the ideal of equal educational opportunity in postsecondary education. As such, the focus of the council is assuring that the least advantaged segments of the American population have a realistic chance to enter and graduate from a postsecondary institution. A secondary purpose of the council is to provide a voice and political vehicle for administrators, counselors, and teachers who are employed in institutionally, state, and federally funded opportunity programs, especially those professionals with TRIO programs.

Publications: Equality, a quarterly national newsletter containing information for professionals who direct, sponsor, or support educational opportunity programs in the United States; *Opportunity Outlook,* published twice a year, a professional journal that profiles successful TRIO programs, professionals, students, and graduates. *Directory of TRIO Programs,* a 60-page national directory, lists all institutions and agencies that sponsor federally funded TRIO programs in America.

National Council of La Raza (NCLR)
810 First Street NE, Suite 300
Washington, DC 20002
202-289-1380
Fax: 202-289-8173
Web site: www.latino.sscnet.ucla.edu/community/nclr.html

The National Council of La Raza exists to improve life opportunities for Americans of Hispanic descent. A nonprofit, tax-exempt organization incorporated in Arizona in 1968, the NCLR serves as an advocate for Hispanic Americans and as a national umbrella organization for 142 formal affiliate, community-based organizations that serve Hispanics in 35 states, Puerto Rico, and the District of Columbia. The NCLR seeks to create opportunities and address problems of discrimination and poverty in the Hispanic community through four major types of initiative: capacity-building assistance to support and strengthen Hispanic community-based organizations; applied research, public policy analysis, and advocacy on behalf of the entire Hispanic community, designed to influence public policies and programs so that they equitably address Hispanic needs; public information efforts to provide accurate information and positive images of Hispanics in the mainstream and Hispanic media; and special catalytic efforts that use the NCLR structure and credibility to create other entities or projects important to the Hispanic community, including international projects consistent with the NCLR's missions.

Publications: Agenda, a quarterly newsletter.

National Education Association (NEA)
1201 16th Street NW
Washington, DC 20036
202-822-7200
202-833-4000
Fax: 202-822-7292
E-mail: KLyons@nea.org
Web site: www.nea.org

The NEA is the nation's oldest and largest organization of professional employees committed to advancing the cause of public education. Founded in 1857 in Philadelphia, the NEA claims 2.4 million members who work at every level of education—from preschool to university graduate programs. At the local level, NEA affiliates are active in everything from conducting professional workshops on discipline and other issues that affect faculty and school support staff to bargaining contracts for school district employees. At the state level, NEA affiliates regularly lobby legislators for the resources schools need, campaign for higher professional standards for the teaching profession, and file legal actions to protect academic freedom. At the national level, NEA's work ranges from coordinating innovative projects to restructuring how learning takes place to fighting congressional attempts to privatize public education. At the international level, NEA is linking educators around the world in an ongoing dialogue dedicated to making schools as effective as they can be. On an individual level, NEA members organize themselves into voluntary groups called caucuses.

Publications: An Educators' Guide to Schoolwide Reform (available on its Web site); *NEA Today* and *NEA Today Online* detail current teaching challenges and solutions; *Thought & Action*, published twice a year, is designed to provide faculty, staff, and students an enlightened balance between theory and practice on issues in higher education. The NEA has published several monographs, including *Mentoring Minorities in Higher Education: Passing the Torch* (1997, second edition).

National Employment Lawyers Association (NELA)
600 Harrison Street, Suite 535
San Francisco, CA 94107
Web site: www.nela.org

The National Employment Lawyers Association is a nonprofit professional membership organization of more than 3,000 lawyers from around the nation who represent employees in employment matters. The association's primary mission is to serve the needs of its members, including providing education and training. NELA also promotes federal and state legislation on employment issues.

Publications: Employee Rights Litigation: Pleading and Practice, Employee Advocate Newsletter, and *Employee Advocate Supplement* (quarterly, distributed to members).

National Organization for Women (NOW)
1000 16th Street NW
Washington, DC 20036
202-331-0066
Fax: 202-785-8576
E-mail: now@now.org or member@now.org
Web site: www.now.org

The National Organization for Women is the largest organization of feminist activists in the United States. Since its founding in 1966, NOW's goal has been "to take action" to bring about equality for all women.

In the past 30 years, NOW has adopted more than a dozen resolutions and stances on an array of issues, including women in poverty, the Equal Rights Amendment, and lesbian rights. The organization has five official priorities: the passing of an equal rights amendment to the U.S. Constitution, opposing racism, advocating for abortion and reproductive rights, supporting lesbian and gay rights, and ending violence against women. Organization leaders have vowed to work to maintain affirmative action. NOW's Web site offers a multitude of information about the organization, including its history, accomplishments, philosophies, and tactics. It includes a section called "Talking about Affirmative Action" that lists various facts and myths about affirmative action.

National Organization for Women (NOW)
Legal Defense and Education Fund
395 Hudson, 5th Floor
New York, NY 10014
212-925-6635
Fax: 212-226-1066
Web site: www.nowldef.org

The NOW Legal Defense and Education Fund strives to achieve equality and improve the lives of women and girls by transforming the institutions and values of society through legal advocacy, public policy development, communications, education, and strategic alliances. The fund pursues equality for women and girls in the workplace, the schools, the family, and the courts through litigation, education, and public information programs. It also provides technical assistance to Congress and state legislatures, distributes fact sheets, and organizes national grassroots coalitions to promote and sustain broad-based advocacy for women's equality.

Publications: A series of legal resource kits cover a range of topics, including sexual harassment in schools, employment discrimination, legal defense, and violence against women. Among them are *An Annotated Summary of the Regulations for Title IX of the Education Amendments of 1972* (1997); *Public Education Programs for African-American Males: A Women's Educational Perspective* (1995); *Secrets in Public: Sexual Harassment in Our Schools* (1993); *Household Workers: Fact Sheet* (1995); *Manual for Survival for Women in Nontraditional Employment* (1994); *Overwhelming Evidence: Reports on Gender Bias in the Courts* (1990); and *National Judicial Education Program Publications List.*

National Partnership for Women and Families
1875 Connecticut Avenue NW, Suite 710
Washington, DC 20009
202-986-2600
Fax: 202-986-2539
E-mail: info@nationalpartnership.org
Web site: www.nationalpartnership.org

The National Partnership for Women and Families is a nonprofit, nonpartisan organization dedicated to improving the lives of women and families. Through public education and advocacy, the National Partnership promotes fairness in the workplace, quality health care, and policies that help women and men meet the dual demands of work and family. Founded in 1971 as the Women's Legal Defense Fund, the National Partnership has grown from a small group of volunteers to a powerful advocate for women and families. The partnership works to improve the nation's civil rights laws and change workplace culture to eliminate discrimination at every level.

Publications: National Partnership News is free to members and is also available via the organization's Web site. Fact sheets on workplace fairness are free and include *Affirmative Action Programs Help Women Shatter the Glass Ceiling, Affirmative Action Opens Doors for Women of Color, What Affirmative Action Is (And What It Is Not), Affirmative Action at Work: Examples of Programs Worth Preserving, White Males Currently Enjoy the Benefits of a Broad Range of Long-standing Preference Programs, Affirmative Action is Good for Business, Affirmative Action Helps Boost Women's Pay and Promotes Economic Security for Women and Their Families, Double Discrimination, Sex and Age Discrimination, Sex and Race Discrimination,* and *Workplace Fairness for Low-Income Women.*

National Women's Law Center (NWLC)
11 Dupont Circle NW, Suite 800
Washington, DC 20036
202-588-5180
Fax: 202-588-5185
E-mail: jappelbaumenwlc.org

The National Women's Law Center is a nonprofit organization that has been working since 1972 to advance and protect women's legal rights. The center focuses on policy areas important to women and their families, including child support, employment, education, reproductive rights and health, child and

adult dependent care, public assistance, tax reform, and social security, with special attention given to the concerns of low-income
women.

Publications: UPDATE, a quarterly newsletter, and various fact
sheets regarding affirmative action. Also, two videos, *Forging a
New Vision of Justice* (1994) and *Fighting for Justice in the 1990's*
(1995).

National Women's Political Caucus (NWPC)
1211 Connecticut Avenue NW, #425
Washington, DC 20036
202-785-1100
Fax: 202-785-3605
E-mail: MailNWPC@aol.com
Web site: www.nwpc.org

Founded in 1971 to encourage women's participation in the political process, the caucus is dedicated to increasing the number
of women in politics. It locates, trains, and supports prochoice female candidates in all levels of government and provides training for young girls and adult women interested in a career in
politics or activism in general.

9to5, National Association of Working Women
231 West Wisconsin, Suite 900
Milwaukee, WI 53203-2308
414-274-0925
Job Survival Hotline: 800-522-0925
Fax: 414-272-2870
E-mail: naww9to5@exedc.com
Web site: www.members.aol.com/naww925

Founded in 1973 by a group of Boston clerical workers, 9to5 is the
nation's largest membership organization of working women. It
has grown from a simple newsletter to a grassroots force of
nearly 15,000 members. The group inspired the movie (and song)
Nine To Five and has made it possible for working women to win
many victories over the years.

The organization provides resources to working women
through its Job Survival Hotline, which links trained organizers
with the women who need them most. The issues most often
raised by hotline callers include sexual harassment, family
leave, and pregnancy discrimination. The group has been on the

forefront of the fight for family and medical leave on the state and national level.

Publications: The 9to5 Guide to Combating Sexual Harassment; Profile of Working Women; Welfare to Work: Obstacles to Job Retention; Moving Forward Project; Office Health and Safety fact sheets; and *9to5 Newsline,* a newsletter published five times a year that sometimes includes articles on discrimination.

Society for Human Resource Management (SHRM)
1800 Duke Street
Alexandria, VA 22314-3499
703-648-3440
800-283-7476
Fax: 703-836-0367
E-mail: shrm@shrm.org
Web site: www.shrm.org

The Society for Human Resource Management represents the interests of more than 100,000 professional and student members from around the world. SHRM provides its members with education and information services, conferences and seminars, government and media representation, on-line services, and publications that equip human resource professionals for their roles as leaders and decision makers within their organizations.

SHRM staff monitors all congressional actions that could affect HR management issues. Working with volunteer leadership, SHRM takes positions on pending legislation and regulatory issues, which are communicated to Congress and governmental agencies.

Publications (available to SHRM members only): *Washington Insider* (monthly); *State Insider* (monthly); *Fact Sheets* (quarterly) contains background and SHRM's position on pending legislation; *Hotline* (weekly) updates on national legislative activity affecting human resource management; and *Developing an Affirmative Action Plan for Minorities and Women: The Required Nuts and Bolts.*

Students of Color Strategy and Policy Department
of the U.S. Student Association (SOCS&PD)
1413 K Street NW, 9th Floor
Washington, DC 20005
202-347-8772
Fax: 202-393-5886
E-mail: ussasocd@essential.org
Web site: www.essential.org/ussa

Through working with campus, state, and national student-run campaigns, the SOCS&PD helps activist students of color (SOCs) and their allies win concrete improvements for communities of color. SOCS&PD works to (1) collect and analyze studies and research on topics affecting SOC access to college, including providing talking points and disseminating some legislation updates for grassroots campaigns involving communities of color; (2) strategize with SOC activists on how to carry out and win campaigns; and (3) train students to effectively implement direct service projects in education, such as early intervention tutoring, mentoring, and college preparation.

Publications: Order copies of the following fact sheets by contacting Vicky Refeau, the Students of Color Strategy and Policy Department coordinator: *People of Color in Higher Education, Federal Financial Aid and Students of Color, Native Americans in Higher Education, African Americans in Higher Education, Asian Americans in Higher Education, Latino/a Americans in Higher Education,* and *Full Time Faculty of Color by Academic Rank.* The SOCS&PD publishes two issue-based organizing manuals focusing on affirmative action and student retention. In addition, it distributes papers on the history and the myths of affirmative action: *The Affirmative Action Organizing Manual for Students of Color* (1996); *Affirmative Action Myth versus Facts* (1997); *Affirmative Action: A Political and Historical Overview* (1997); and *II Advance: The Retention Organizing Manual for Students of Color* (1996).

Union Privilege
815 16th Street NW
Washington, DC 20006
202-637-5390
Fax: 202-508-6902
Web site: www.aflcio.org

Union Privilege is a nonprofit organization that provides various benefits to union members, including legal assistance and insurance. Membership is automatic for members of American Federation of Labor-Congress of Industrial Organization (AFL-CIO) local unions. The organization offers a nationwide legal services plan free to most members of the AFL-CIO.

United Auto Workers Union—Women's Department
8000 East Jefferson
Detroit, MI 48214
313-926-5212

The goals of the UAW Women's Department are to help bring women into active participation in their local unions, to encourage women to run in union elections, to teach women skills for bargaining, and to develop leadership and education. Although the Women's Department still conducts some workshops on discrimination and sexual harassment, it is currently developing revised written and video training materials and new workshops for UAW and other union members.

Wider Opportunities for Women, Inc. (WOW)
815 15th Street NW, Suite 916
Washington, DC 20005
202-638-3143
Fax: 202-638-4885
Web site: www.w-o-w.org

Wider Opportunities for Women works to achieve economic independence and equality of opportunity for women and girls. It is recognized for its skills training models, technical assistance, and advocacy for women workers; for encouraging nontraditional employment for women and implementing self-sufficiency; and for its 500-member Workforce Network. For more than 30 years, WOW has helped women with programs emphasizing literacy, technical and nontraditional skills, welfare-to-work transition, and career development.

Publications: A variety of guides, resource manuals, and training materials are targeted at employers, human resource personnel, and union locals. Fact sheets include *Teen Parents and Welfare Reform* (1994); *Women and Nontraditional Work* (1993); *Women, Work and Family* (1991); *Overview: Women in the Workforce* (1997); and *Women, Work and Child Care* (1989).

Women Employed
22 West Monroe, Suite 1400
Chicago, IL 60603
312-782-3902
Fax: 312-782-5249
E-mail: women-employed@msn.com

Founded in 1973, Women Employed is a not-for-profit member/donor organization dedicated to the economic advancement of women through service, education, and advocacy. Through research, analysis, and advocacy, Women Employed promotes strong enforcement of federal equal opportunity laws, increased access to vocational training for higher paying jobs, and effective corporate equal opportunity programs. Women Employed also develops model direct service programs designed to enable economically disadvantaged women and girls to move toward economic self-sufficiency. The organization provides comprehensive career and professional development for women at all employment levels and involves women in advocacy on key employment-related issues. Areas of expertise include affirmative action, balancing work and family, economic status of women, equal opportunity, glass ceiling barriers and solutions, nontraditional employment, pay equity, sexual harassment prevention, and welfare reform.

Publications: Fact sheets include *Workfare Is Not the Answer to Welfare; Filing an Employment Discrimination Charge with the EEOC; Rhetoric and Reality: The Debate about Affirmative Action; The Glass Ceiling, Sexual Harassment and Your Rights on the Job; Employment Rights; Pregnancy Rights on the Job;* and *Facts about the Family and Medical Leave Act.* Books include *Reinventing the EEOC: Barriers to Enforcement* (1997); *Pathways & Progress: Corporate Best Practices to Shatter the Glass Ceiling* (1996, Chicago Area Partnerships); *Two Sides of the Coin: A Study of the Wage Gap between Men and Women in the Chicago Metropolitan Area* (1994); *Sexual Harassment: The Problem That Isn't Going Away* (1994); *Job Training as a Path out of Poverty* (1993); and *Occupational Segregation: Understanding the Economic Crisis for Women* (1988), which includes a current statistical update.

Women's Bureau
U.S. Department of Labor
Office of the Secretary
Washington, DC 20210
202-219-6652
Fax: 202-219-5529 or 219-3904
E-mail: westbound-wwc@dol.gov
Web site: www.wwc@dol.gov

The Women's Bureau is the only federal agency responsible for promoting the interests of working women. Created by congressional mandate in 1920, the agency is one of the oldest in the Department of Labor and is charged with "formulating standards and policies that shall promote the welfare of wage earning women, improve their working conditions, increase their efficiency, and advance their opportunities for profitable employment." Today, the advocacy agency works to provide working women with practical resources to balance work and family needs and to empower more women to get employment or improve their employment through education, training, freedom from discrimination, and equity in employment hiring and payment structures.

Publications: Single copies of available publications may be obtained free of charge from the Women's Bureau. Send a self-addressed mail label with the order. Mail the request to the closest regional office or to U.S. Department of Labor, Women's Bureau, Attn: Publications, 200 Constitution Ave NW, Washington DC 20210. Some publications are available on the Internet at http://www.dol.gov/dol/wb or http://www/dol.gov/dol/wb/welcome.html. The bureau does not have any publications that specifically address affirmative action, but several publications, including the *Don't Work in the Dark* series, address issues of discrimination. Also available are *What Works! The Working Women Count Honor Roll Final Report*—a selection of programs and policies that make work better; *Working Women Count! A Report to the Nation, Executive Summary,* results from a national survey of over 250,000 working women detailing what they like about their jobs, what they do not like, and what they want to see changed (1994); and *A Working Woman's Guide to Her Job Rights* (1992) (purchase from the Government Printing Office, Stock Number 029-002-00001-9, $2.50).

Women's Rights Litigation Clinic
Rutgers School of Law—Newark
15 Washington Street
Newark, NJ 07102-3192
201-648-5637

Founded as a temporary student-initiated undertaking in 1972 and institutionalized as a permanent enterprise in 1973, the clinic has focused on litigation and legal counseling relating to women's rights. Open to both second and third-year students, the Women's Rights Litigation Clinic offers a legal-practice experience to students who, working with attorney-instructors, have achieved a number of important victories, particularly in the area of gender equality.

Publications: Stop Sexual Harassment in Housing, a flyer, published in English and Spanish.

Selected Print Resources

As in other chapters of this book, an attempt has been made to present all points of view on the issue of affirmative action. The number of books and monographs available on this issue, as well as the law, changes rapidly, and many works may be quickly outdated. Some of these are still listed in this chapter because they present a particular point of view or because they are of historical significance. Before relying upon the facts or legal precedent in any particular work, however, check the date it was published.

Anthologies

Beckwith, Francis J., and Todd E. Jones. *Affirmative Action: Social Justice or Reverse Discrimination?* Amherst, N.Y.: Prometheus Books, 1997. 250 pp. Bibliography. ISBN 1-57392-157-2 (paper).

Francis Beckwith, an associate professor of philosophy, culture, and law at Trinity Graduate School of Trinity International University as well as a Senior Research Fellow at the Nevada Policy Research Institute, and Todd Jones, an associate professor of philosophy at the University of Nevada, serve as the editors of a diverse collection of works about the issue of affirmative action. The essays include, for example, President Johnson's 1965 Howard University commencement speech as well as essays by Thomas Sowell and Shelby Steele and classic pieces from moral philosophers such as Ronald Sworkin. The authors sought to offer essays that used rational discussion and analysis rather than emotional debate of this sensitive issue.

The works were collected in response to the 1996 decision by California voters to eliminate most forms of state-sanctioned affirmative action (this is still tied up in court); the authors themselves disagree about the issue and sought to offer "nuance positions" as well as more serious philosophical and public policy defenses and critiques. Part I of the book covers the public policy debate over affirmative action, and Part II, the philosophical discussions about the issue. There are also extensive introductions to each section and an extensive bibliography. Although they admit that there is some overlap, the authors find the philosophical justification of affirmative action is logically prior to the public policy justification, though the defense of a public policy proposal may appeal to as well as employ philosophical argument. The authors' introductions and commentary tend to be academic and philosophical but useful. This book represents one of the most well researched and balanced collections available. As the authors describe their own worthy goals with this book, "although our views differ, we both take to heart, and we hope the reader does as well, the words of Martin Luther King, Jr., 'We will not be satisfied until justice rolls down like waters and righteousness like a mighty stream.'"

Bibliographies

Dworaczek, Marian. *Affirmative Action and Minorities: A Bibliography.* Monticello, Ill.: Vance Bibliographies, 1988. 63 pp. ISSN 0193-970X and ISBN 1-55590-638-9.

This extensive and useful list is now quite out of date, but it is included as one of the few available bibliographies exclusively on the subject of affirmative action. Its list of books and articles is useful; however, there is no summary for each listing—merely the author, title, and ordering information. The book includes a section on A/V materials but no electronic publications. Most of the videos and slides listed are even more dated and are not readily available. A number of Canadian resources are included in addition to the United States listings.

Nordquist, Joan. *Affirmative Action: A Bibliography.* Santa Cruz, Calif.: Contemporary Social Issues: A Bibliographic Series, No. 41. 1996. 68pp. ISSN 0887-3569.

One of a series of current and accurate information on a variety of contemporary social issues, this bibliography is not just a long list of books, journals, and articles on the subject of affirmative action but an arrangement of entries under useful categories divided into 13 main subject areas. Categories include the philosophy of affirmative action, the effects of affirmative action, attitudes about affirmative action, and affirmative action and education. Also included are useful and hard-to-find directories, bibliographies, activist organizations, and periodicals on the topic. The list represents a variety of viewpoints ranging from the general to the scholarly. The bibliography includes sources from social, political, economic, philosophical, legal, feminist, and multicultural literature from a wide variety of publishers, including alternative publishers, small presses, feminist presses, and activist organizations. Unfortunately, each listing includes merely the title, author, publisher, and date rather than any summary description of the work. Still, this work represents the most comprehensive and accurate resource available on the subject.

Books, Monographs, and Selected Articles and Reports

Bergmann, Barbara R. *In Defense of Affirmative Action.* New York: Basic Books, 1996. 213 pp. Index, bibliographical references. ISBN 0-465-09833-9.

This book allows a distinguished economist to cut through the rhetoric and provide a well-reasoned defense of affirmative action. Bergmann persuasively demonstrates why she believes there are no effective substitutes to affirmative action as a solution to the persistent race and sex discrimination in our society. She argues that critics who suggest we "just enforce the laws against discrimination" are misinformed and misguided. Bergmann reminds us that many others in our society, such as wealthy white children, receive special consideration for the best schools and jobs, but none claims that makes them incapable, as is frequently argued for the beneficiaries of affirmative action. Unlike other defenders of affirmative action, Bergmann directly confronts the issue of quotas, acknowledging that affirmative action does involve paying attention to the numbers hired by race and sex; otherwise, she insists, prejudice or habits would lead to a preference for white males in most openings. She believes we are naive or even dishonest if we insist that if we do away with affirmative action we will be left with a system that is sex-blind and race-blind. Rather, Bergmann insists, affirmative action is needed to move us to a society in which merit truly rules.

The book includes a thorough discussion of the pros and cons of affirmative action as well as potential alternatives. In addition to underscoring the reasons for more blatant discrimination, Bergmann also discusses the more benign kind: "Patterns of occupational segregation by race and sex tend to persist in part because people have good reason to be cautious in making hiring and promotion decisions. These decisions are the most crucial to any organization's success. Employers have an understandable tendency to move cautiously and to continue doing what has worked well previously. Hiring candidates of a different race or sex is likely to be seen as risky or asking for trouble."

Bergmann is a professor of economics at American University and has served on the staff of President Kennedy's Council of Economic Advisors and as president of the American Association of University Professors. She is also the author of *The Economic Emergence of Women*.

Bolick, Clint. *The Affirmative Action Fraud: Can We Restore the American Civil Rights Vision?* Washington, D.C.: The Cato Institute, 1996. 170 pp. Index, bibliographical references. ISBN 1-882577-27-2 (cloth); ISBN 1-882577-28-0 (pbk.)

Bolick, the vice-president and director of litigation at the Institute for Justice (founded to engage in constitutional litigation, protecting individual liberty, and challenging the regulatory welfare state), argues in this book that the civil rights establishment has failed because of its "preoccupation" with group entitlement rather than individual justice. He believes that democracy is the answer to inequality in our society and that being against discriminatory affirmative action is not the same as being against racial reform. He argues that affirmative action is "trickle-down" civil rights: benefits are bestowed upon the most-advantaged members of designated groups in the name of the least advantaged, who do not reap those benefits. Those programs, he believes, reinforce the propensity of individuals to define themselves in terms of race. Bolick has worked on developing civil rights litigation programs to eliminate barriers to opportunity, focusing on the efforts of low-income people to gain greater entrepreneurial and educational opportunities. Unlike race-preference programs, he argues, these efforts are not racially divisive, even though the people who benefit are primarily minorities, because, he believes, those efforts focus on opening opportunities to the economically disadvantaged rather than redistributing opportunities on the basis of race.

Bolick made headlines when he publicly opposed President Clinton's nomination of law professor Lani Guinier as assistant attorney general for civil rights. He writes extensively about that battle in his book.

Bowen, William G., and Derek Bok. *The Shape of the River: Long-Term Consequences of Considering Race in College and University Admissions.* Princeton, N.J.: Princeton University Press, 1998. 472 pp. Index, bibliographical references. ISBN 0-691-00274-6.

One of the few books on affirmative action that does not consist mainly of clashing opinions, *The Shape of the River* contains a wealth of empirical evidence to bear on the heated debate about how race-sensitive admissions policies actually work and what effects they have on students of different races.

The authors are the economist William Bowen, president of the Andrew W. Mellon Foundation and former president of Princeton University, and Derek Bok, former president of Harvard University and former dean of the Harvard Law School. These well-credentialed and worldly academicians argue that we can only pass an informed judgment on the wisdom of race-sensitive admission if we understand in detail the college careers and then the lives of students. They rely upon a metaphor from Mark Twain, arguing that we must learn the shape of the entire river. The basis for the book is an unprecedented study of the academic, employment, and personal histories of more than 45,000 students of all races who attended academically selective universities from the 1970s to the early 1990s.

The study and this book demonstrate that affirmative action increases the likelihood that blacks will be admitted to selective universities, and they show the effect elimination of the program would have on the number of minority students. The study proves these students have performed as well as their peers in subsequent careers as well as in civic and community affairs. The book also details the views of these students.

The authors respond to critics who claim that such policies harm their intended beneficiaries by forcing them to compete with academically superior classmates. They also examine the various alternatives. Even though they publish extensive studies and data to back up their opinions, the authors do not shrink from a positive conclusion: "There is certainly much work for colleges and universities to do in finding more effective ways to improve the academic performance of minority students. But, overall, we conclude that academically selective colleges and universities have been highly successful in using race-sensitive admissions policies to advance educational goals important to them and societal goals important to everyone. Indeed, we regard these admissions policies as an impressive example of how venerable institutions with established ways of operating can adapt to serve newly perceived needs." This book is undoubtedly the most well-researched and best-written examination of the thorny issue of race-sensitive admission policies available today.

Browne-Miller, Angela. *Shameful Admissions: The Losing Battle To Serve Everyone in Our Universities.* San Francisco: Jossey-Bass Publishers, 1996. 276 pp. Index, bibliographical references. ISBN 0-7879-0182-2.

Browne-Miller, a lecturer in three departments at the University of California–Berkeley, wrote this book in the wake of the summer 1995 decision to end affirmative action admission policies at the university. An insiders' look at how and why, Browne-Miller believes we can blame affirmative action for creating an educational system that no longer delivers. The author argues that no four-year institution can meet the goal of rebalancing a lifetime of social inequalities. Although she believes that affirmative action has not caused or created the real challenges posed by an increasingly diverse student population, she concludes that they distracted us from the more important issue of a fragmented and overextended university system. Instead, she argues, we should be focusing on the issue of who should go to college and where. Browne-Miller proposes that we empty our traditional colleges and universities and encourage, instead, a new "communiversity" that would serve local people, the community, and regions in which they are based; that would exempt no students; and that would focus on lifelong learning. The former universities, she suggests, should become think tanks and research, trade, and professional schools. She advocates that this would go a long way toward a new social justice. Currently, she asserts, we have no way of knowing which student admitted is really more qualified. This book provides a thoughtful and different view of the underlying issues relating to affirmative action.

Browne-Miller is also the author of *The Day Care Dilemma, Learning to Learn,* and *Intelligence Policy.*

Caplan, Lincoln. *Up against the Law: Affirmative Action and the Supreme Court.* Twentieth Century Fund, 1997. 75pp. Index. ISBN 0-87078-409-9.

Caplan, an attorney and journalist, examines the role the U.S. Supreme Court has played in recent decades and provides an explanation of the actual practices and consequences of representative affirmative action programs. He explores the ambiguities and contradictions in key decisions and identifies the current balance among the justices on this subject. Caplan concludes that campaign sloganeering has contributed to the public's current misunderstanding of the issues.

In truth, however, as he points out, the Court has also been confused. In none of the dozen affirmative action cases that the Supreme Court has decided since the 1978 *Bakke* ruling have the decisions been unanimous. Most have been decided by a single vote, and many involve three or more opinions. Caplan traces this lack of unity to deep-seated misunderstandings on the Court and throughout society about the genesis of affirmative action, the wide variety of efforts that the term entails, and the purposes that different efforts aim to accomplish. As he argues, because the affirmative action program for any particular agency, private company, university, or other institution is unique, attempts to draw legal lines around such efforts create complications. The author argues that the benefits of letting "a thousand flowers bloom"—which is the history of affirmative action—has been undermined by the Court's mishandled efforts to plow away weeds. Rather than framing the debate as between conflicting principles—as with many modern debates such as abortion—he believes that the current debate involves "different understandings of the same concepts—of the problem of discrimination that affirmative action was designed to address, of the goal of equality it was meant to serve, and of other basic elements."

Caplan is a former staff writer of *The New Yorker* and is now assistant managing editor of *U.S. News and World Report.* He is the author of four previous books: *Skadden: Power, Money and the Rise of a Legal Empire; An Open Adoption; The Tenth Justice: The Solicitor General and the Rule of Law;* and *The Insanity Defense and the Trial of John W. Hinckley.*

Carter, Stephen L. *Reflections of an Affirmative Action Baby.* New York: Basic Books, 1991. 286 pp. Index, bibliographical references. ISBN 0-465-06871-5.

Carter, a law professor at Yale University, former clerk to Supreme Court Justice Thurgood Marshall, and one of the nation's leading experts on constitutional law, starts this provocative book by proclaiming, "I got into law school because I am black." Admitting that he has gained from affirmative action, he draws on his own experiences to confront the problems that race has spawned. He is particularly critical of those who would require black intellectuals to conform to one "politically correct" way of thinking and being black: "To be black and an intellectual in America is to live in a box. So I live in a box—not of my own making—and on the box is a label—not of my own choosing. Most of those who have not met me, and many of those who have, have seen the box and read the label and imagine that they have seen me."

In Part I of his book, Carter chronicles his own story; in Part II, he examines the growing disagreement among blacks over the issues raised by affirmative action; and in Part III, he suggests ways to build a consensus over solutions. Carter argues not so much that affirmative action has gone too far but that it hasn't gone far enough to undo the nation's moral obligations from its legacy of slavery. He argues that affirmative action reinforces racist stereotypes by promoting the idea that blacks cannot aspire to more than being "the best black." He suggests that affirmative action must not be abandoned but returned to its roots: providing educational opportunities for those who might otherwise not have them. After opportunities have been provided, he urges that the recipients must be held to the same standards as anyone else. Carter's book provides a highly personal, well-written, and proactive look at the issue.

Cose, Ellis. *Color-Blind: Seeing beyond Race in a Race-Obsessed World.* New York: Harper Collins, 1997. 260 pp. Index, bibliographical references. ISBN 0-06-017497-8.

Cose, a contributing editor for *Newsweek* magazine and former chairman of the editorial board and editorial page editor of the *New York Daily News,* has also served as a fellow for a variety of think tanks, including the Joint Center for Political Studies. This book seeks to answer the question, Is a truly race-neutral society possible? Cose wonders if the United States can wipe the slate clean and forget its past racism. He questions whether color-blindness is just "another name for denial."

Cose, the author of *The Rage of a Privileged Class,* rejects both sides of the current race debate: one side claiming that discrimination is at the root of all of America's racial problems, the other maintaining that prejudice has practically disappeared. Neither view, Cose believes, is accurate. Exploring race in South Africa and Latin America, he illustrates why the United States can't move directly from a country where discrimination is sanctioned to a race-neutral society. Instead, Cose offers 12 necessary steps to help America achieve its true potential, ranging from No. 1, "We must stop expecting time to solve the problem for us," to No. 12, "We must stop looking for one solution to all our racial problems."

Provocative and practical, this book relies extensively on well-documented research, including the work of psychologist John Dovidio, who found that people who work together on the same team can "begin to see beyond skin color." Thus, though Cose believes that we must "keep the conversation [about race] going" (step 10), he emphasizes that we must also seize opportunities for interracial collaboration. "If you can establish a sense of groupness, of being on the same team even artificially and temporarily, that begins to create a foundation on which people can have more personal, deeper discussions and understandings," observes Dovidio.

Color-Blind provides one of the most sensible and balanced looks at the thorny problem of race in America. The problem with affirmative action, Cose observes, is not that it has failed but that it has never been given a real chance. The policy was never intended to solve all the ills of race in our society; for example, the fact that it benefits more middle-class blacks just means that we need to have more initiatives aimed at the poor. Also, Cose believes we have not really had affirmative action for 30 years—as argued by some critics—but for more like ten; it was resisted and not widely implemented for the first 20. The reality, Cose concludes, is that critics have not really come up with anything better.

Federal Glass Ceiling Commission. *Good for Business: Making Full Use of the Nation's Human Capital.* Washington, D.C.: U.S. Government Printing Office, 1995. 243 pp. Bibliography.

This fact-finding report of the Federal Glass Ceiling Commission, chaired by former labor secretary Robert Reich, was mandated by Congress in the Glass Ceiling Act, Title II of the Civil Rights

Act of 1991. The act established the bipartisan Glass Ceiling Commission with 21 members diverse in terms of politics, ethnicity, age, and gender. The act set forth the commission's mission: to conduct a study and prepare recommendations on "eliminating artificial barriers to the advancement of women and minorities" to "management and decision-making positions in business."

The report confirmed the "glass ceiling metaphor," first coined in a *Wall Street Journal* article that identified an invisible barrier between women and the executive suite. The report found that 97 percent of the senior managers of *Fortune 1000* industrial and *Fortune 500* companies are white—94 to 97 percent are male. The research also confirmed that when women and minorities did reach the upper levels of business, their compensation was lower. The report dispelled the myth that the limited numbers were temporary. The commission also found that few women and minorities were in the "pipeline" to the executive suite—those jobs that would soon lead to the next level.

The commission found that the world at the top does not "look like America" in that two-thirds of the population of the United States and 57 percent of the working population are female, minorities, or both. By the year 2005, women and minority men will make up 67 percent of the workforce.

Many CEOs interviewed by the commission recognized that the current situation was not good for businesses that need to reflect the marketplace and their customers as well as to respond to trading partners that are becoming more global and diverse. They echoed a 1993 study of *Standard and Poor's 500* companies that showed that firms that succeed in shattering their own glass ceilings racked up stock market records nearly two and a half times better than comparable companies. The report urges the country to "learn from the success stories"—to study the companies that have boosted profits while eliminating barriers for diverse workforces.

Packed with statistics and suggestions as well as history about the problems and barriers to women and minorities in corporate America, the Glass Ceiling Report serves as a useful, well-written reference for researchers interested in the problem of executive suite access and potential solutions.

Fiscus, Ronald J. *The Constitutional Logic of Affirmative Action.* Durham, N.C.: Duke University Press, 1992. 150 pp. Index, bibliographical references. ISBN 0-8223-1206-9.

This book attempts to clarify the argument for a constitutional rationale of affirmative action, addressing the moral and legal ramifications of this subject. Fiscus draws a distinction between compensatory and distributive justice, arguing that the former doesn't provide an appropriate basis for justifying broader programs of affirmative action but instead is the principle underlying efforts to provide remedies in specific cases of discrimination. Distributive justice, Fiscus's proposed remedy, avoids the pitfalls of the current approach with the suggestion that a stipulated assumption of equality begins at birth. With that assumption, there would be a distribution of opportunity proportionate to society's racial and gender composition. In a society without discrimination, for example, if 20 percent of the population were black, then 20 percent of all jobs, promotions, college acceptances, and so on, would go to blacks. Any deviation from this distribution could only be attributed to discrimination.

Fiscus counters the argument that in "reverse discrimination" cases, whites—particularly white males—are "innocent victims" of affirmative action plans. He argues that proportional quotas do not produce "innocent victims" because those holding positions in excess of what proportionality would provide are not entitled to them. In fact, he argues in a straightforward fashion for quotas—but only quotas that are proportionate to the racial composition of society. As the author stated in his concluding chapter:

> Life has always been unfair. It is unfair now. And it will always be unfair. People have treated people unfairly through the ages, whether the mechanism has been social class and economic inequality, ethnic or racial or gender-based prejudice, physical appearance, xenophobia, simple thoughtlessness or meanness of spirit, or any of a host of other factors that people have mistakenly believed were valid indicators of how other people should be treated.

In any case, one may concede that life is and will continue to be unfair without undermining in the slightest the assumption that diminishing unfairness is a basic task of law and society. What can reasonably be done must be done, for how can we ever hope to attain the just society if we accept injustices along the way?

This book provides a provocative stance on the debate with a reasoned and intellectual argument.

Glazer, Nathan. *Affirmative Discrimination: Ethnic Inequality and Public Policy.* New York: Basic Books, 1975. 248 pp. Index, bibliographical references. ISBN 0-465-02076-3.

This book, though dated, is included because of is value in providing a historical perspective on affirmative action and its original goals. Glazer, then a professor of education and social structure at Yale and editor of *Public Interest Magazine*, noted that until the early 1970s, affirmative action meant to seek out and prepare members of minority groups for better jobs and educational opportunities. At that time, Glazer explained, affirmative action came to mean more than advertising opportunities, actively seeking out those who might not know of them, and preparing those who might not yet be qualified. This is when, he argued, affirmative action came to mean the setting of statistical requirements based on race, color, and national origin for employers and educational institutions, threatening our concern for individual claims for justice and equity and replacing them with a concern for rights publicly determined and delimited racial and ethnic groups. An early critic of this trend, Glazer questioned the wisdom and equity of the then-new policy. He argued against abandoning this first principle of a liberal society, that the individual's interests and welfare are the test of a good society, for we now attach benefits and penalties to individuals simply on the basis of their race, color, and national origin.

Glazer has modified his views somewhat (see Glazer biography in Chapter 3), but his 1975 book remains important for serving as one of the first academic critiques of affirmative action.

Greene, Kathanne W. *Affirmative Action and Principles of Justice.* Westport, Conn.: Greenwood Press, 1989. 184 pp. Index, bibliography. ISBN 0-313-26678-6.

This book, now somewhat out of date, provides a solid historical framework for the legal and political background of affirmative action. Greene is an assistant professor of political science at the University of Southern Mississippi in Hattiesburg. She identifies her biases up front, defining herself as a staunch defender of affirmative action, noting that even some members of her family have asked her not to speak about the subject because it is too emotional. Greene believes that "these individuals, like so many others, are unwilling to face up to what any discussion of affirmative action exposes—prejudice, oppression, and injustice. . . . Prejudice, oppression, and injustice do not simply go away with time. They must be recognized before they can be changed, and change requires effort. I see affirmative action as a necessary step toward change."

This book provides solid coverage of the legislative history of Title VII, the early employment discrimination case law, and more recent affirmative action cases as well as policymaking and statutory cases. The book concludes with the author's own explanation about the philosophical basis of affirmative action as well as a useful (although dated) list of references. It is a good contribution to the debate for its careful, historical perspective.

Guernsey, JoAnn Bren. *Affirmative Action: A Problem or a Remedy?* Minneapolis: Lerner Publications Company, 1997. 112 pp. Index, bibliography, glossary. ISBN 0-8225-2614-X.

In this balanced work on the pros and cons of affirmative action, the author points out that one reason we have such difficulty resolving the debate is that it involves conflicting American principles: "On the one hand, citizens believe that everyone deserves equal opportunities; on the other hand, they hold firmly to the principle that hard work and merit—not involuntary membership in some group—should determine who prospers and who does not."

In clear language for young people and with easy-to-follow notes and suggested sources, Guernsey covers the topic from a definition of the issue to a brief history, and she includes a more extensive discussion of racial discrimination, gender discrimination, and California as a case study. She also tries to predict the future of affirmative action. The list of resources, bibliography, and notes are limited but serve as a good start for further research.

Guinier, Lani, and Susan Sturm. *The Future of Affirmative Action: Reclaiming the Innovative Ideal. California Law Review* 84 (1996): 952-1005.

Law professor Lani Guinier, well known for President Clinton's unsuccessful nomination of her as the head of the U.S. Attorney General's Office of Civil Rights, and her colleague, Susan Sturm, attack head-on the opponents of affirmative action. They debunk both the legal and policy arguments against affirmative action as well as arguing that—far from doing too much—affirmative action, in fact, seeks to accomplish far too little.

Suggesting that the proponents of affirmative action have allowed the critics to frame the argument, the authors instead argue that "it is necessary to change the paradigm." They continue:

Certainly we must challenge out loud the basic assumption that affirmative action is a departure from an otherwise sound meritocracy. At the same time, we must challenge existing add-on practices of affirmative action as too conservative a remedy. The experience of women and people of color offers insights beyond showing how and why those particular people have been excluded. We need to show that the current one-size-fits-all ranking system of predicting 'merit' is no longer justified or productive for anyone.

The authors argue that the current system doesn't predict actual job performance and does "violence to the fundamental principles of equity and 'functional merit.'" They believe that patterns of exclusion experienced by women and people of color are "signals" rather than a sign that the rest of the system is fair to others. Instead, they argue for a performance-based criteria of selection, premised upon a nuanced and complex system of performance evaluations and probationary periods for jobs, rather than selection by grades or test scores.

The article is well written, provocative, and well researched. ' It offers an innovative way of thinking about the ongoing debate.

Lawrence, Charles R. III, and Mari J. Matsuda. *We Won't Go Back: Making the Case for Affirmative Action.* New York: Houghton Mifflin Company, 1997. 314 pp. Index, bibliographical references. ISBN 0-395-79125-1.

In this honest "meditation" on affirmative action, two of the country's leading teachers on the issue make a strong case for a more humane understanding. Their story is told from the personal and sometimes divergent perspectives of an African American man and an Asian American woman. They conclude that affirmative action should be expanded as a gain for the whole society.

The authors struggle with some of the thorniest parts of today's debate on points such as "How do African Americans feel about Clarence Thomas?" "Why do most women remain silent on affirmative action?" "Do Asian Americans need the policy?" and "How should issues of hate speech and political correctness be addressed?" They also interview and discuss other Americans who have dealt with affirmative action to help us understand which people are "in the room" because of affirmative action. The authors do not shrink from the spiritual issues and values behind affirmative action. They ask, for example, "What is it that we Americans value?" "Do we want to live in a world where there is no sense of caring or community?"

The authors are professors at Georgetown University and speak on race issues and affirmative action around the country. They are also the authors of *Words That Wound: Critical Race Theory, Assaultive Speech* and *The First Amendment.*

Leshin, Geraldine. *Equal Employment Opportunity and Affirmative Action in Labor-Management Relations: A Primer.* Los Angeles: Institute of Industrial Relations, University of California, 1982. (Updated periodically.)

Written as a textbook for students of labor-management relations, this work covers the basics of discrimination and affirmative action, including cases and analysis under collective bargaining, equal employment opportunity, the equal pay act, Title VII, employment discrimination, age discrimination, and affirmative action. A compilation of useful information from various sources, it does suffer somewhat from differences in style of the various sources. Before using any of the material, check to determine if it has been republished recently. The book does contain a useful glossary.

Lynch, Frederick R. *Invisible Victims: White Males and the Crises of Affirmative Action.* New York: Praeger, 1991 (paper); Westport, Conn.: Greenwood Press, 1998 (cloth). 237 pp. Index, bibliography. ISBN 0-275-94102-7 (pbk.); ISBN 0-313-26496-1 (cloth).

Lynch, a senior research associate at the Salvatori Center, Claremont McKenna College, writes that close scrutiny of race-related topics is a new taboo. He calls the present era the "new McCarthyism" and argues that race and gender goals and quotas have produced conflict, resentment, and other problems. "Affirmative action should no longer be regarded as an article of political faith," Lynch says; "rather, it should be seen as a major social revolution to be studied sociologically." Lynch believes that the major quantitative studies differ on the effect of affirmative action policies, so he instead uses a case-study method, interviewing 32 individuals he believes were affected by affirmative action.

The books consists mostly of Lynch's own interviews of these 32 people as well as media extracts and other quotes. Hardly scientific, the work provides a human face and vibrant voices to illustrate Lynch's admittedly biased and conservative viewpoint on the subject.

Malamud, Deborah C. *Class-Based Affirmative Action: Lessons and Caveats.* Texas Law Review 74(1996): 1847-1900.

Malamud, an assistant professor of law at the University of Michigan, argues that the "class, not race" conservative war cry in contemporary American politics put forth by opponents of affirmative action ignores some fundamental issues. One of those, she suggests, is that legal thinkers on the left have long sought the legal recognition of economic inequality or "class" as a force in American life. In addition, she suggests that most American institutions, especially the courts, have endorsed the fiction that the United States is without a class system and suggests that the debate over affirmative action opens the door to a real discussion about that issue.

Specifically, Malamud presents the United States Supreme Court decision in *Adarand v. Pena* as opening the door to such an analysis, but she wonders if the courts can "get it right." She explains that what she means by that phrase is not just for the programs to be "technically adequate" but also to advance the public discourse on the question of economic inequity.

Malamud goes to considerable length in this article to demonstrate the complexity of the measurement of economic inequality and expresses pessimism about the capacity of the legal system to probe deeply into the "social phenomenon of economic inequality for purposes of class-based affirmative action." She suggests that the debate should focus beyond the "conventional questions" of legitimacy of such a system to the "cultural impact of their programs on societal understandings of economic inequality."

Sedmak, Nancy J. *Primer on Equal Employment Opportunity.* 5th ed. Washington, D.C.: BNA Books, 1991. 201 pp. Index. ISBN 0-87179-684-8.

This book (updated periodically since the first edition in 1978) provides a comprehensive overview of the field of equal employment opportunity. Part I lists the relevant laws, order, regulations, and guidelines—on the state, local, and federal levels—as well as the federal agencies involved in the enforcement and coverage of employers, employees, and unions under the various federal laws. Part II analyzes and describes the laws according to each type of discrimination involved. The often complex policy and practice issues involved in recruiting, hiring, promotion, employment testing, and reverse discrimination are outlined in Part

III. Part IV provides a discussion of the enforcement and administrative aspects of equal opportunity law. Although somewhat dated, the work is a good overview of the issues and is included because it is widely available in most libraries.

The material is presented in a readable, clear format, suitable for readers without much legal training. Each case, statute, and regulation is summarized without a great deal of technical jargon. The book is a good source of citations to cases, statues, EEO decisions, and regulation for further research.

Uforsky, Melvin. *The Supreme Court and Affirmative Action.* New York: Charles Scribner's Sons, 1991. 270 pp. Index, bibliographical references. ISBN 0-684-19069-9.

Uforsky, a professor of history and constitutional law at Virginia Commonwealth University and author of *A Mind of One's Own*, a biography of Justice Louis Brandeis, profiles one important United States Supreme Court case on affirmative action in this book. *Johnson v. Transportation Agency, Santa Clara County*, decided in 1988, was a landmark decision that meant that public and private employers could voluntarily adopt hiring and promotion goals to benefit minorities and women. The author makes the case and the issues both readable and compelling.

He starts the story with the phone call Diane Joyce places to an affirmative action officer in order to get a job as a road dispatcher in California's Santa Clara County Transportation Agency. Uforsky next tracks the path of this case through the lower courts and into the Supreme Court. Although the book provides an extensive and useful background on affirmative action, the stories stand out, as Uforsky writes:

> Interestingly, when I interviewed Paul Johnson and Diane Joyce in the summer of 1989, both of them said they wanted fairness, they wanted equal opportunity, they wanted to be judged on their own merits. They came at these ideals from different angles, but in an ideal world one would not find the two of them very far apart. They are pretty much old-fashion Americans who believe fervently in their country and in its promise of equality for all under the law.
>
> Ultimately, it was their human stories, and not the broader issue of affirmative action, that drew me to write this book. In teaching constitutional history, I try to remind my students—and me—that while "great

cases may enunciate important legal principle," they start with people, men and women who for one reason or another believe that they have not been treated rightly, and appeal to the law for help.

Whether *Johnson v. Transportation Agency, Santa Clara County* ever takes its place among the "great" cases, it deals with an important issue, and we can understand that issue better if we can place it in a human context. This book is a worthy addition to that important goal.

Yates, Steven. *Civil Wrongs: What Went Wrong with Affirmative Action.* San Francisco: Institute for Contemporary Studies, 1994. 276 pp. Index, bibliographical references. ISBN 1-55815-292-X.

Yates argues that racial problems are worse rather than better in this country, in large part because of the failure of affirmative action and other policies of race and gender. He believes that "hundreds" of ordinary people, particularly minorities, have been harmed by reverse discrimination. Yates claims that affirmative action has worsened racial tension on campus and throughout society, that affirmative action is directly linked to multiculturalism and "political correctness," and that the policy fosters a victim's mindset and reinforces the worst racial stereotypes.

Yates claims in this work to return to the philosophical roots of affirmative action to prove the why behind what he sees as its lack of success. He claims that the goals of President Kennedy's Executive Order No. 10925, which first ordered "affirmative action," have been undermined. Yates believes that the force behind affirmative action is the philosophy of social engineering that is deeply antagonistic to the principles on which this country is founded and similar to totalitarian ideologies. He argues instead for something he calls the "philosophy of social spontaneity," which he believes will demonstrate that civil rights can be upheld without detrimental government intervention while offering women and minorities the opportunity to rise on their own merits.

Yates's book focuses on philosophical and political arguments based on individual examples rather than on studies or other empirical evidence. He concludes that "affirmative action is one of several policies in contemporary American society that are pursued zealously in the face of growing evidence of many negative, and few positive, results."

Yates is a visiting professor of philosophy and has written

for academic publications. This book is an outgrowth of the policy study *Beyond Affirmative Action,* which he wrote for the Heartland Institute.

Zelnick, Bob. *Backfire: A Reporter's Look at Affirmative Action.* Washington, D.C.: Regnery Publishing, Inc., 1996. 415 pp. Index, bibliographical references. ISBN 0-89526-455-2.

Zelnick, an ABC News reporter with more than 29 years experience who is also an attorney and lifelong civil rights supporter, found himself surprised by his own conclusions after he closely examined the issue of affirmative action. Although acknowledging the good intentions of affirmative action, he concludes that the policy: favors the less qualified over the more qualified, endangers public safety in such areas as crime and fire prevention and medical care; has made it impossible for businesses and government to use objective merit selection criteria in hiring and promotion; brings few benefits to those most in need of help; and distracts from the real cause of inner-city black problems. The policy continues, he believes, because the issue has developed powerful constituencies in business and government and has been broadened for political purposes to include beneficiaries who want relief but lack the historical claim of blacks. Zelnick also argues that affirmative action panders to the darker instincts of racial animosity and has proven immune to evidence that it is counterproductive.

He traces the origin of affirmative action from what he believes should have been a short-term program designed to expand employer awareness of qualified job applicants to the policy he sees today as a coercive network of race-conscious laws, regulations, quotas, preferences, and entitlement programs. Zelnick concludes with an in-depth, behind-the-scenes report on the affirmative action battle in California.

An extensive, although far from politically neutral, look at the issue, Zelnick's book quotes Shelby Steele, who has called affirmative action an icon that people are afraid to question. Zelnick concludes: "But a hard look at affirmative action today shatters the icon. There is no moral virtue in supporting a policy that corrupts the values it purports to serve. Nor is there any power in clinging to the rafters of a sinking ship."

Selected Nonprint Resources

7

Films and Videos

Affirmative Action and Reaction

Type: Videocassette
Length: 27 minutes
Date: 1996
Cost: $89.95
Source: Films for the Humanities
and Sciences
12 Perrine Road
Monmouth Junction, NJ 08852
800-257-5126
Web site: www.films.com

Journalist Ben Wattenberg, known for his *Think Tank* specials, interviews Lani Guinier, professor of law at the University of Pennsylvania and Present Clinton's controversial and unsuccessful nominee for assistant attorney general for civil rights, in this program to pursue a broader sense of affirmative action and legitimate reaction. This one-on-one setting produces an intimate excavation into the factors that constitute affirmative action and the effect it has on everyone in its wake. Some of the questions addressed by a confident and impressive Guinier are how blacks and whites differ in their perception of affirmative action, if the policy is still necessary to remedy past discrimination, and what changes might be needed in order to insure success of the program. Another issue Guinier questions is the fallacy of a two-party system to command a real debate. She discerns rather that politics has become consumed with reelectability instead of accountability and says she would like to see more "fight to resolve" issues, not a "fight to win."

Guinier is undoubtedly in support of affirmative action; she insists it is actually a conservative approach to the problems it works to heal. The information discussed and revealed in this conversation, however, will prove useful for anyone researching the debate who is looking for a discussion of the less common attributes of the controversy. This is a professionally produced video resource where the climate of the exchange is refreshingly relaxed in contrast to the many disputes between individuals whose passion fuels fiery and often vengeful confrontation.

Affirmative Action for Men
Type: Videocassette
Length: 28 minutes
Date: 1993
Cost: $89.95
Source: Films for the Humanities and Sciences
            12 Perrine Road
            Monmouth Junction, NJ 08852
            800-257-5126
            Web site: www.films.com

This is a commercial-free recording of a Phil Donahue television talk show in which the audience meets Diane Joyce and Paul Johnson, who were involved in an affirmative action suit in Santa Clara, California. Both workers applied for the same position in the Transportation Agency, and Johnson was offered the job—allegedly because he was more qualified. Joyce, in an effort to redress some of the past discrimination she had incurred, took her case to a district court, which ruled in Johnson's favor. Joyce continued her fight and brought her appeal to the United States Supreme Court, which overturned the previous judgments and handed Joyce the spot Johnson thought he had secured. Johnson believes he was denied the rank he had earned because he was a white man and because affirmative action was an established policy in California.

Donahue mediates an extremely obstinate crowd and finds—rather humorously—that no one in the audience supports Joyce in her efforts for equal opportunity. An informal poll of the audience indicates that though some members are indeed on Joyce's side, they aren't willing to back her up when she comes under attack.

This video represents a side of society that doesn't discern the relevance of affirmative action and believes that those institutions affected by the policy should have the freedom to hire, fire, elect, and admit as they see fit—not even necessarily based on merit. *Affirmative Action for Men* represents the perspective of conservatives on this issue.

Affirmative Action: The History of an Idea

Type: Videocassette
Length: 56 minutes
Date: 1996
Cost: $129 (Order #AVE6552)
Source: Films for the Humanities and Sciences
            12 Perrine Road
            Monmouth Junction, NJ 08852
            800-257-5126
            Web site: www.films.com
            Widely available in libraries

This video opens with shots of political debris from the affirmative action debate and moves quickly through an overview of the evolution of government-legislated antidiscrimination laws and into talk show format under the premise of a *Think Tank* special to dissect the essential elements of the issue. The host, Ben Wattenberg, leads his guests, Harvard Professor of Law Christopher Edley, Senior Fellow at the Manhattan Institute Abigail Thernstrom, Duke Professor of Law Stanley Fish, and Research Fellow at the American Enterprise Institute Dinesh D'Souza, in a discussion on the history and relevance of affirmative action. Their dispute is spliced with clips of interviews and speeches by advocates of civil rights and critics of affirmative action.

From these fragments, the host delineates three distinct perceptions of affirmative action: equality of opportunity, equality of results, and diversity. The panel speaks specifically to these differences and raises more questions about racial nepotism and the measure of merit. The guests passionately argue the topic, and it is obvious they all have strong feelings about affirmative action; in fact, their enthusiasm sometimes becomes verbose and difficult to interpret without a strong familiarity with the issues and politics in general.

The special presents examples where affirmative action has

been incorporated or eliminated—for example, in the United States military, the Chicago Police Department, and the University of California. These models provide a more tangible understanding of affirmative action. This video is well produced and thorough, although it might work better as a more intensive exploration of the debate after the researcher first gains a broad sense of its history.

Affirmative Action under Siege: What's at Stake for Our Campuses, Careers, and Communities?
Type: Videocassette
Length: 120 minutes
Date: 1995
Cost: $250
Source: Black Issues in Higher Education
            Cox, Matthews and Associates, Inc.
            10520 Warwick Avenue, Suite B8
            Fairfax, VA 22030-3136
            800-783-3199; 703-385-1839
            Web site: www.blackissues.com

Black Issues in Higher Education (BIHE) invited six panelists to meet and discuss on live satellite some of the problems affirmative action programs attempt to solve and how these policies help or hinder antidiscrimination efforts. Panelists include Elaine Jones, director-counsel, NAACP Legal Defense and Educational Fund; Patricia Ireland, president, National Organization for Women; Everett Winters, president, American Association for Affirmative Action; Michael Forrest, executive director, National Association of Colleges and Employers; Stephan Balch, director, National Association of Scholars; and Errol Smith, vice-chairman, California Civil Rights Initiative. BIHE, an organization and news magazine devoted to minority issues in higher education, offers this open forum to answer questions such as, "How would the abolishment of affirmative action affect campus diversity and multicultural programs?" and "Would the policy lessen attempts to work toward equal opportunity on campuses, in communities, and careers?" The panel discussion is interspersed with outside perspectives from previous interviews with Dinesh D'Souza from the American Enterprise Institute, Ward Connerly from the University of California Board of Regents, and the authors of the California Civil Rights Initiative as well as comments from callers and audience members watching the show live.

Despite a few initial bumps in the introduction, this program maintains a smooth, professional level of production that elicits deep-seated emotions among the panelists, coupled with hard facts and historical segments. Julianne Malveaux effectively moderates a lively bunch who sometimes insult each other through their banter. Generally, their arguments are significant and frequently visited topics: the systemic nature of the problem, the semantics of affirmative action versus "race" or "group" preference, possible political motives, dismantling the "good ole boy network," and better preparation at the primary and secondary education levels. As usual in this kind of format, few problems are solved and many questions are raised. The program does succeed in elevating the awareness level of the viewer—an important element in understanding affirmative action and how it affects everyone.

Affirmative Action versus Reverse Discrimination:
The Constitution—That Delicate Balance (Part 12)
Type: Videocassette
Length: 60 minutes
Date: 1984
Cost: $29.95
Source: Media and Society Seminars and the
             Annenberg/CPB Project
             Columbia University
             School of Journalism
             New York, NY 10027
             800-LEARNER (532-7637)

As the twelfth segment of a 13-part series on the Constitution, this video opens with Fred W. Friendly of the Columbia University School of Journalism talking with U.S. Justice Potter Stewart about the Fourteenth Amendment, also known as the Equal Protection Clause of 1896, and how it came to be through the work of people like Thomas Jefferson. As they discuss the implications of the amendment and the changes that followed, the pair introduce a forum comprised of several recognizable representatives of the law, government, media, and academia. The assembly is guided through a hypothetical situation to examine the positives and negatives of affirmative action. The director of this exercise appoints three members of the group to hold teaching positions at a university where they have all just become eligible for tenure. The candidates are a black man, a white man, and a white woman, and their supervisors are two white men and a white woman. As they progress through the exercise, the debate includes a riveting discussion of constitutionality, personal experience, statistics, and even some humorous legal and political banter.

Although the arena may sound dry, the design of this program is engaging. The format allows for an equal representation of the many sides of the controversy and provides the opportunity to discuss the core of the debate. The participants cover some of the most common questions raised about affirmative action, including the measure of merit, a color-blind institution, and at what point they believe the policy becomes reverse discrimination. The video serves as an excellent tool to grasp the vast number of opinions and illustrates circumstances where affirmative action becomes a point of contention.

A Peacock in the Land of Penguins
Type: Videocassette
Length: 10 minutes
Date: 1995
Cost: $495 purchase, $125 rental (includes guide, index, and Peacock profile instruments)
Source: CRM Films
            2215 Faraday Avenue
            Carlsbad, CA 92008
            800-421-0833

This short, award-winning video based on the animated fable by Barbara "B. J." Hateley and Warren H. Schmidt uniquely presents the basics of an issue everyone has or will face upon entering the workforce. Without minimizing the difficulty of the issue, this video offers a rare simplicity absent from most attempts to produce an educational tool on diversity. The accessibility of the complex message makes this a relevant piece in introducing or inspiring awareness about diversity.

The story depicts a society in which penguins are the ruling class and have laid ground rules and standards for everyone else in their bird society. The penguins control everything that goes on from the workplace to home. Predictably, someone resists and tries to break out of the norm. "Peacock" is introduced and moves from an initial acceptance period to a wall of intolerance and eventual ostracism due to his colorful exuberance and aggressive nature. Peacock is one of a handful of birds who make it to the top with their proficiency only to be beaten down because of their differences and unwillingness to conform. The moral of this story comes out in the climax, where wolves plan to attack the penguins, but the outlaws hear of the plan and work with their foes to fight back, coming together despite everyone's differences.

Although the simple nature of this tale might insult some viewers' knowledge of the issue, it illustrates the basics of effective communication and teamwork and will appeal to those with little experience working in the context of diversity. Although the parallel to today's society seems clear with the penguin representing the white male, younger viewers might not recognize that point. The video could serve to initiate a classroom discussion for students beginning to understand their diverse classmates and surrounding environments.

A Time for Justice: America's Civil Rights Movement
Type: Videocassette/film (b/w)
Length: 38 minutes
Date: 1989
Cost: $30 for individual purchase of video and text kit
          $2.75 for *Free At Last,* 104-page illustrated supplement
          (available at bulk rates)
Source: Teaching Tolerance
          400 Washington Avenue
          Montgomery, AL 36177-9621
          334-264-0285
          Web site: www.teachingtolerance.com
          Widely available in libraries

Charles Guggenheim, in association with the Southern Poverty Law Center, creates in this film a well-balanced and succinct historical reminder of the events and efforts of a time—less than 50 years ago—that we now refer to as the American civil rights movement. Clips of speeches by civil rights leader Martin Luther King, Jr. are integrated with scenes of demonstrations, riots, marches, and trials in a colorful collection of the life and death that fueled African Americans' struggle for justice. As a witness to a major fulcrum point in the evolution of affirmative action, *A Time for Justice*—winner of an Academy Award—helps explain the reasons behind antidiscrimination laws.

Although the video stands alone in its superior quality of production and content, it can be used in combination with a companion teacher's guide and 104-page supplement, *Free at Last: A History of the Civil Rights Movement and Those Who Died in the Struggle,* to form an excellent educational package. The guide offers day-by-day adaptable lesson plans, and the supplement complements both the video and the guide with elaborate historical navigations of profiles, photos, and personal narratives of the civil rights movement. Teaching Tolerance, the department at Southern Poverty Law Center dedicated to education and responsible for this tutorial package, distributes the kit (one per institute) at no cost to schools, university departments, or community organizations upon written request.

A Time for Justice will appeal to anyone who craves a historical perspective on affirmative action; the video presents an intimate look at the trenches of a "peaceful" war against hate. Although the film does not deal with affirmative action, it answers some of the obvious and not-so-obvious questions researchers face in addressing today's issues of discrimination in schools and the workplace.

Choices: A Training Program in Equal Employment Opportunity

Type: Videocassette
Length: Part I, Modules 1 through 5, 54 minutes
            Part II, Modules 6 through 12, 23 minutes
Date: 1992
Cost: $400 per module
Source: BNA Communications
            9439 Key West Avenue
            Rockville, MD 20850-3396
            800-233-6067; 301-948-0540
            Web site: www.bna.com/bnac

Updated and revised in 1992, *Choices* has the flexibility and adaptability to survive over time as a useful guide for companies and organizations in establishing and maintaining equal employment opportunity policies. Accompanying this two-part video set of 12 modules is a facilitator's guide and participants' manuals, which are imperative for the program to be effective. Without the guides, the modules would lack introduction and clarity. The manuals contain substantial reference material and complement the video by explaining all the possible implications in EEO liability. Also included in the guide is a glossary of EEO terms, suggested guidelines to revisit in every employment routine, and overviews of the laws affecting every organization's responsibilities. The facilitator has the freedom with these manuals to explore the matter displayed in the dramatizations as intensively or briefly as the group needs. Each vignette illustrates an idea from which the viewers can extract a list of questions and generalizations that have corresponding analyses in the guidebook. There are many levels of exercises to gain resolution for each concept as well as a review and summary at the end of each segment.

Choices was designed to provide managers with a proficient understanding of equal employment opportunity so that they can apply those principles to all management decisions. To convey this message as thoroughly as possible, the producers demonstrate several situations for each practice. One vignette confronts discrimination based on race, gender, age, and national origin in recruiting, hiring, promoting, and the general working environment. *Choices* addresses affirmative action policies in several of the modules as they become pertinent and would be a reliable source in developing and implementing an appropriate affirmative action plan.

Destination: Diversity
Type: Videocassette
Length: 26 minutes
Date: 1994
Cost: Single tape $495 corporate, $395 nonprofit
Four-part series $1,195 corporate, $995 nonprofit
Both single and series $1,595 corporate,
$1,295 nonprofit
Free ten-day, no obligation preview tape available
Source: Schorr Communications, Inc.
1109 First Avenue, Suite 400
Seattle, WA 98101-2945
800-672-4677; 206-233-0135

Destination: Diversity (the single-tape version), presented by workplace diversity trainer and clinical psychologist Alice Hunter, is a concise summary of a four-part diversity training series. The series begins by defining diversity with a group of 30 representatives from all sects of society, who then discover their own differing levels of biases and eventually determine ways in which they can begin to move from awareness to behavior change. The single-tape, edited version offers an effective taste of how the complete series will approach diversity in the workplace and whether a more in-depth inquiry into these methods will help a specific company or organization.

Hunter delivers a convincing summation of the facts about discrimination in today's workplaces and the costs of bias. Although the discussion among the participants in the diversity training workshop, which takes place on Blake Island in Washington state, is insightful, intelligible, and motivational on its own, a 44-page facilitators' guide and 20-page participants' workbook are included at no extra charge with the single tape, and a 76-page guide and 36-page workbook are included with the four-part series. These guides contain suggested agendas for workshops ranging from one hour to a full day of various exercises.

Destination: Diversity contains important information about improving communication in a culturally diverse workplace. Although many diversity training programs tend to be very literal and systematic, this one lets the participants' own study guide them to a deeper understanding of the issue. Although diversity will happen with or without affirmative action, this program provides useful information for an organization that seeks to accept and incorporate a growing number of diverse workers into the workforce.

Exploring Race and Affirmative Action

Type: Videocassette
Length: 27 minutes
Date: 1996
Cost: $59.95
Source: Close Up Foundation
            44 Canal Center Plaza
            Alexandria, VA 22314-1592
            800-765-3131

The Close Up Foundation began in 1970 as a nonprofit, nonpartisan organization to inspire responsible participation in the democratic process, encouraging youth, educators, and citizens from every realm to individually and collectively understand and affect public policy. That goal led them to facilitate this project in which they have promoted four young Americans to investigate action through interviews with policy experts whose views tended to differ from their own. Among those interviewed are attorneys Ralph Neas and Ceclie Counts Blakey, syndicated columnist Robert Novak, and Robert Woodson of the National Center for Neighborhood Enterprise. The interviewers are asked to reconvene in a round-table exchange with chronicled footage of the birth of affirmative action laws from the struggle for civil rights as they consider the victories and failures of its programs along the way.

Some of the questions raised in the group regard the legitimacy of a meritocracy without first establishing an equal playing field, and whether Martin Luther King, Jr. was truly interested in a color-blind society when he spoke of judging others by the content of their character, not the color of their skin. The participants also look at the difference between quotas and goals or time tables, the supposed need to lower the barriers minorities must climb on their way to success, and what they might say about role models in their cultures. This is yet another reputable resource that seeks to reach a wide range of people by showing the full spectrum of opinion regarding affirmative action policy.

The Fairness Factor Series: (1) How to Recruit, Interview, and Hire to Maximize Effectiveness and Minimize Legal Liability; (2) How to Manage Performance and Discipline to Maximize Productivity and Minimize Legal Liability; (3) How to Manage Employee Termination to Minimize Legal Liability

Type:	Videocassette
Length:	20 minutes each
Date:	1998
Cost:	$849 for series purchase, $420 for series rental
	$395 single video purchase, $195 single rental
Source:	CRM Films
	2215 Faraday Avenue
	Carlsbad, CA 92008
	800-421-0833

This three-part series works well as a training guide for companies to move through each stage of employment as successfully and free of legal liability as possible. The format is geared toward managers looking for effective ways to recruit, interview, hire, evaluate, discipline, and terminate employees while minimizing charges of unfair practices. Attorney Rita Risser serves as the legal eye in each section to ensure a clear understanding of the equal opportunity laws being addressed. *The Fairness Factor* is essentially a how-to video in impartial employment habits and avoiding lawsuits, but it doesn't discount the need for the law. On the contrary, both Risser and the narrator make a point to impress their support of the policies.

Each section of vignettes is preceded with a step-by-step key to the employment action. They enact both incorrect and correct ways of executing a task. Throughout each section, a narrator brings up one or more—depending on relevance—of the five various "fairness factor" questions; for example, "Am I basing decisions solely on business-related criteria?" The video emphasizes the necessity of documenting everything from a description of the job qualities before hiring to finalizing a termination with an exit interview. Following the guidelines will help protect against litigation, and the steps also can assist in enhancing a diverse workplace and maintaining a level playing field.

Certainly this video series won't work for everyone since the approach is a business-oriented framework, but its consistent tone and methods will be effective in helping design fair and legal company employment policies.

How Can We Be Fair? The Future of Affirmative Action

Type: Videocassette
Length: 13 minutes
Date: 1996
Cost: $12
Source: Kendall/Hunt Publishing Company
          4050 Westmark Drive
          Dubuque, IA 52004-1840
          800-228-0810

This video, produced by the National Issues Forums Institute, delivers a brief introduction to affirmative action while posing an inquiry for the future. The reporter provides a concise summary of the inception of affirmative action to redress past discrimination and aggressively recruit minorities to fill positions where they were previously exempted. The host frames the issue in terms of the fairness of the policy and breaks the debate down into three possible approaches: (1) people—not government—can ensure fairness; (2) level the playing field, but don't fix the game; or (3) we need to finish the job we started. The video reviews each option entirely, citing the support and criticism of each viewpoint and illustrating how the various plans of action would affect the future of the policy. At the end, the viewers are asked to choose.

This product should be used as a beginning piece to know the basics of affirmative action as it now stands. The dialogue is tight and refined to address a complicated issue in a short period of time. As the debate continues and circumstances change, the validity of this presentation may become questionable. However, the video will retain its universal voice and sharp quality until something dramatic alters the essence of affirmative action.

Keeping the Door Open: Women and Affirmative Action

Type: Videocassette
Length: 13 minutes
Date: 1997

Cost: $15 for video; $2 for booklet
Source: Equal Rights Advocates
          1663 Mission Street, Suite 550
          San Francisco, CA 94103
          415-621-0672
          Web site: www.equalrights.org

Equal Rights Advocates (ERA), a women's law center fighting since 1974 for women's equality, produced *Keeping the Door Open* to answer the question, Why should women support affirmative action? They provide numbers regarding the past and continuing exclusion of women from many professions and use groundbreaking cases against the San Francisco Fire Department, Allstate Insurance Company, and the U.S. Forest Service to exemplify the headway made over the years toward a more equal representation and opportunity for women in those careers. Indicative of the title, their aim is this award-winning product is to show evidence of advancement and also to create urgency to support a work in progress.

This is a tight, deftly edited collection of interviews and facts that will sustain the viewer's interest in the impact of affirmative action on women's lives. They talk with women business owners, lawyers, firefighters, physicians, contractors, and others in positions where women have been generally underrepresented. Although the video is easy to follow and can be used independent of the corresponding booklet, ERA provides an associative text to reaffirm and expand the basics of the video by supplying statistics to dispel the myths surrounding affirmative action.

Again, their intent is clear—to keep the door wide open for women and to explain the basis on which women were included in affirmative action. Because ERA believes some people assume that women's fight for equality was over long ago, this piece was developed to contradict that supposition.

The Keys to the Kingdom
Type: Videocassette
Length: 60 minutes
Date: 1989
Cost: $49.95 (Sold for educational purposes only; PBS offers
          one free copy to educational institutions. Contact PBS
          for more information.)
Source: PBS Video
          1320 Braddock Place
          Alexandria, VA 22314

800-645-4727
Web site: www.pbs.org
Widely available in libraries

Blackside, Inc., produced *The Keys to the Kingdom* (1974–1980) as part of a sequel series, *Eyes On the Prize II,* which meets America at the racial crossroads from 1965 to 1985. This particular video is the only one in the extensive series that explores the genesis of affirmative action in education and politics. This documentary-style investigation of the alliance between the law and the cultural struggles to integrate the promise of equality focuses on the employment force and schools in Boston, Massachusetts, and later in Atlanta, Georgia. The video illustrates the heated and often violent contingency that plagued Boston in 1974 when Judge W. Garrity ruled that the district's schools begin desegregation practices by busing black students to predominantly white neighborhood schools and vice versa. Because this was the first real effort in Boston to institute the desegregation laws that had originally been passed 20 years prior and revamped again in 1964 and 1965, the confrontations were immense—as depicted in this documentation—with common scenes of riots and demonstrations. Captured here is the development of affirmative action and the basic components that would lead its advocates to offer it as a necessary tool for realizing an equal society.

While the divided Boston community works on funding resolutions, the focus of the presentation shifts to Atlanta in 1973, where Maynard Jackson is the first black mayor ever elected. Although affirmative action was already federally regulated at the time, Jackson made it city policy and used the legal remedy to ensure black involvement in the construction of a new airport—not without resistance. From this show of backlash, the video moves to another significant fight against affirmative action as Allan Bakke takes his case against the University of California at Berkeley all the way to the U. S. Supreme Court.

All of these events are well blended and skillfully produced to present a strong framework of affirmative action. *The Keys to the Kingdom* will speak to anyone who is interested in knowing some of the background of today's complicated affirmative action programs.

Legislating Morality: Affirmative Action and the Burden of History
Type: Videocassette
Length: 29 minutes

Date: 1996
Cost: $89.95
Source: Films for the Humanities and Sciences
           12 Perrine Road
           Monmouth Junction, NJ 08852
           800-257-5126
           Web site: www.films.com

Opening with background on the Declaration of Independence, this program undertakes the difficult task of following the Constitution into present-day politics while at the same time exploring history. A collage of past wrongdoing by the government and society is verbally woven into the video to present a powerful case for positive compensation in order to level the playing field. Although the components of history that encourage current preferential treatment are upheld by several constituents in this video—Mario Cuomo, former governor of New York; Roy Innis, chairman of the Congress on Racial Equity; and Charles Willie, professor of Education at Harvard—the rebuttal argument is solidly defended as well. Ward Connerly, regent of the University of California, who opposes what he calls "race preference" practices, insists that focusing on the outcome by engineering diversity through governmental legislation sets a dual standard for discrimination.

The producers of this program have created an exceptional balance by countering each point with a clip of an interview from one of several educated experts in support of an opposition to affirmative action. They bring up common questions in discussing the process of attaining equality, such as, "What would Martin Luther King, Jr. think of affirmative action?" "Why aren't these equal opportunity practices applied in professional sports?" and "How can we take from one to give to another without calling the practice reverse discrimination?" Although they use higher education—specifically the University of California—to discuss the pros and cons of affirmative action, their ideas can be applied to any institution. They provide enough information and examples for the viewer to make an educated choice regarding his or her own position on affirmative action. The video concludes with the assertion that people, not government, will have to honor the spirit of the law if it is to be effective.

**Recruitment and Admissions Dilemmas
in Higher Education: What's Next for Students of Color?**
Type: Videocassette

Length: 120 minutes
Date: 1998
Cost: $300
Source: Black Issues in Higher Education
Cox, Matthews and Associates, Inc.
10520 Warwick Avenue, Suite B8
Fairfax, VA 22030-3136
800-783-3199; 703-385-1839
Web site: www.blackissues.com

One of the more current videos on affirmative action, this recorded conference of panelists explores the changing politics of recruitment and admission standards as well as the reality of decreasing numbers of minorities attending institutions in districts where race as a provision in the selection process has been excluded. The panel consists of: Joyce Smith, executive director, National Association for College Admission Counseling; Anthony Carevale, vice president, Education Testing Service; Nancy Cantor, executive vice president, Academic Affairs at the University of Michigan; Bob Schaffer, public education director, National Center for Fair and Open Testing; Don Brown, commissioner, Texas Higher Education Coordinating Board; and Bradford Wilson, executive director, National Association of Scholars. All panelists agree, as do most experts, that the ultimate goal of diversity is a valid and essential one for the nation to succeed economically and evolve as a whole. Yet, they are left struggling with how to achieve diversity without excluding someone in the process.

Carol Randolph, Court TV anchor and a practicing attorney, does a superb job of moderating and directing this forum to cover a range of concerns. The panelists address demographics of college admissions in the late 1990s as well as the motives and origin of interest groups advocating individual rights rather than group rights. Among their discourse, they consider the scope of factors influencing admissions, such as the validity of standardized tests in comparison to overall GPA, class rank, counselor and teacher recommendations, essay samples, extracurricular activities, socioeconomic background, bilingualism, and the ability to pay. Although the opinions and statistics being thrown around in this debate can be overwhelming and mind-boggling, they present reputable strategies for people at all levels of higher education to contemplate when thinking about recruitment and the admission of students of color.

The Road to Brown

Type: Videocassette
Length: 50 minutes
Date: 1989
Cost: $195
Source: California Newsreel
149 Ninth Street, Suite 420
San Francisco, CA 94103
415-621-6196
Web site: www.newsreel.org

This documentary takes its audience on a trip to the roots of affirmative action from the time following the abolition of slavery, when so many newly freed African Americans were lynched and the country suffered a violent rift. Depicted here is the story of Charles Hamilton Houston, "the man who killed Jim Crow," a black lawyer of unusual privileged class who, after serving time in a segregated World War I, devoted his entire life to fighting for civil rights. After presenting a synopsis of the Thirteenth, Fourteenth, and Fifteenth Amendments and the cases that followed in response—*Dred Scott v. Sanford* and *Plessy v. Ferguson*—the tale continues to follow Houston and his progress in the courts as he lays the groundwork to ensure protection against discrimination and segregation. Houston argued that "separate but equal" was impossible and avoided equality for all. This video portrays the legwork of a long road of legal battles, including the African American's right to vote, that led to the critical 1954 case of *Brown v. Board of Education*. This event set a standard in education practices that would spread to institutions in all sectors of America.

Brown set the precedent for today's affirmative action policies. Houston's persistent efforts to secure justice and freedom for everyone—not just an equal share for blacks—laid the groundwork for the historic civil rights struggle. California Newsreel is dedicated to creating films of African American studies and other social issues; they offer in *The Road to Brown* more conclusive evidence on the legal unfolding of affirmative action.

Shattering the Silences

Type: Videocassette
Length: 86 minutes
Date: 1997
Cost: $195

Source: California Newsreel
             149 Ninth Street, Suite 420
             San Francisco, CA 94103
             Web site: www.newsreel.org

Shattering the Silences begins with narrator Lynn Thigpen prefacing an in-depth look at a selection of eight minority professors from universities across the country and their experiences in predominantly white institutions. In its quest to demonstrate the benefits of a diverse faculty, the film offers a powerful account of the campus struggle to create a rich and colorful climate in the classroom. The professors raise interesting dilemmas about affirmative action and its shortcomings and inadequacies while asserting that the battle for racial justice is crucial, as it affects everyone. The intimacy of the stories shared in this program is at times emotional and often piercing, but it is always intelligibly portrayed. These professionals are deeply affected by the inequalities that still exist on U.S. campuses today. Only one professor questions the reasoning of affirmative action, which he claims demands that universities hire less-qualified minorities and women in accordance with the required quotas. The film's objective is straightforward: to give a voice to faculty of color and provide the opportunity for other campuses to use this film as a catalyst for institutional change to increase the pool of diverse role models.

Some of the specific issues discussed are departmental policies, cultures, curricula, and the institution's responsibilities in recruitment, promotion, and retention of faculty of color. Naturally, the participants consider individual attitudes as well as look closely at student interaction and opinion in regard to their professors and overall education.

Also offered with the video is a text framework for group facilitation that contains adaptable levels of questions and lesson plans. The video can also be used alone to reach its viewers. The faculty chosen for this program are carefully candid as they build a foundation for diversity and break down some of the misconceptions about minorities in academia. *Shattering the Silences* has the potential to be an integral part of a university's efforts to diversify their educational environment.

The Speeches Collection: Martin Luther King, Jr.
Type: Videocassette (b/w)
Length: 60 minutes
Date: 1990
Cost: $19.98

Source: MPI Media Group
16101 South 108th Avenue
Orland Park, IL 60467
800-323-0442
Widely available in libraries

This collection represents the well-known speeches of Martin Luther King, Jr. from his time as a pastor to a speech just days before his assassination when he predicted his own death, clarifying the impact he had on America during the birth of the civil rights movement. Although a 60-minute synopsis of a man who led a "free nation" to be a "freer nation" hardly fills his shadow, this video offers a sense of King's power and how his accomplishments helped prepare America for the potentially endless battle for equality. Historical footage of critical developments in the civil rights movement bracket a chronologically arranged collection of King's addresses to the nation, with each speech introduced and dated.

Martin Luther King, Jr. preempted the heart of his country in peaceful revolution and continues to affect anyone who seeks to address the question of race and discrimination. Advocates as well as opponents of affirmative action pull quotes by King in debate on the topic. Although it is impossible to know what he would have to say about affirmative action, many have taken on the challenge of deriving from his memoirs how he would approach the issue. This video presents the opportunity for such discussion by reducing affirmative action to its organic beginnings and imparting a general knowledge of its constituents.

Although the format of *The Speeches Collection: Martin Luther King, Jr.* is modest and somewhat dated, the video adequately serves the point of acquainting the audience with some of the staple information on a movement that eventually led America to conceive affirmative action.

Story of a People, Volume IV: Affirmative Action on Trial
Type: Videocassette
Length: 50 minutes
Date: 1998
Cost: $19.98
Source: Xenon Entertainment Group
1440 9th Street
Santa Monica, CA 90401
310-451-5510
Widely available in libraries

Bob Dockery, known for his issues-based black audience programming, and Xenon Video engineer an exceptional assortment of interviews pieced together to form a comprehensive view of the heated match over affirmative action. Excerpts of street interviews are interwoven with in-depth interviews to proffer a wide range of beliefs on the topic. Hosted by the personable and soft-spoken actor Danny Glover, the many sides of affirmative action are outlined and displayed. The audience is introduced to a particular group of characters who depict the elemental problems and advantages of affirmative action. The owner of Adarand Constructors, who brought a lawsuit against the City of Denver (Colorado) over the affirmative action policies that allegedly had denied him business, pleads his case along with a woman in the construction business who claims that she—like many other woman—would never have found a place in that trade without affirmative action. A conservative black radio show host adamantly defends his theory that affirmative action is immoral and should be abolished. His account, along with tales of a doctor and several scholars and professors of law, portray the compelling and contradictory sides of the debate.

The flowing and balanced production will add insight and encourage a follow-up discussion for most audiences as they grapple with their own feelings about affirmative action. *The Story of a People* concludes with a meeting of the interviewees, who would have benefited from a more disciplined facilitator as they proceed to verbally attack one another at free will. Although this isn't a sound example of how to conduct a discussion, it shows how invested people are in the issue and what to avoid in managing such a debate.

Internet Resources

Affirmative Action
E-mail: pilot@infi.net

This site offers a four-page report regarding the affirmative action debate. It discusses the role of affirmative action in higher education and makes predictions about the future of this area of law.

Affirmative Action and Diversity
Carl Gutierrez-Jones
Department of English, UCSB

Santa Barbara, California
E-mail: carlgi@humanitas.ucsb.edu
Web site: http://humanitas.ucsb.edu/aa.html

This site is an academic resource. It provides articles and theoretical analyses, policy documents, current legislative updates, and an annotated bibliography of research and teaching materials. New links and documents are continually added. The site presents diverse opinions regarding affirmative action topics; rather than taking a singular pro or con position, it is designed to help lend many different voices to the debates surrounding the issues of affirmative action. Visitors are encouraged to E-mail suggestions.

American Civil Liberties Union
Web site: http://www.aclu.org

This site provides access to, among other things, the ACLU's briefing paper on affirmative action, which contains a brief history of events leading to the enactment of affirmative action law, statistical examples of affirmative action results, and advice on setting up an affirmative action program. It also differentiates affirmative action from quota systems and presents the results of affirmative action in the university setting. The site provides links to other pages concerning minority issues, and it contains a search engine that provides access to all of the ACLU's Internet resources, including news articles.

Americans United for Affirmative Action
E-mail: auaa@netgainec.com
Web site: http://www.auaa.org

Americans United for Affirmative Action is a national, nonprofit organization committed to educating the public on the importance of maintaining affirmative action programs and the principles of equal opportunity in employment and education. This site provides updates concerning affirmative action issues broken down by executive, legislative, judicial, and state news.

Berkshire Associates, Inc.
Web site: http://www.berkshire-aap.com

This site is maintained by Berkshire Associates, Inc., a consulting firm that specializes in setting up affirmative action plans. It is directed toward business owners and provides software and training to implement affirmative action plans.

California Civil Rights Institute
Web site: http://www.solipsism.com/insomweb/Politics/
AA/ aff-faw_old.html

This site provides links and references to multiple articles and newspaper stories regarding affirmative action law. It also provides a somewhat conservative view of myths and realities surrounding affirmative action issues.

Department of Labor Employment Standards Administration
Office of Federal Contract Compliance Programs (OFCCP)
Web site: http://www.dol.gov/dol/esa/public/regs/
compliance/ofccp/aa/htm

This site is maintained by the Department of Labor and describes the federal government's efforts to comply with Executive Order 11246. It covers every aspect of affirmative action in federal contracts, provides examples of affirmative action programs, and illustrates their results.

Diversity Database: University of Maryland
E-mail: diversity@umail.umd.edu
Web site: http://www.inform.umd.edu/diversity

This site is provided by the University of Maryland. It offers an informative question and answer page, and it links to other affirmative action sites. The information provided in this site is generally favorable to affirmative action programs.

Equal Employment Opportunity Commission
E-mail: GPOaccess@gpo.gov
Web site: http://www.eeoc.gov

The EEOC is the government agency that administers employment discrimination laws and litigates some discriminatory actions. An employment discrimination claim must be filed with the EEOC before legal action can be taken. This site offers information regarding the commission's activities, employment discrimination facts, and the process of filing a claim with the EEOC.

Equal Rights Advocates
E-mail: information@equalrights.org
Web site: http://www.equalrights.org/AFFIRM/INDEX.htm

This site is primarily concerned with affirmative action issues surrounding California Proposition 209. Despite this narrow scope, this site also offers coverage of legislative initiatives in every state and provides arguments about why affirmative action is still necessary. It explains the effects that affirmative action programs have on women and provides stories of people who have been affected by affirmative action programs. This site has links to other affirmative action sites, briefs of relevant case law, and access to a publication list.

Executive Office of the President
Email: President@WhiteHouse.gov
Web site: http://www.whitehouse.gov/WH/EOP/hmtl/
aa/aa-index.html

This site is maintained by the federal government. It contains a report to President Clinton regarding the status of the government's affirmative action programs as well as a summary of the history, goals, and effects of affirmative action in government programs and also remarks on the need to continue with affirmative action programs. This information applies only to public affirmative action programs and not those enacted voluntarily in private business.

Fox Performance Training and Human Resource Associates
Web site: http://www.foxperformance.com/affirmative.html

This site explains affirmative action programs from the perspective of private employers. It explains how to create a successful affirmative action plan and why it is important to have such a plan. This site is updated regularly with advice on how to adjust to the latest changes in the law.

General Services Administration Office
of Equal Employment Opportunity
Web site: http://www.gsa.gov.eeo7b.htm

This site explains many common and not so common terms and concepts used in the law of affirmative action and the affirmative action debate.

Leadership Conference on Civil Rights
E-mail: komar@civilrights.org
Web site: www.civilrights.org

This site includes diverse information about the Leadership Conference on Civil Rights, including its legislative priorities, vital issues, and links to background materials on affirmative action.

Maryland Association of Affirmative Action Offices
Web site: http://www.jhuapl.edu/maaao/index.htm

This site does not address affirmative action directly, but it contains numerous links to national organizations dedicated to civil rights.

Students of Color and Policy Department
E-mail: ussasocd@essential.org
Web site: http://www.essential.org/ussa/foundati/
aamyths. html

This site is provided by the United States Student Association. It explains a number of myths about affirmative action. It conveys a strong view in favor of such programs but is quite informative regarding important affirmative action criticisms.

United States Information Agency
Web site: http://www.usia.gov/usa/race/affirm.htm

This site provides three articles that discuss issues in the affirmative action debate. The articles discuss the role of affirmative action today, outline how to correct any current problems, and offer possible alternatives to the present system.

Glossary

apartheid: the government policy in South Africa that required people of different races to live separately; the word is often used to indicate separateness or segregation in general.

civil rights: the rights to personal liberty and equal opportunity established by several of the amendments to the Constitution of the United States; the social and political movement to end racial discrimination.

defendant: the person, employer, or entity (such as a school) charged with the complaint or wrong; usually an individual employee, student, or supervisor will be accused because of his or her own conduct; an employer or school may be liable through respondeat superior or agency theories.

discrimination: prejudicial outlook, action, or treatment.

disparate impact: in discrimination cases, discriminatory effect that results unintentionally from the use of a requirement—for example, a preemployment test—that on its face is neutral.

ethnicity: relating to a group of people's unity that is based on shared race, language, religion, or culture.

integration: the act or process of incorporating individuals of different groups, such as races, into society as equals.

meritocracy: a system that is based strictly on rewarding individual merit (excellence) or achievement, not showing preference based on group membership.

plaintiff: the person bringing the lawsuit or claim; usually the victim in an affirmative action case.

prejudice: a preconceived judgment or opinion formed without just grounds or sufficient knowledge.

quota: a numerical expectation or requirement; in the realm of affirmative action, quotas are fixed percentages of minorities or women to be hired by employers or admitted to schools to create a diverse population.

stereotype: a standardized mental picture that is held in common by members of a group and that represents an oversimplified opinion or prejudiced attitude toward members of another group.

stigma: a mark of shame or discredit.

Index

211

Lynne Eisaguirre is an attorney, author, and entrepreneur who helps organizations solve employee relations problems through training, speaking, and consulting. She is the author of *Sexual Harassment*, second edition.